DISCOURSES OF COUNSELLING

DISCOURSES OF COUNSELLING

HIV Counselling as Social Interaction

DAVID SILVERMAN

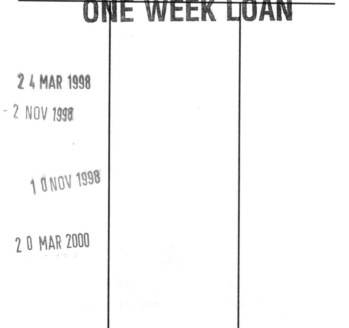

© David Silverman 1997

This edition first published 1997

SAGE Publications Ltd
6 Bonhill Street
London EC2A 4PU

SAGE Publications Inc
2455 Teller Road
Thousand Oaks, California 91320

SAGE Publications India Pvt Ltd
32, M-Block Market
Greater Kailash - I
New Delhi 110 048

British Library Cataloguing in Publication data

A catalogue record for this book is
available from the British Library.

ISBN 0 8039 7661 5
ISBN 0 8039 7662 3 (pbk)

Library of Congress catalog record available

Typeset by Type Study, Scarborough, North Yorkshire
Printed in Great Britain by Biddles Ltd, Guildford, Surrey

Kiitos Anssi

Contents

Preface and Acknowledgments

This book is the product of research that began in 1988. It is based largely on transcripts of tape-recordings of the counselling and advice-giving received by people who request an HIV test (sometimes loosely called an 'AIDS test'). These transcripts were then analysed to identify recurrent features in terms of how all parties organized their talk.

The method of analysis derives from a sociological and sociolinguistic approach called 'conversation analysis' (CA). For the non-specialist, CA is described in Chapter 2 of this book. For the moment, it might be worth stating that CA directs the analyst's attention to how talk is locally processed by interactants on a turn-by-turn basis to produce order and meaning.

CA focuses on what people are doing in their talk. As such, it specifically avoids any attempt to interpret talk in terms of what participants might be thinking. Rather its warrant for its interpretations resides in how a participant demonstrably monitors a previous turn of talk. This means that the conversation analyst usually begins by noting some 'outcome' in talk (e.g. a certain understanding or response produced by one speaker) and then works backwards through the talk to understand the trajectory which might have produced that outcome.

Because of this focus on the organization of talk between professionals and clients, I hope this book will be of interest to social scientists and sociolinguists. At the same time, I have consciously tried to make the writing accessible to those of you actually involved with HIV and AIDS, as well as to people practising or teaching within the burgeoning field of counselling.

The attempt to write for multiple audiences is obviously fraught with difficulty. I have tried to meet the needs of the practitioner (and, indeed, client) audience by highlighting the practical implications of my analysis. I am also encouraged by the responses of practitioners around the world to the many workshops that I have held about this research. Without exception, HIV counsellors have been fascinated by looking at detailed transcripts of what HIV counselling is *in practice*. In this way, they tell me that they have learned more both about other people's practice and about their own i.e. what they were doing, usually skilfully, without always realizing it.

The international character of my data will also, I hope, make this book of interest beyond the shores of Great Britain. In particular, I should like to point out to American counsellors that Chapters 5 and 8 are entirely based on US HIV counselling interviews, while Chapter 9 compares 'family therapy' based counselling in a US and a British centre.

The book begins with the contentious issue of the relationship between 'counselling' and the more general health promotion goals of much HIV test counselling. In the first chapter, I argue for the relevance of this data to some matters that concern counsellors outside this kind of health setting. Chapter 2 sets out the methodological issues involved in studying counselling by the analysis of tapes and transcripts. In particular, it compares this approach to alternative methods of evaluating counselling.

Chapters 3 to 8 offer the central, data-analysis part of the research. Chapter 3 sets out a way of understanding HIV counselling in terms of two stable ways of structuring communication between professionals and clients. In Chapters 4 and 5 I examine how the parties produce certain matters, at certain moments, as observably 'delicate' and how they manage that 'delicacy'. Chapter 5 is specifically focused on the delivery of the HIV test result in post-test counselling.

Chapters 6 to 8 are devoted to various aspects of the delivery and reception of health-related advice in HIV counselling. In particular, Chapter 7 examines how client resistance arises and is mitigated, while Chapter 8 looks at a device through which professionals can conceal the advice-like character of what they say to clients.

The last two chapters examine more general issues. Chapter 9, as already noted, compares certain aspects of 'family therapy' style counselling in a UK and a US centre. Its particular focus is on how counsellors encourage clients to talk about their troubles and how such 'troubles talk' may make counselling a double-edged 'discourse of enablement'. Finally, Chapter 10 summarizes the practical implications of this research for counsellors, while appendices provide information on how the data was gathered and some background on the centres whose counselling is discussed here.

I know from my own experience that people often read an academic text in a different way to a novel – in particular, one rarely reads from beginning to end. If you are most interested in the practical issues discussed, I suggest that you might begin by reading Chapters 1 and 10. Then, if your appetite is whetted, you might want to look in more detail at the data analysis chapters (3–8) and maybe Chapter 2 on methodology and Chapter 9 on what might loosely be called 'the politics of counselling'.

I gratefully acknowledge the help of workers and patients at a number of centres who made this research possible. I particularly thank Riva Miller and Eleanor Goldman (Royal Free Hospital Haemophilia Centre) and Robert Bor and Heather Salt (late of the Royal Free Hospital District AIDS Unit) for some of the data used in Chapters 3 and 9. Grateful thanks are offered to Doug Maynard, Sociology Department, University of Indiana, Bloomington, for providing me with data used in Chapter 8 and to Gale Miller for the US family therapy data used in Chapter 9. Many other HIV counsellors who offered considerable help and kindness must remain anonymous. I can only hope that they feel that this book does justice to their work. The English Health Education Authority and Glaxo Holdings plc funded the research upon which this book is based and I am delighted to acknowledge their support.

I would particularly like to thank my co-worker, from 1988 to 1992, Anssi Peräkylä, now Associate Professor, Sociology Department, Helsinki University. Without Anssi's insights, I would have achieved little. His close readings of earlier drafts of this book have been of tremendous help. This book is dedicated to Anssi as a token of thanks for his friendship and support.

Among other colleagues whose comments have, at some stage, been helpful, I would like to mention Paul Acourt, Paul Drew, David Greatbatch, Christian Heath, John Heritage, Doug Maynard, Ilmari Rostila, Nicolas Sheon and Vicki Taylor. In addition, I was helped in writing Chapter 5 by the comments on some of the data by members of data-session workgroups at the Workshop on Institutional Interaction (supported by the Academy of Finland) Suitia, Finland, August 1995 and members of a data workshop at the Department of Sociology, University of Nottingham, January 1996. Greer Rafferty, Postgraduate Secretary, Sociology Department, Goldsmiths' College, has helped me overcome many of the glitches that occur in preparing the manuscript. Naturally, I alone am responsible for the version presented in this book.

Almost twenty papers have been produced by myself and/or Anssi Peräkylä as a result of this research. Inevitably, some of the material that follows is a revised version of some of these papers. In particular, Chapter 3 is a revised version of a paper, jointly written with Anssi Peräkylä, 'Reinterpreting Speech-Exchange Systems: Communication Formats in AIDS Counselling' that originally appeared in *Sociology*, 25(4): 627–51, 1991. Chapter 9 is a revised version of Gale Miller and David Silverman, 'Troubles Talk and Counseling Discourse: a Comparative Study', *The Sociological Quarterly*, 36(4): 725–47, Fall 1995.

In addition, some material has been taken from my earlier publications as follows: Chapter 2 draws in part on David Silverman, 'Analyzing Naturally-occurring Data on AIDS Counselling: some methodological and practical issues', in M. Boulton (ed.), *Challenge and Innovation: Methodological Advances in Social Research on HIV/AIDS*, London: Falmer Press, 1994 and my book *Interpreting Qualitative Data*, Sage: London, 1993; Chapter 4 incorporates some of David Silverman 'Describing Sexual Activities in HIV Counselling: the Co-operative Management of the Moral Order', *Text*, 14(3): 427–53, 1994 and Chapter 5 uses parts of D. Silverman, R. Bor, R. Miller and E. Goldman, 'Advice-Giving and Advice-Reception in AIDS Counselling', in P. Aggleton, P. Davies and G. Hart (eds), *AIDS: Rights, Risk and Reason*, London: Falmer Press, 1992.

London
March 1996

Abbreviations

AIDS	Acquired immune deficiency syndrome
AIS	Advice-as-Information Sequence
BAC	British Association for Counselling
C	Counsellor
CA	Conversation analysis
CBA	Category-bound activity
GUM	Genito-urinary medicine
HEA	English Health Education Authority
HIV	Human immunodeficiency virus
HV	Health visitor
ID	Information delivery
IV	Interview format
MA	Marked acknowledgment
MCD	Membership categorization device
NHS	National Health Service
P	Patient
PDS	Perspective display sequence
POTS	Proposal of the situation
RT	Response token
SRP	Standard relational pair
STD	Sexually transmitted disease
UA	Unmarked acknowledgment

PART ONE
INTRODUCTION

Part One contains two chapters which are introductory in character. Chapter 1 deals with the theoretical, professional and organizational context of HIV counselling, using examples from Britain and the USA. It is concerned with how far the concept of 'counselling' is appropriate to describe the health promotion activities involved in the work of HIV health professionals.

In Chapter 2 I consider methodological issues in researching and evaluating medical practice, with particular reference to HIV and AIDS counselling. In this chapter, I offer an introduction to conversation analysis. I also discuss the appropriate role of social research in relation to my attempt to understand professionals' skills rather than to locate their failures.

1

What is HIV Counselling?

As this chapter will show, there is no simple answer to the question: what is HIV counselling? Indeed, if there were such a simple answer, then the research on which this book is based would be unnecessary.

In this chapter I set out to clarify the context in which HIV counselling occurs. Initially, this will involve simple definitions of AIDS, HIV and an HIV 'test'. I then look at why policy-makers and health practitioners began to connect the HIV-antibody test with counselling. This leads into the central part of the chapter: the generic definition of 'counselling' and its relation to the sometimes narrower, health promotion aims of HIV counselling. Finally, the chapter addresses what this research might contribute to the analysis of counselling 'skills'.

AIDS and HIV

Acquired immune deficiency syndrome (AIDS) is identified by the presence of one or more of a set of opportunistic infections and tumours. The human immunodeficiency virus (HIV), which causes AIDS, is spread by body fluids, particularly semen and blood. Subject to a 'window period' during which antibodies to the virus may not appear (thought to be up to six months in length), a test can establish the presence of the HIV virus.

A simple definition of an HIV test is as follows:

> The test for HIV antibodies is a diagnostic indicator of whether an individual has been infected with HIV. It alone does not indicate or predict whether, or when, that person will develop AIDS, although an increasing number of HIV-infected people are likely to develop AIDS over time. (Bor et al., 1992: 62).

In most Western societies, people are expected to receive counselling both before and after an HIV test. In Britain, for instance, since 1985, the Department of Health requires such counselling (Beardsell et al., 1995: 53).

But why has counselling become associated with the HIV test? Put in another way what is the 'mandate' for counselling?

The mandate for HIV counselling

Amidst the polemics of what Watney (1987) has called 'AIDS commentary', there is general agreement on three issues. First, that 'AIDS is primarily a *social* phenomenon with urgent and consuming medical issues attached'

(Miller, 1988: 130). Second, that, short of a medical breakthrough, the most effective response to HIV infection is via cultural and behavioural change. Third, such change will depend upon communication processes that are complicated and little understood.

While there is some support for health promotion programmes based simply on information (World Heath Organization, 1988: 15), most researchers and community workers argue that knowledge itself does not change behaviour (Stoller and Rutherford, 1989; Nelkin, 1987; Aggleton, 1989; Greenblat, 1989) and that fear-arousal is largely ineffective (Sherr, 1989). However, it remains difficult to isolate those factors which are effective in changing people's behaviour. For instance, a review of studies of the impact of HIV testing on behaviour reveals great uncertainties about the salient factors – is it testing, learning the result of one's test or testing with counselling that is most effective in behaviour change? (Miller and Pinching, 1989).

It seems that the answer we give to these questions depends upon which wave of the epidemic we are talking about. Early research had suggested the effectiveness of a positive test result in producing behaviour change among gay men (Miller et al., 1986; Peterman and Curran, 1986; Richards, 1986). However, this may have had a lot to do with the effective role of peer-endorsed safer sex ethics among the gay community. Testing alone is unlikely to be as effective with intravenous drug abusers and heterosexuals (Miller and Pinching, 1989: S187).

Where people lack a supportive peer network, writers associated with the World Health Organization have argued that HIV counselling is a key component of prevention strategies, 'complementing and supporting information, education and communication strategies, and as a *sine qua non* of clinical management' (Carballo and Miller, 1989: 117).

So it is argued, particularly in Britain, that there is a need to counsel all patients at genito-urinary medicine (GUM) clinics about HIV (Quinn, 1988) and that, in any event, counselling must precede the antibody test (Miller et al., 1986). It is suggested that this is not just a matter of health education but also of social support – cases of suicide have been reported among people who have the HIV test without pre-counselling (Miller, 1988).

These issues are reflected in the provision of counselling in the United States, although this provision is more diverse than in Britain. In the USA, pre-test counselling is by no means the norm. Many centres only provide post-test counselling with clients being provided with a questionnaire and a group meeting prior to the test – as with Centre US1 discussed in this book. The gains and losses of this approach are discussed in Chapter 10.

What is HIV counselling?

Simply calling for counselling in relation to HIV and AIDS fails to clarify exactly what 'counselling' is. So, in the next three sections, we consider issues which arise in relation to this contentious term:

1 how 'counselling' in general is defined;
2 the character of HIV 'counselling';
3 how closely (2) fits (1).

What is counselling?

Let us begin with the definition of 'counselling' provided by the leading British professional body:

> Counselling is the skilled and principled use of relationships which develop self-knowledge, emotional acceptance and growth, and personal resources. The overall aim is to live more fully and satisfyingly. Counselling may be concerned with addressing and resolving specific problems, making decisions, coping with crises, working through feelings and inner conflicts, or improving relationships with others.
>
> The counsellor's role is to facilitate the client's work in ways that respect the client's values, personal resources, and capacity for self-determination. (British Association for Counselling definition, quoted in Bond, 1990: 5).

Here is an authoritative version of what counselling is. It characterizes the counsellor as an enabler – enabling clients to cope with life and to understand themselves. In particular, we can note that the emphasis on the active role of the client ('the client's work') implies rejection of a model of the client as a passive recipient of the counsellor's solutions.

Now, of course, we can quibble at such a definition. For instance, we can search it in vain for any account of exactly *how* a counsellor might actually fulfil the roles described. However, this really is only a quibble, for two reasons. First, no definition of a profession can, in a few short sentences, convey all the skills required to practise it. If this could be achieved in a definition, then one could become a counsellor just by reading a textbook; training courses and, above all, professional experience would not be needed.

Second, a single definition of any profession will immediately fall foul of the varying contexts in which the profession is practised: institutional, theoretical and political. Let me spell out the relevance of these three contexts for the profession of counselling.

The institutional context Counselling today takes place in a variety of different institutional contexts which give it different meanings. Feltham (1995: 5) notes that, in the context of personnel management, counselling can have a disciplinary intent 'where the willingness of the "counsellor" to be a listener is strictly limited'. Equally, in the medical settings where AIDS counselling often takes place, 'counselling is commonly understood as a prescriptive and directive process' (Bond, 1990: 5).[1] This medical view is reflected in the title 'Health Adviser' given to professionals in many British hospitals who carry out what is still called 'counselling' around the HIV test.

The theoretical context Like several relatively new professions (including sociology!), counselling has no agreed body of theory. Instead, counselling is in what the philosopher of science Thomas Kuhn (1962) called a 'pre-paradigmatic' state, in which several models (or paradigms) compete for authority. The variety of theories that underlie counselling include:

– behaviouralism and cognitive behaviour therapy, which involve restructuring behaviour so as to manage problems;
– humanistic therapies which stress empathy and 'person-centredness';
– systemic therapies which attempt to locate troubles within social systems and use theoretically defined, non-humanistic techniques (e.g. circular questioning) to help to develop clients' skills at resolving such troubles (see Feltham, 1995: 78–92).

The political context   Emerging professions, like counselling, need to lay claim to some secure body of knowledge. Hence the accreditation of counsellors by the British Association for Counselling (BAC) and the occasional turf warfare between 'counsellors', 'psychotherapists' and 'psychoanalysts'.[2]

In a book entitled *What is Counselling?*, Feltham (1995: 9) attempts to circumvent some of these difficulties with this more extended definition of counselling:

> Counselling is viewed . . . as principled (an ethical endeavour with strict boundaries); which draws upon theories of psychotherapy and personality (it is a serious, professional activity resting partly on knowledge from the social sciences); which is practised according to certain learned (not innate or casually acquired) interpersonal skills; but which nonetheless includes the values of practical, personal experience and intuition. It should not be confused with advice-giving, but neither should it be thought inferior to, or even essentially different from, psychotherapy. . . . Its main target group is the distressed and confused but it is also an educative endeavour.

Of course, as Feltham himself recognizes, his definition, although more detailed than the definition with which we began, equally falls foul of the varying contexts of practice. In relation to its theoretical context, Feltham's reference to psychological theories would be opposed by some schools of counselling. For instance, the 'systemic method' of counselling is more based on social systems than personality theories (see Bor et al., 1992).

However, in the context of this book, the most interesting part of Feltham's definition is his distinction between counselling and 'advice-giving'. As we shall see, in the health-related context of counselling around the HIV-antibody test, advising is being done in the name of counselling.

Having briefly discussed how counselling in general is defined, it is now time to focus on HIV counselling. Bearing in mind Feltham's distinction between 'counselling' and 'advice-giving', we will then return to the issue of whether what goes on in HIV test counselling interviews is properly understood as 'counselling'.

Counselling around the HIV-antibody test

How is HIV counselling organized? Who does it? And what are its aims?

As there is no single answer to these questions, I will simplify my answer in two ways. First, I will, for the moment, confine myself to pre-test counselling. Second, I will discuss only the most common way in which such counselling is organized in Britain. Later in this chapter, I will present variations in this format represented by the range of data analysed in this book. In the course of this later presentation, I will discuss US centres, post-test counselling and different styles of HIV counselling in Britain.

Pre-test counselling in Britain usually takes place in the agency which conducts the HIV-antibody test. In this section, I focus on the organization of such counselling in genito-urinary medicine clinics of British hospitals. However, counselling also takes place in drug dependency clinics, general practice, prisons and private sector testing centres (Bond, 1990: 52). Additionally, given the transmission of the HIV virus through contaminated blood products in the late 1970s and early 1980s, HIV counselling is also conducted at many haemophilia centres (see Peräkylä, 1995).

Pre-test counselling at GUM clinics is conducted by health advisers, sometimes after a prior interview with a doctor. Many of these health advisers are nurses who, with the onset of AIDS, have shifted from other activities, such as 'contact-tracing' of cases of other sexually transmitted diseases. Invariably, such nurses, along with health advisers from non-nursing backgrounds, will have attended specialized training courses in counselling in relation to HIV infection. Such courses are held at a number of specialist training centres in the UK. They last for a minimum of one week and provide information about the HIV virus as well as opportunities for role-play.

The main aims of HIV test counselling have been set out in an authoritative text as shown in Table 1.1:

Table 1.1 *Aims of HIV test counselling*

1. To identify and clarify people's concerns and their risk for HIV
2. To check their understanding of how HIV is transmitted, how transmission can be prevented, and the meaning of the antibody test
3. To help people make more informed decisions by weighing up the benefits and disadvantages for them of having the test
4. To help people consider what might be their greatest concern if they were either HIV negative or HIV positive
5. To provide them with information about the personal, medical, social, psychological and legal implications of being diagnosed either HIV positive or HIV negative
6. To help prepare people for difficulties they may face in the future and to provide support for them, their family and their contacts

Source: Bor et al., 1992: 64.

Many of the items in Table 1.1, particularly those concerned with helping to identify the client's own concerns, will be familiar to counsellors well outside the AIDS field. However, there are elements here which may cause raised eyebrows. Notice, for instance, how the fifth item on the list above incorporates a reference to the provision of 'information'. In other contexts, counselling is often defined more in terms of the development of 'self-knowledge' rather than the delivery of information (see the British Association for Counselling definition, quoted on p. 5 above).

Now Bor, Miller and Goldman are respected counsellors who practise and teach one of the main counselling methods ('systemic' theory). So the presence of the 'information-giving' item on their list should be viewed not as some kind of normative 'error' but as telling us something of the specifics of *HIV* counselling.

In particular, we may note two features which may distinguish HIV counselling from counselling in many other environments. First, unlike a great deal of counselling, HIV counselling, in perhaps the majority of cases, is delivered to people who have not specifically requested it. It simply comes as part of the package if you request an HIV test. The clients of HIV counsellors may not have brought 'problems' that they wish to talk about and so may often adopt a more 'passive' role. So, speculatively, we might suggest that many such clients, unless specifically incited to talk by counsellors' questions, may orient themselves to be the passive recipients of information.

The second distinctive feature of HIV counselling is the medical environment in which it takes place – either deriving from the hospital setting or from the blood-taking involved in an HIV test. This carries two clear implications. First, the counsellor is aware that her client (or patient) is likely to lack some of the medical knowledge about the character and implications of HIV testing. Second, relatedly, the pre-test counselling interview will need, in part at least, to turn on the issue of obtaining 'informed consent' to the taking of blood for the test (see Chester, 1987: 34; Bond, 1990: 54 and Beardsell et al., 1995: 53). Indeed, unless such counsellors have provided 'proper' information, prior to an HIV test, they lay themselves and the physicians involved open to criminal charges of assault (Beardsell et al., 1995: 57).

So it is this specifically medical (and legal) environment which dis-tinguishes HIV counselling from much other counselling, particularly in relation to the provision by counsellors of information. Moreover, such information-giving is not just a defensive response to legal constraints. The medical environment means that counsellors must think in terms of 'health promotion', often defined in the narrow 'information delivery' sense approved by some official bodies (e.g. World Health Organization, 1988).

Indeed, if we examine how the overall aims of HIV counselling are often defined, we can see the regular presence of a sense that clients' behaviours need to be changed. Sometimes, this health promotion dynamic is expressed in direct, even authoritarian, terms, as in Chester's account of the basic purposes of HIV counselling: 'to guide the client towards a safer life style and to sources of help . . . to curtail the spread of infection by seeking compliance in risk-reduction behaviour' (Chester, 1987: 34).

Sometimes Chester's discussion of the need for 'compliance' gives way to apparently more client-centred versions of behaviour change, as in Bond's version of the aim of HIV test counselling: 'to give someone an opportunity to discuss confidentially the ways in which they can adjust their behaviour to minimise the risk of their becoming infected with HIV and to avoid infecting others' (Bond, 1990: 54).

Elsewhere, Chester's 'authoritarian' orientation is combined with Bond's 'client-centredness'. For instance, Bor, Miller and Goldman write that 'Counselling provides an opportunity to educate people about the risks of transmission and to promote behaviour change that will prevent the further transmission of HIV' (1992: 62). Here, the language of 'education' and 'behaviour change' suggest that health promotion conceived as information delivery is to the fore. However, in their very next paragraph, these writers revert to a language of client choice which is quite compatible with how both counselling and health promotion are defined elsewhere. They write: 'Counselling can help people to make informed decisions by considering the advantages and disadvantages of being tested for HIV' (ibid.).

Two points need to be made about these different positions. First, it would be naive to assume that such 'client-centred' counselling, while less obviously authoritarian than the more medically oriented models, is necessarily free from the effects of power. As I show in Chapter 9, non-directive counselling exercises power through what we call its 'incitement to speech'. However, we should also note that this is not intended as a criticism of 'client-centredness' but simply as a recognition that any form of professionalism cannot be too distant from the exercise of power – an exercise which sometimes all parties might recognize as appropriate and indeed useful.

My second point is that these strains between what we have crudely called one kind of (relatively authoritarian) 'health promotion' orientation and more familiar, non-directive versions of counselling are apparent outside the pages of textbooks. For instance, Beardsell, Hickson and Weatherburn's (1995) survey of British HIV counsellors found both versions well represented.

On the more limited, 'health' end of the spectrum, they elicited the following interview response from one counsellor:

> It's about informed consent not counselling. One of the problems is that counsellors will go down the rape line, the mother-in-law line, the marital line. . . . We get people with huge other problems coming in and [we've] got to be very sure how to deal with these people. (Beardsell et al., 1995: 54).

Yet another counsellor, however, explicitly wanted to take up what she called 'wider' issues:

> You need to take up the wider counselling issues. I feel strongly that you need to be qualified. People often mix up careers counselling, educational counselling, giving

information etc. with psychological therapy type counselling and I think it's necessary to have proper training. *Test counselling isn't just about assessing risk and getting informed consent.* (ibid., my emphasis)

In the chapters that follow, we will see these different emphases playing themselves out in the context of actual counselling interviews. For the moment, I would simply suggest that we see such differences as reflecting how, in their dealings with clients, HIV professionals are pulled in two, potentially different directions: health promotion (conceived as information-giving) and non-directive counselling. Given the information- and advice-giving aspects of HIV counselling, how far is it properly referred to as 'counselling'?

Advice-giving and counselling

It will at once be apparent that, whatever its official title, any description of professional–client communication around the HIV-antibody test as 'counselling' would be highly contested. The uncertain character of this activity arises out of the medical environment in which so much HIV counselling occurs.

As Bond (1990) has pointed out, there is an apparent conflict between the aims of certain types of health promotion (expressed in the World Health Organization's Global Programme on AIDS' reference to *prevention* counselling) and the non-directive thrust of most professional conceptions of counselling (represented in the BAC's stress on the need to 'respect the client's values'). Accordingly, Feltham (1995: 17) suggests that most counsellors distinguish between 'telling clients what they should do and facilitating their own efforts to arrive at their own decisions'.

Hence counselling is usually synonymous with a *non-directive* intervention based on assumptions about the dangers of advice-giving, most notably:

that it may constitute a form of collusion (reinforcing the client's false belief in his own helplessness or confusion); that it fails to note, unearth and work with the psycho-dynamics underlying requests for advice; and that it cheats the client of a valuable opportunity of discovering his or her own potent decision-making resources. (ibid., 18)

Although Feltham notes various grounds on which advice-giving by a counsellor may be appropriate and situations in which advice is, in fact, given but concealed, the prevailing professional assumption, as he notes, is that advice-giving 'may be incorrect or unwise and may backfire' (ibid.).

The apparent conflict between advice-giving and professional conceptions of counselling is reflected in an earlier study of HIV counselling in the UK which sought to distinguish various activities, as shown in Table 1.2.

Given the health promotion goals attached to HIV counselling, Table 1.2 shows how Chester characterizes many of the activities that take place between professionals and clients as 'advice' and 'support' rather than 'counselling' as professionally defined.

Table 1.2 *What is HIV counselling?*

Advice – the imparting of authoritative information, explanation, guidance, clarification of options.
Support – the provision of encouragement, enhancement of morale, maintenance of sociability etc., together with specific practical assistance.
Counselling – the skilled and principled use of (a) relationship to facilitate self-knowledge, emotional acceptance and growth, and the optimal development of personal resources.

Source: Chester, 1987: 7

This book, of course, draws its research data from HIV counselling. Moreover, much of the data to be discussed derive from counselling around the HIV-antibody test during which health promotion goals are often foremost. Does this mean that we are not really dealing with 'counselling' at all?

Certainly, this was the view of one academic teacher of counselling to whom I showed an early draft of one chapter. Equally, a recent British study of HIV professionals found that they were concerned about the use of 'counselling' as a 'catch-all' term to describe their work and that in HIV care: 'claims that counselling is provided are not . . . self-evident in meaning and may lead to misunderstanding' (Bond, 1990: 8).

One way round this apparent impasse is to treat the activities that we are dealing with here as not necessarily 'counselling' but as forms of communication in which 'counselling skills' may be used and/or may be relevant. So, for instance, 'giving general information', 'giving advice', 'befriending/buddying', 'client advocacy' and 'crisis intervention' may all be seen as 'ways of helping which are not counselling but would be better practised in conjunction with the use of counselling skills' (Bond, 1990: 8).

Despite its understandable need to draw boundary lines around what constitutes 'counselling', the British Association for Counselling has, as Bond points out, sanctioned the identification of 'counselling skills' in activities which it is not prepared to define as 'counselling'. Its code states that

> 'counselling skills' are distinguished from 'listening skills', and from 'counselling'. . . . What distinguishes the use of counselling skills from these other activities is the intention of the user, which is to enhance performance of their functional role. (quoted ibid.)

In the BAC's sense, then, we may say that, although this book is not about activities that would always be professionally defined as 'counselling', it is about activities (from advice- and information-giving to elicitation of the client's perspective) in which 'counselling skills' are relevant. However, even if the counselling audience is prepared to accept the above assertion, we are still no clearer as to a precise understanding of what these skills are. More specifically, we need to understand something about the skills deployed in HIV counselling.

Counselling skills

If we are to advance the discussion, we need to look more closely at normative accounts of such skills set out by policy-makers and practitioners. In this context, I will then turn to what my research can offer.

Normative accounts of HIV counselling

Most normative accounts properly pay attention to the form of HIV counselling as well as its content. Some normative definitions take account of the social relationship between counsellor and client. For instance, Miller and Pinching argue that:

> the counsellor in HIV must remain a person offering a trusting, implicitly and explicitly supportive, ongoing and confidential relationship that rises above the rhetoric, the hype, the unrealistic expectations and the hidden agendas embraced by . . . public discussions. (1989: S191)

However, while few counsellors would disagree with this statement, it is not immediately clear how it could be carried out in practice or what are the mechanics through which such a 'trusting' relationship could produce a communication format able to generate client uptake and changed behaviour.

Some of the answers to these questions are contained in two recent, theoretically based accounts of HIV counselling (Miller and Bor, 1988; Bor et al., 1992). Using a 'systemic' model of counselling which locates both counsellor and client within a network of social systems, these books clearly lay out a set of communication techniques designed to encourage clients to define the issues that face them now and in the future. Prominent among these are 'circular' and 'hypothetical' questions which encourage clients to think about possible future states and the perceptions of significant others (Bor et al., 1992: 9–37).

In my view, such an approach comes closer than other normative accounts to actually discussing the 'nuts and bolts' issues of communication in HIV counselling. In relation to our earlier discussion, by defining a 'client-centred' version of professional practice, concerned more with what clients can do for themselves than what counsellors can do for them, the 'systemic' model accommodates HIV counselling much more closely to how counselling is usually perceived.[3]

However, such detailed discussion of different ways in which counsellors can construct questions is a rare exception to a literature which largely confines itself to generalities. Reading the available literature, one is struck by the prevalence of well-meaning nostrums based on commonsense, liberal assumptions rather than on research. Fenton's (1987) emphasis on 'feeling comfortable' when discussing sex and on the counsellor knowing the right information is a case in point.

Two further factors, discussed in many reports, make this situation particularly worrying. First, large numbers of references are made to the current practical problems of HIV counselling – from staff 'burnout' (Carballo and Miller, 1989) to the pressures produced by media campaigns (Thompson and McIver, 1988; Beck et al., 1987; Sonnex et al., 1987) and the related problem of counselling an increasing group of 'worried well' patients (Miller, D., 1987; Salt et al., 1989). Second, the training needs among groups as diverse as health advisers (Sadler, 1988) and social workers (Shernoff, 1988), as well as among general practitioners and in the whole field of primary care (Henry, 1988; Goedert, 1987; Hodgkin, 1988), seem immense and largely unsatisfied.

The lack of a soundly based counselling practice is acknowledged in some of the literature. For instance, Carballo and Miller (1989) recognize that, despite normative definitions, what counts as counselling remains problematic. As they suggest, the *ad hoc* character of counselling practice is a common feature of examples elsewhere of crisis intervention:

> As a result, counselling strategies have often had to be innovative and hastily derived and, to date, much of the HIV/AIDS counselling support being provided continues to be the result of the personal commitment and interests of individual clinicians and other health care staff. As such, its characterisation, definition, role and content is variable and lacking in training support and institutionalised continuity. (Carballo and Miller, 1989: 119)

The possible contribution of this research

The weakness in normative definitions of counselling is due both to the varying contexts of practice and to the limits of textbook definitions of 'counselling'. Even Bor, Miller and Goldman's (1992) otherwise exemplary text uses 'tidied up' extracts from HIV counselling interviews as well as invented examples.

The limits of normative versions of counselling not based on analysis of real-time counselling interviews is seen most clearly in the training of counsellors. Conventional training courses seek to impart many of the following skills noted by Feltham:

> attentive listening, accurate understanding, an ability to articulate what one has heard and understood and to know how to paraphrase and to summarize another's concerns expressed through conversation, an ability to engage emotionally with others and so on. (Feltham, 1995: 23)

However, in teaching such skills through normative instruction or role-plays, one can easily miss some of the complexities of actual counselling practice – both the problems that counsellors encounter and the practical solutions they find in the constraints of routine counselling practice.

In this book, I seek to argue that the theoretically guided analysis of detailed transcripts of actual counselling interviews can make a significant contribution to counselling practice. This contribution can be seen in three related ways, set out in Table 1.3.

Table 1.3 sets out a body of strong claims. Rather than embellish them at this early stage, I leave the reader to judge how far these claims are justified

Table 1.3   *Claims of this research*

---

1. It makes available for analysis the seen but unnoticed skills used by counsellors.
2. It reveals that a focus on counselling skills can overlook the active skills of clients. Counselling, like any other form of socially organized activity, can thus be viewed as the co-operative accomplishment of all parties.
3. It demonstrates that counselling skills are, at best, embellishments of everyday conversational skills.[4] Hence it shows how counselling (and counselling theory) needs to be re-connected to its basis in what we do already.

---

by the chapters that follow. The theoretical and methodological bases of these claims are set out in the following chapter, while Chapters 3 to 9 present the relevant data analysis. I will return to these practical issues in Chapter 10.

Notes

1 The degree of divergence between the BAC's definition of counselling and medical views is vividly illustrated in this statement by a general practitioner quoted by Bond (1990: 5): 'a great deal of general practice is concerned with counselling, which is now the popular term for *giving advice* to people' (my emphasis).

2 Occasionally, according to Feltham, this can lead to the politicization of definitions of professional activities where counselling veers between the quasi-medical respectability of psychotherapy and the appeal to non-medical, more 'democratic' claims (Feltham, 1995: 6).

3 As I note at the end of this chapter, some of the data discussed here involve Miller, Bor and Goldman as well as other counsellors who have learned from them 'systemic' practice. For a brilliant, detailed examination of how such communication functions, see Peräkylä (1995).

4 This point is recognized by Feltham (1995: 23) who writes: 'Counselling is based to a large extent on pre-existing interpersonal, verbal skills, in the same way that advanced athletic performance is based on pre-existing mobility skills'.

2

Basic Methodological Issues

This chapter seeks to set out the methodological background to the data-analysis chapters that follow. Its main aim is to explain why our research was based on analysing tape-recordings and transcripts of actual counselling interviews and to introduce some elements of the theory of interaction (conversation analysis) that animated this analysis. I also attempt to deal fairly directly with the debate about the relevance of such social research for practitioners in the fields of counselling and health promotion.

The chapter is organized in terms of the following issues:

- the debate about how counselling may best be evaluated;
- the related issue about what contribution social science research can make to practice;
- a simplified introduction to conversation analysis;
- a discussion of the methodological and practical implications of this kind of CA-based research.

At times, parts of this chapter may read quite polemically. Where this happens, it is a regrettable consequence of the need to telescope quite complicated issues within a few paragraphs. However, I hope it will also be clear to the reader that I do not set out with the belief that there is only one 'right' way of proceeding in either social science or counselling. Instead, I entirely agree with the conventional wisdom that, in such matters, everything depends upon what you are trying to do.

Strategies for evaluating counselling

John McLeod has recently reminded us that 'almost all counselling and psychotherapy research has been carried out from the discipline of psychology' (1994: 190). One consequence has been a focus on quantitative studies concerned with the attributes of individuals. This has meant that linguistic and sociological issues, such as language use and social context, have been downplayed (see Heaton, 1979).

Such a psychological focus has also had an impact on research design, leading to the dominance of experimental and/or statistical methods favoured in psychology. Of course, no research method is intrinsically better than any other; everything will depend upon one's research objectives. So it is only a question of restoring a balance between different ways of conceiving counselling research.

In this light, perhaps it is time now, as McLeod suggests, to pose the following strategic question about research on counselling:

> Can useful knowledge be best achieved by accurate, objective measurement of variables or by respecting the complexity of everyday language? (1994: 9)

My use of tape-recordings of counselling sessions was just such an attempt to 'respect the complexity of everyday language'. As we shall see, by doing so, I have been able to generate some unexpected findings. However, my style of research also found a particular answer to a further question raised by McLeod:

> by what criteria are the validity of research findings to be judged? (ibid.)

We can expand (and explain) McLeod's question by relating it to the debate in social science about the status of any claim to depict 'reality'. The issue of validity is posed in terms of what constitutes a credible claim to truth. Thus Denzin and Lincoln discuss the following four criteria applied by 'conventional positivist social science' (including most psychological studies of counselling) to 'disciplined inquiry':

> *internal validity*, the degree to which findings correctly map the phenomenon in question; *external validity*, the degree to which findings can be generalized to other settings similar to the one in which the study occurred; *reliability*, the extent to which findings can be replicated, or reproduced, by another inquirer; and *objectivity*, the extent to which findings are free from bias. (Denzin and Lincoln, 1994: 100)

If we take seriously the demands of validity and reliability, there are three obvious ways of evaluating counselling:

1 Measuring clients' response to counselling by means of research interviews which elicit their knowledge and reported behaviour. This would involve a longitudinal study, following a cohort of patients. The study could have either an experimental or non-experimental design.
2 Measuring clients' response to counselling by means of objective behavioural indicators. This also would involve a longitudinal study, following a cohort of patients.
3 Measuring the degree of fit between actual counselling practice and certain agreed normative standards of 'good counselling'.

Focusing on HIV/AIDS counselling, I review each strategy below. In doing so, we will see that each raises both methodological and analytic questions. I shall suggest that, in terms of either of or both these questions, none of these three strategies is entirely satisfactory.

The research interview

This might have either an experimental or non-experimental design.

In the experimental design, we might randomly assign clients to two groups. In Group 1, clients are counselled, while in Group 2, the control group, no counselling is provided. Both groups are then interviewed about their knowledge of AIDS and how they intend to protect themselves against the disease. This interview is followed up, some months later, with a further interview examining their present behaviour compared to their reported behaviour prior to the experiment.

In a non-experimental design, existing counselling procedures are evaluated by a cohort of patients. Again, we might follow up a cohort some time later.

The advantage of such research designs is that they permit large-scale studies which generate apparently 'hard' data, based on unequivocal measures. However, a number of difficulties present themselves.[1] Let me list a few:

(a)   How seriously are we to take patients' accounts of their behaviour? Isn't it likely that clients will tend to provide answers which they think the counsellors and researchers will want to hear (see McLeod, 1994: 124–6)?

(b)   Doesn't the experimental design ignore the *organizational* context in which health-care is delivered (e.g. relations between physicians and other staff, tacit theories of 'good counselling', resources available, staff turnover, etc.)? Such contexts may shape the nature and effectiveness of counselling in non-laboratory situations.

(c)   Even if we can overcome the practical and ethical problems of not providing, say, pre-test counselling to a control group, may not the experience of being allocated to a control group affect the reliability of our measures and the validity of our findings (see McLeod, 1994: 124)?

(d)   Don't both studies treat subjects as 'an aggregation of disparate individuals' who have no social interaction with one another (Bryman, 1988: 39)? As such, they give us little hold on how counselling is organized as a local, step-by-step social process and, consequently, we may suspect that we are little wiser about how counselling works in practice.

The non-experimental study seeks to identify qualitative research on counselling with the attempt: 'to enter, in an empathic way, the lived experience of the person or group being studied' (McLeod, 1994: 89).

This pursuit of 'lived experience' means that many qualitative researchers favour the open-ended interview (see Silverman, 1993: ix). Even when tape-recording actual interactions is contemplated, attention is deflected from analysing the local organization of talk. For instance, while McLeod calls for a study of 'the interior of therapy', he also cites favourably attempts at 'interpersonal process recall' where participants are played back the tape 'to restimulate the actual experience the person had during the session' (1994: 147). Thus, in common with many qualitative researchers, what matters most for McLeod is what people think and feel rather than what they do.

Both the 'in-depth' accounts apparently provided by the 'open-ended' interview and the apparently unequivocal measures of information-retention, attitude and behaviour that we obtain via laboratory or question-naire methods have a tenuous basis in what people may be saying and doing in their everyday lives. Moreover, if our interest is in the relation of counselling to health-related behaviour, do such studies tell us how people actually talk with professionals and with each other as opposed to via responses to researchers' questions?

An example makes the point very well. At a recent meeting of social scientists working on AIDS, much concern was expressed about the difficulty of recruiting a sample of the population prepared to answer researchers' questions about their sexual behaviour. As a result, it was suggested that a subsequent meeting should be convened at which we could swap tips about how to recruit such a sample.

Now, of course, this issue of recruiting a sample is basic to survey research. And, for potentially 'delicate' matters, like the elicitation of accounts of sexual behaviour, survey researchers are quite properly concerned about finding willing respondents. At the same time, it is generally acknowledged that the best chance of limiting the spread of HIV may be by encouraging people to discuss their sexual practices with their partners. This implies something about the limits of survey research. Such interview-based research necessarily focuses on finding people prepared to talk about their sexuality in an interview. However, it can say nothing about how talk about sexuality is organized in 'naturally occurring' environments such as talk between partners or, indeed, talk about sexuality in the context of real-time counselling interviews.

Behavioural indicators

This method seeks to elicit behavioural measures which reliably report the effectiveness of counselling. Its advantage is that, unlike the research interview, it does not depend upon potentially unreliable client perceptions and self-reports of behaviour and behavioural change. Moreover, by eliminating concern with the information that clients may acquire from counselling, it takes on board the research which shows that acquired knowledge does not have any direct link with behavioural change.

In relation to HIV test counselling, it has been suggested that an appropriate behavioural indicator is seroconversion.[2] Presumably, then, we would need to study a cohort of patients who test seronegative and are counselled. We would then re-test them after a further period, say twelve months, to establish what proportions from different counselling centres and with different counsellors have seroconverted. In this way, it would be claimed, we could measure the effectiveness of counselling in relation to promoting safer behaviour.

The advantage of this approach is that it generates apparently objective behavioural measures. However, like the research interview, its reliability also has serious shortcomings:

(a) How do we know that the counselling alone is the variable that has produced the reported behaviour? Although we may be able to 'control' for some gross intervening variables (like gender, age, sexual preference, drug use, etc.), it is likely that some non-measured variables may be associated with the reported behaviour (e.g. access to other sources of information, availability of condoms or clean injecting equipment).

(b) How do we know that an initial seronegative test means that the client is not infected with the HIV virus? The problem is created by the fact that there is a 'window period' of up to six months during which the body does not produce antibodies despite the presence of the virus. Consequently, if any of the cohort has been exposed to risk of infection during that period, any negative result would have a dubious status.[3]

(c) A major problem for many counsellors in using behavioural measures is that such measures do not fit with how the purposes of counselling are usually defined. As we shall see, 'effective' counselling is often defined in terms of criteria which are either only indirectly linked to behavioural change or relate to behavioural changes other than particular physical outcomes. Hence lack of seroconversion could not be treated as a reliable measure of effective counselling.

Meeting normative standards

To many counsellors, the only sensible means of evaluating their work is to start from their own objectives. These objectives will reflect their normative theories of 'good practice'.

Like sociology, counselling has been a site for many competing theoretical orientations (see McLeod, 1994: 142–64). The post-war dominance of 'client-centred' theories (Rogers, 1957) now seems to have been displaced by 'therapeutic alliance' theory (Horvath and Greenberg, 1986) and theories deriving from the quasi-sociological 'systemic' approach of the Milan School (Selvini-Palazzoli et al., 1980).

In relation to our data on HIV counselling, two main normative approaches were found. In one British centre (see Peräkylä, 1995) and, to a lesser extent, in the US centres, counsellors used some variant of the 'systemic' approach. Indeed, in this British centre, some of the practitioners were authors of major texts which explained how the approach could be used in HIV counselling (Miller and Bor, 1988; Bor et al., 1992). In practice, this commitment to theory-based counselling was seen, among other things, in the use of 'circular' questions, often based on hypothetical situations and by the avoidance or delay of direct advice-giving (see Peräkylä, 1995).

An example of pre-HIV test counselling at this centre is given in Extract

2.1 below. Transcript symbols are given in Appendix 3. The counsellor (C) has just asked her male patient (P) how he would feel about a positive HIV test result:

>   Extract 2.1 (UK4)
> 1   P: found out I was [posi- positive I was going die.=
> 2   C: [Ri:ght.
> 3   P: =Because I wouldn't lie to (them) because I heard
> 4   about er oh a thing .h where: i- uh: some Frenchman
> 5   (0.4) er left a note to-to- to his boyfriend the
> 6   following morning that .hhh er: wu- welcome to the:
> 7   to the ai:ds uh:m (0.5) virus.
> 8   =An[d this chap went ba:ck .h and found=
> 9   C: [Right.
> 10   P: =that this chap had infected him.
> 11   C: Right.
> 12   P: Now I think that's nasty. That is really is er:
> 13   C:a   So you think you'd probably be fairly k- (.) keen to
> 14   try and (.) not pass it on to other [people.
> 15   P: [Oh yeah
> 16   definite[ly. I couldn't- I couldn't live-
> 17   C:b   [( ) d'you think perhaps (.) if-
> 18   if- what would happen if an urge came on d'you think
> 19   possibly you might be able to
> 20   P: We::[ll
> 21   C: [(be safe) or something (.) [to try and get=
> 22   P: [Yeah.
> 23   C: =rid of the urge.
> 24   (.)
> 25   P: I'd try t[o but-
> 26   C:c   [And is that the situa:tion?
> 27   P: (   )
> 28   (0.5)
> 29   P: Those kinds- those sort of situations is- it's very
> 30   har[d to know what you're going=
> 31   C: [Mm
> 32   P: =actually do:. (0.7) At that moment in time.=
> 33   C: =Right.
> 34   (1.0)
> 35   P: I could say one thing and maybe (.) I could be-
> 36   it could be the (.) complete reverse type of thing.
> 37   C:d   Sure. .hh I mean uh say- say if it comes back
> 38   negative a:nd er
> 39   (1.1)
> 40   P: I'd pr[obably
> 41   C: [You haven't been re-tested so we don't

```
42              know::
43    P:        Y[eah
44    C:          [what's going to happen:, do you think that'll
45              change anything in your relationships with other
46              people.=Do you think you'd carry o:n having sex with
47              them: without protection or:?
48    P:e       I think I'll still be carrying o:n (0.5) er sex
49              without protection. (0.5) u-Because I- I (.) because
50              I believe that you can take more (    ) and test and
51              they maybe in three or five- five months or (the
52              same).
```

Notice here, after P completes his answer (line 12), C offers a candidate summary of what P has been saying (**a**). This is immediately confirmed by P (lines 15–16). However, rather than changing topic or giving further information, C now asks P a hypothetical question about what P might do (shown as **b**), using a term ('urge') supplied earlier by P (data not shown). When P's answer now indicates hesitancy about his earlier position, C requests more specification (shown as **c**).

P's answer now casts further doubt on his earlier position and C asks an additional hypothetical question, requiring P to assume that his test turned out to be negative (beginning at **d**). P's answer to this question (shown at **e**) confirms that he would be unlikely to engage in safer sex whatever the result of his HIV test.

In the other British centres, where counselling was mainly done by nurses in sexually transmitted diseases clinics, a primarily 'medical model' dominated. This meant that, after a brief 'history-taking', the counsellor spent most of her time delivering information to the client with the avowed aim of ensuring that the HIV test only took place with the client's informed consent.

Extract 2.2 shows such a counsellor giving advice to a female patient about safer sex after a negative HIV test result:

```
      Extract 2.2 (UK1)
1     C:        .hhhh Now when someo:ne er is tested (.) and they
2               ha:ve a negative test result .hh it's obviously
3               ideal uh:m that (.) they then look after themselves
4               to prevent [any further risk of=
5     P:                   [Mm hm
6     C:        =infection. .hhhh I mean obviously this is only
7               possible up to a point because if .hhh you get into
8               a sort of serious relationship with someone that's
9               long ter:m .hh you can't obviously continue to use
10              condoms forever. .hh Uh:m and a point has to come
11              where you make a sort of decision (0.4) uh:m if you
12              are settling down about families and things that you
13              know (0.6) you'd- not to continue safer sex.
```

```
14              [.hhhh Uh:m but obviously: (1.0) you=
15    P:        [Mm:
16    C:        =nee:d to be (.) uh:m (.) take precautions uhm (0.3)
17              and keep to the safer practices .hhh if: obviously
18              you want to prevent infection in the future.
19    P:        [Mm hm
20    C:        [.hhhh The problem at the moment is we've got it
21              here in ((names City)) in particular (.) right across
22              the boar:d you know from all walks of life.
23    P:        Mm hm
24    C:        Uh::m from you know (.) the sort of established high
25              r- risk groups (.) now we're getting heterosexual
26              (.) [transmission as well. .hh Uhm=
27    P:            [Mm hm
28    C:        =so obviously everyone really needs to careful. .hhh
29              Now whe- when someone gets a positive test result
30              er: then obviously they're going to ke- think very
31              carefully about things.
```

Let me make three observations about Extract 2.2. First, unlike Extract 2.1, C delivers advice to P. Second, this advice is offered without a perceived problem having been elicited from P. Reasons of space do not allow me to include what immediately precedes this extract but it concerns another topic (the meaning of a positive test result) and no attempt is made to question P about her possible response to this topic, i.e. how she might change her behaviour after such a test result. Third, C does not personalize her advice. Instead of using a personal pronoun or the patient's name, she refers to 'someone' and 'they' (lines 1–4) and 'everyone' (line 28).[4]

In principle, it should be possible to evaluate HIV counselling, like that shown in Extracts 2.1 and 2.2, according to how far it meets the normative standards supported by counsellors. So we might evaluate any given counselling interview, as appropriate, by whether it followed a 'systemic' method or whether it properly achieved 'informed consent'.

For instance, in Extract 2.2, we might note that P only produces minimal uptake in the form of various utterances of 'mm hmm'. While these may indicate that P is listening, they do not mark what C is saying as advice. Hence, at the very least, they do not show P uptake and may also be taken as a sign of passive resistance (see Heritage and Sefi, 1992). Conversely, in Extract 1, by using hypothetical questioning, C seems to get P to think through his likely future behaviour and to revise his initial responses. Although C will later deliver advice (data not shown), it is likely to be well grounded in P's own perspective.

Here we seem to be on the way to developing a firmly based evaluation of these extracts. Unfortunately, in practice, it has proved difficult to establish reliable measures to evaluate counselling. As McLeod (1994: 150–64) has noted, several problems have confronted attempts at evaluation by means of normative standards:

(a)   Observers find it difficult to differentiate different measures (e.g. 'congruence', 'empathy' and 'acceptance') and instead rate counsellors according to 'their image of a "good therapist"' (McLeod, 1994: 150).

(b)   *Ad hoc* decisions are often made about which part of a counselling interview should be assessed. The scope extends from a whole counselling interview (or even several interviews with the same client) down to a micro-segment of one interview. The latter, narrow approach may gain in precision but at the cost of understanding the context of the surrounding talk. The broader approach may find it hard to make detailed assessments of whole interviews.

(c)   Even if such measures are reliable and precise, the result 'assesses only the presence or absence of a mode, and not the skilfulness with which it is delivered' (ibid. 151).

Such problems in attempts to use internal, 'normative' standards of evaluation look even worse when viewed in the context of studies which seek to relate such measures to particular outcomes. As McLeod (ibid.) notes, one such study (Hill et al., 1988) found that only 1 per cent of variance in client responses was related to observed measures of counsellor behaviour!

However, the problems we have found in each of these three attempts to evaluate counselling need not lead to the abandonment of the project. Apart from anything else, any professional practice, including counselling, in principle stands to gain from a sympathetic dialogue with social science researchers.

One way out of the impasse is to stand back a little from methodological details and to examine the assumptions about social research from which our three methods of evaluating counselling may derive.

Orthodoxies in social science research

I have suggested elsewhere (Silverman, 1994a) that there are two potentially dangerous orthodoxies shared by many social scientists and by policy-makers who commission social research like the three evaluative studies we have been considering. The first orthodoxy is that people are puppets of social structures. According to this model, what people do is defined by 'society'. In practice, this reduces to explaining people's behaviour as the outcome of certain 'face-sheet' variables (like social class, gender or ethnicity).

We will call this the Explanatory Orthodoxy. According to it, social scientists do research to provide explanations of given problems, e.g. why do individuals engage in unsafe sex? Inevitably, such research will find explanations based on one or more 'face-sheet' variables.

The second orthodoxy is that people are 'dopes'. Interview respondents' knowledge is assumed to be imperfect, indeed they may even lie to us. In the same way, practitioners (like doctors or counsellors) are assumed always to depart from normative standards of good practice. This is the Divine Orthodoxy. It makes the social scientist into the philosopher-king (or queen) who can always see through people's claims and know better than they do.

What is wrong with these two orthodoxies? The Explanatory Orthodoxy is so concerned to rush to an explanation that it fails to ask serious questions about what it is explaining.

There is a parallel here with what we must now call a 'post-modern' phenomenon. It seems that visitors to the Grand Canyon in Arizona are now freed from the messy business of exploring the Canyon itself. Instead, they can now spend an enlightening hour or so in a multi-media 'experience' which gives them all the thrills in a pre-digested way. Then they can be on their way, secure in the knowledge that they have 'done' the Grand Canyon. This example is part of something far larger. In contemporary culture, the environment around a phenomenon has become more important than the phenomenon itself. So people are more interested in the lives of movie stars than in the movies themselves. Equally, on sporting occasions, pre- and post-match interviews become as exciting (or even more exciting) than the game itself. Using a phrase to which we shall shortly return, in both cases, *the phenomenon escapes*.

This is precisely what the Explanatory Orthodoxy encourages. Because we rush to offer explanations of all kinds of social phenomena, we rarely spend enough time trying to understand how the phenomenon works. So, for instance, we may simply impose an 'operational definition' of 'unsafe sex' or a normative version of 'good counselling', failing totally to examine how such activities come to have meaning in what people are actually doing in everyday (naturally occurring) situations.

This leads directly to the folly of the Divine Orthodoxy. Its methods preclude seeing the good sense of what people are doing or understanding their skills in local contexts. It prefers interviews where people are forced to answer questions that never arise in their day-to-day life. Because it rarely looks at this life, it condemns people to fail without understanding that we are all cleverer than we can say in so many words. Even when it examines what people are actually doing, the Divine Orthodoxy measures their activities by some idealized normative standards, like 'good communication'. So, once again, like ordinary people, practitioners are condemned to fail.

Both kinds of research are fundamentally concerned with the environment around the phenomenon rather than the phenomenon itself. In quantitative studies of 'objective' social structures and qualitative studies of people's 'subjective' orientations, we may be deflected from the phenomenon towards what follows and precedes it (causes and consequences in the 'objective' approach) or to how people respond to it (the 'subjective' approach). This is illustrated in Figures 2.1 and 2.2.

causes > the phenomenon >
> consequences

Figure 2.1 *Objectivism*

perceptions > the phenomenon
> responses

Figure 2.2 *Subjectivism*

In both approaches, the phenomenon with which ostensibly we are concerned disappears. In 'objectivism', it is defined out of existence (by fiat, as Cicourel, 1964 puts it). Equally, what I have called 'Subjectivism' is so romantically attached to the authentic rush of human experience that it merely reproduces tales of a subjective world without bringing us any closer to the local organization of the phenomena concerned.

Summary: relevance to counselling research

At this point, the reader might rightly have two questions. First, how does this, increasingly abstract, discussion of orthodoxies in social research relate to the more concrete issues of evaluating counselling with which we began? Second, since destruction is always easier than construction, what alternative, if any, is proposed?

Both questions will be answered below. However, it is probably easiest to attempt to begin with my answer to the first question. In this way, we will tidy up the 'destructive' part of this chapter in order to be able to concentrate better on its 'constructive' argument.

In brief, my suggestion is that counselling research based on measuring clients' response can fall prey to the Explanatory Orthodoxy, through a focus on the *consequences* of counselling. On the other hand, using normative standards to assess counselling practice derives from the Divine Orthodoxy because it has a pre-defined sense of the character of counsellors' skills (and of their likely deficiencies).

In all three of the approaches that we considered earlier, the search for reliable measures of outcome (approaches 1 and 2) or counsellors' behaviour (approach 3) may create fresh, seemingly intractable methodological difficulties. Thus outcome measures may be contaminated by the artificial situation of the research interview or made problematic by their uncertain relationship to counsellors' own aims. Equally, trying to apply normatively derived measures of 'good' counselling practice may result in problematic tabulations where the skills of counsellors in using a particular method cannot be evaluated.

More to the point, in terms of Figures 2.1 and 2.2 above, all three approaches risk missing the phenomenon of counselling itself. The first approach, using research interviews, follows what we have called 'subjectivism'. Its focus on clients' perception of counselling and response to it gets us no closer to understanding what has happened in the counselling interview itself. The second approach, using objective behavioural indicators, reflects an 'objectivist' methodology. Its concern with the consequences of counselling does not allow us to comprehend which features of the counselling interview may be associated with such consequences.

Our third approach has the merit of focusing on actual counselling practice. But, to some extent, the 'phenomenon' still 'escapes' because pre-defined measures cannot do justice to the skills *in situ* that counsellors deploy.

These assumptions are summarized in Table 2.1:

Table 2.1   *Counselling research: measures and assumptions*

Measure	Orthodoxy	The 'phenomenon'
Interviewing clients	Explanatory	Escapes – only looks at consequences
Clients' behaviour	Explanatory	Escapes – only looks at consequences
Normative standards	Divine	Escapes – pre-defined version of skills

Conversation analysis

It is now time to lay my cards on the table and to offer the alternative approach on which my research is based – conversation analysis (henceforth CA). CA is centrally concerned with the organization of talk, although its concern with social organization leads it to describe its subject-matter as 'talk-in-interaction'.

Equally, counsellors, by definition, treat talk as a non-trivial matter. However, even if we concede the centrality of talk to social life, why should counselling researchers give priority to recording and transcribing talk? Given the usefulness of other kinds of data derived, say, from observations of behavioural change or interviews with clients, what is the special value of transcripts of tape-recordings of conversation?

One way to start to answer this question is to think about how research based upon data which arises in subjects' day-to-day activities can seek to preserve the 'phenomenon' of interactions like counselling interviews. Although such 'naturally occurring' data is never uncontaminated (for instance it may need to be recorded and transcribed), it usually gives us a very good clue about what participants usually do outside a research setting.

Conversely, in research interviews, as Heritage puts it: 'the verbal formulations of subjects are treated as an appropriate substitute for the observation of actual behaviour' (Heritage, 1984: 236). The temptation is then to treat respondents' formulations as reflections of some pre-existing social or psychological world.

But if we follow this temptation in counselling research, we deny something that all counsellors recognize: that talk is itself an activity. Although this is recognized in many normative versions of counselling, to base our research on such versions would be to narrow our focus to those activities which we already know about.

An alternative is to investigate how counselling interviews actually proceed without being shackled by normative standards of 'good' communication. In this way, we might discover previously unnoticed skills of both counsellors and clients as well as the communicational 'functions' of apparently 'dysfunctional' counsellor behaviour.

Detailed transcripts of conversation overcome the tendency of transcribers to 'tidy up' the 'messy' features of natural conversation. In Appendix 3, I provide a simplified set of the transcription symbols used in our research.[5]

It should not be assumed that the preparation of transcripts is simply a technical detail prior to the main business of the analysis. As Atkinson and Heritage (1984) point out, the production and use of transcripts are essentially 'research activities'. They involve close, repeated listenings to recordings which often reveal previously unnoted recurring features of the organisation of talk. The convenience of transcripts for presentational purposes is no more than an added bonus.

Heritage (1984: 237) has noted the gains of working with tape-recordings and transcripts. His observations can be summarized as follows:

1   It is very difficult for an observer working with fieldnotes to record such detail.
2   The tape-recording and the transcript allow both analyst and reader to return to the extract either to develop the analysis or to check it out in detail.
3   What may appear, at first hearing, to be interactionally 'obvious' can subsequently (via a transcript) be seen to be based on precise mechanisms skilfully used by the participants.

It is worth concluding with Heritage's summary of the advantages of transcripts:

> the use of recorded data is an essential corrective to the limitations of intuition and recollection. In enabling repeated and detailed examination of the events of interaction, the use of recordings extends the range and precision of the observations which can be made. It permits other researchers to have direct access to the data about which claims are being made, thus making analysis subject to detailed public scrutiny and helping to minimise the influence of personal preconceptions or analytical biases. Finally, it may be noted that because the data are available in 'raw' form, they can be re-used in a variety of investigations and can be re-examined in the context of new findings. (Heritage, 1984: 238)

The transcription symbols used in this research derive from CA. CA is based on an attempt to describe people's methods for producing orderly social interaction. CA's concern with the *sequential* organization of talk means that it needs precise transcriptions of such (commonsensically) trivial matters as overlapping talk and length of pauses. As Sacks put it:

> What we need to do . . . is to watch conversations . . . I don't say that we should rely on our recollection for conversation, because it's very bad. . . . One can invent new sentences and feel comfortable with them (as happens in philosophy and linguistics). One cannot invent new sequences of conversation and feel happy with them. You may be able to take 'a question and answer', but if we have to extend it very far, then the issue of whether somebody would really say that, after, say, the fifth utterance, is one which we could not confidently argue. One doesn't have a strong intuition for sequencing in conversation. (1992, Vol. 2: 5)

However, one cannot assume that transcripts which do not record such details as length of pauses are necessarily imperfect. There cannot be a *perfect* transcript of a tape-recording. Everything depends upon what you are trying to do in the analysis, as well as upon practical considerations involving time and resources.

CA sets out to analyse three fundamental features of talk (Heritage, 1984: 241–4):

1 *The structural organization of talk*: talk exhibits stable, organized patterns, demonstrably oriented to by the participants. These patterns 'stand independently of the psychological or other characteristics of particular speakers'. This has two important implications. First, the structural organization of talk is to be treated as on a par with the structural organization of any social institution, i.e. as a 'social fact', in Durkheim's terms. Second, it follows that it is illegitimate and unnecessary to explain that organization by appealing to the presumed psychological or other characteristics of particular speakers.
2 *Sequential organization*: 'a speaker's action is *context-shaped* in that its contribution to an on-going sequence of actions cannot adequately be understood except by reference to its context . . . in which it participates'. However, this context is addressed by CA largely in terms of the preceding sequence of talk: 'in this sense, the context of a next action is repeatedly renewed with every current action'.
3 *The empirical grounding of analysis*: the first two properties need to be identified in precise analyses of detailed transcripts. It is therefore necessary to avoid premature theory-construction and the 'idealization' of research materials which uses only general, non-detailed characterizations.

Heritage sums up these assumptions as follows:

> Specifically, analysis is strongly 'data-driven' – developed from phenomena which are in various ways evidenced in the data of interaction. Correspondingly, there is a strong bias against *a priori* speculation about the orientations and motives of speakers and in favour of detailed examination of conversationalists'

actual actions. Thus the empirical conduct of speakers is treated as the central resource out of which analysis may develop. (1984: 243)

In practice, Heritage adds, this means that it must be demonstrated that the regularities described 'are produced and oriented to by the participants as normatively oriented-to grounds for inference and action' (ibid.: 244). Further, as we shall shortly see, deviant cases, in which such regularities are absent, must be identified and analysed.

The presence of deviant cases reminds us that CA specifically avoids a purely mechanical view of conversation: 'conversation is not an endless series of interlocking adjacency pairs in which sharply constrained options confront the next speaker' (Heritage, 1984: 261).

For instance, the phenomenon of adjacency works according to two non-mechanistic assumptions:

- an assumption that an utterance which is placed immediately after another one is to be understood as produced in response to or in relation to the preceding utterance;
- which means that, if a speaker wishes some contribution to be heard as *unrelated* to an immediately prior utterance, he or she must do something special to lift assumption 1 – for instance by the use of a prefix (like 'by the way') designed to show that what follows is unrelated to the immediately prior turn at talk.

As Atkinson and Heritage put it: 'For conversational analysts, therefore, it is sequences and turns-within-sequences, rather than isolated utterances or sentences, which are the primary units of analysis' (1984: 3).

CA and institutional talk

So far we have been examining ordinary, or casual, conversation. However, our focus in this book is specifically on counselling interviews. What contribution can CA make to the analysis of talk in such an institutional setting?

In the course of his published lectures, Sacks (1992) occasionally ponders what might specifically distinguish 'institutional' talk. For instance, using Schegloff (1968), he notes how a caller has to engage in considerable work to transform the meaning of a called-defined 'business call' (1992, Vol. 1: 200–1). He also notes that a candidate-feature of institutional talk is the absence of 'second stories'. For instance, 'it is absolutely not the business of a psychiatrist, having had some experience reported to him, to say "My mother was just like that, too"' (1992, Vol. 1: 259).

CA uses the practices found in ordinary conversation as a baseline from which to analyse institutional talk. It can then examine how particular sequence types found in conversation 'become specialised, simplified, reduced, or otherwise structurally adapted for institutional purposes' (Maynard and Clayman, 1991: 407).

Viewed in this light, one minimal way to describe counselling interviews is to examine their modified use of certain properties of everyday conversation. A basic sequence of actions in a recognizable interview is a series of questions and answers (Silverman, 1973). After a question, as Sacks puts it, 'the other party properly speaks, and properly offers an answer to the question and says no more than that' (Sacks, 1972: 230). However, after the answer has been given, the questioner can speak again and *can* choose to ask a further question. This chaining rule can provide 'for the occurrence of an indefinitely long conversation of the form Q-A-Q-A-Q-A . . .' (ibid.).

Although question–answer sequences do arise in mundane conversation, they seem to provide a defining characteristic of many counselling interviews, as we saw in our discussion of Extract 2.1. The chaining rule gives a great deal of space to the counsellor to shape the flow of topics, while most clients' questions are positioned after the counsellor has invited them to ask a question.[6]

There is not the space here for detailed exegesis of CA studies.[7] One example of a study of institutional talk, based on data from medical consultations, but particularly relevant for counselling research, will suffice.

Using data from paediatric settings, Maynard (1991) neatly demonstrates the previous point about the adaptation of ordinary conversational practices in institutional talk. One such practice is to elicit an opinion from someone else before making one's own statement. Maynard gives this example:

>   Extract 2.3 (Maynard, 1991: 459)
> 1   Bob: Have you ever heard anything about wire wheels?
> 2   Al: They can be a real pain. They you know they go outta line
> 3   and--
> 4   Bob: Yeah the-- if ya get a flat you hafta take it to a
> 5   special place ta get the flat repaired.
> 6   Al: Uh-- why's that?

Notice how Bob's report (lines 4–5) is preceded by an earlier sequence. At lines 1–3, Bob asks Al a question on the same topic and receives an answer. Why not launch straight into his report?

Maynard suggests a number of functions of this 'pre-sequence':

1   It allows Bob to monitor Al's opinions and knowledge on the topic before delivering his own views.
2   Bob can then modify his statement to take account of Al's opinions or even delay further such a statement by asking further questions of Al (using the 'chaining' rule).
3   Because Bob aligns himself with Al's preferred 'complaint' (about wire wheels), his statement is given in a 'hospitable environment' which implicates Al.
4   This means that it will be difficult (although not impossible) for Al subsequently to dispute Bob's statement.

Maynard calls such sequences a 'perspective display sequence' (or PDS). The PDS is 'a device by which one party can produce a report or opinion after first soliciting a recipient's perspective' (ibid.: 464). Typically, a PDS will have three parts:

a question from A
an answer by B
a statement by A

However, 'the PDS can be expanded through use of the probe, a secondary query that prefigures the asker's subsequent report and occasions a more precise display of recipient's position' (ibid.).

In the paediatric clinic for children referred for developmental difficulties, the use of PDS by doctors is common. Extract 2.4 is one such example:

> Extract 2.4 (Maynard, 1991: 468)
> 1 Dr E: What do you see? as– as his difficulty.
> 2 Mrs C: Mainly his uhm– the fact that he doesn't understand
> 3   everything and also the fact that his speech is very
> 4   hard to understand what he's saying, lots of time
> 5 Dr E: Right
> 6 Dr E: Do you have any ideas WHY it is? are you-- do you?
> 7 Mrs C: No
> 8 Dr E: Okay I think you know I think we BASICALLY in some
> 9   ways agree with you, insofar as we think that D's
> 10   MAIN problem, you know, DOES involve you know
> 11   LANGuage.
> 12 Mrs C: Mm hmm

The basic three-part structure of the PDS works here as follows:

Question (line 1)
Answer (lines 2–4)
Statement (lines 8–11)

Notice, however, how Dr E expands the PDS at line 6 by asking a further question.

As Maynard points out, doctors are expected to deliver diagnoses. Often, however, when the diagnosis is bad, they may expect some resistance from their patients. This is particularly true of paediatrics, where mothers are accorded special knowledge and competence in assessing their child's condition. The function of the PDS in such an institutional context is that it seeks to align the mother to the upcoming diagnosis. Notice how Dr E's statement on lines 8–11 begins by expressing agreement with Mrs C's perspective but then reformulates it from 'speech' to 'language'. Mrs C has now been implicated in what will turn out to be the announcement of bad news.

Of course, as Maynard notes, things do not always work out so easily for the doctor. Sometimes parents display perspectives which are out of line with the forthcoming announcement, for example by saying that they are quite happy with their child's progress. In such circumstances, Maynard shows how the doctor typically pursues a statement from the parent which acknowledges *some* problem (e.g. a problem perceived by the child's teacher) and then delivers his diagnosis in terms of that.

Maynard concludes that the PDS has a special function in environments requiring *caution*. In ordinary conversations, this may explain why it is seen most frequently in conversations between strangers or acquaintances where the person about to deliver an opinion is unlikely to know about the other person's views. In the paediatric setting discussed, the functions of the PDS are obvious:

> By adducing a display of their recipients' knowledge or beliefs, clinicians can potentially deliver the news in a hospitable conversational environment, confirm the parents' understanding, coimplicate their perspective in the news delivery, and thereby present assessments in a publicly affirmative and nonconflicting manner. (Maynard, 1991: 484)

Maynard's work shows how medical encounters may, in part, involve the use of mechanisms, like the PDS, which occur in ordinary conversation. By using such conversation as a baseline, CA allows us to identify what is distinctive about institutional discourses.

In addition, a distinctive contribution of CA is to ask questions about the *functions* of any recurrent social process. So Maynard examines how his PDS sequences work in the context of the delivery of bad news.

By focusing on the turn-by-turn organization of talk, CA has shown the distinctive features of the sequential organization of talk that organize institutional settings. It has also suggested the functions of this organization in each institutional context.

Methodological implications

In many respects the kind of research discussed here is very different from the mainstream of both quantitative *and* qualitative social research. To discuss why we have proceeded in this manner, we must touch upon two further, basic methodological issues.

First, conventional experimental or interview studies of counselling presumably take seriously the issue of the validity of their descriptions and the reliability of their research instruments (see McLeod, 1994: 97–101). How far does our non-mainstream, CA-based approach take on board such matters? Or does it represent a move away from conventional scientific standards of adequacy?

Second, given that our research is based mainly on recordings of counselling interviews, how is it able to make any claims about the wider constraints on both counselling and people's behaviour?[8]

Validity

To what extent does our research allow generalizable observations to be made? I take it that few readers have the stomach for any remaining qualitative researchers who might maintain that our only methodological imperative is to 'hang out' and to return with 'authentic' accounts of the field (but see McLeod, 1994: 101 for contrary evidence). Conversely, I argue that issues of validity and reliability are relevant to any form of social research.

We will deal first with the issue of reliability. Attempts to bypass this issue by appealing to the different ontological position of field research (e.g. Marshall and Rossman, 1989) are unconvincing. As others have pointed out:

> Qualitative researchers can no longer afford to beg the issue of reliability. While the forte of field research will always lie in its capability to sort out the validity of propositions, its results will (reasonably) go ignored minus attention to reliability. For reliability to be calculated, it is incumbent on the scientific investigator to document his or her procedure. (Kirk and Miller, 1986: 72)

Kirk and Miller suggest that the conventionalization of methods for recording fieldnotes offers a useful method for addressing the issue of reliability. However, we need only depend upon fieldnotes in the absence of audio- or video-recordings. As argued above, the availability of transcripts of such recordings, using standard conventions, satisfies Kirk and Miller's proper demand for the documentation of procedures.

Fortunately, there is no dispute that validity is a serious issue in field research. Although academic journals are still prepared to publish papers based on no more than a few carefully chosen 'examples', their authors need to further demonstrate the validity of their claims (see Bloor, 1978; Mitchell, 1983; Silverman, 1989b, 1993). So our analysis, in subsequent chapters, of, for instance, the co-production and management of potentially 'delicate' issues or of advice sequences has been developed by following the standard methods of case-study research, based upon the constant comparative method and the identification of deviant cases in order to revise and strengthen our analysis. Because these methods often involve inducing hypotheses from data, they are sometimes called 'analytic induction' (see Silverman, 1993: Ch.7).

The method of analytic induction encourages us to generate and then to test hypotheses in the course of research. Note that this method, coupled with a close attention to the local organization of the phenomenon *in situ*, means that we can be more confident that deviant cases derive their status from a comparison with knowledge of participants' routine practices rather than with idealized conceptions of those practices. The latter is a frequent concomitant of deploying hypotheses, couched in 'operational definitions' of variables, *prior to* entry into the field.

The revised analysis can subsequently be applied to tapes of counsellor–client consultations gathered at many centres, allowing for further revision. Indeed, one of the fascinating upshots of our current research is the degree of invariance that we are discovering in the local management of delicacy, using settings as apparently diverse as Britain, the USA and Trinidad (see Silverman and Bor, 1991). This reveals that the comparative method has no less a place in the detailed analysis of naturally occurring situations than in more conventional experimental, interview or life-history methods. So, contrary to the assumption of many social scientists, as well as funding bodies, validity need not be a problem in case-study research.

Having dealt with the issue of validity, we now move on to our second question. How far does a close analysis of communication in counselling allow us to go beyond to the broader behavioural and structural issues involved in the institutional contexts of talk?

Institutional contexts: how? and why?

The kind of detailed research on counselling that we call for lays itself open to the charge that it deals 'only' with talk. The implication is that, because it supposedly refuses to look beyond the talk, it is unable to offer adequate explanations of its findings.

Of course, I have already offered a critical review of this approach in our comments on the Explanatory Orthodoxy. Nonetheless, I do *not* want to suggest that it is always improper to look beyond talk-in-interaction. Instead, my position is that we are not faced with either/or choices but with issues largely of *timing*.

My assumption is that it is usually necessary to refuse to allow our research topics to be defined in terms of, say, the 'causes' of 'bad' counselling or the 'consequences' of 'good' counselling (the Explanatory Orthodoxy). Such topics merely reflect the conceptions of 'social problems' as recognized by either professional or community groups. Ironically, by beginning from a clearly defined analytical perspective, I show how we can later address such social problems with, I believe, considerable force and persuasiveness.

My argument suggests that one's initial move should be to give close attention to how participants locally produce contexts for their interaction. By beginning with this question of 'how', we can then fruitfully move on to 'why' questions about institutional and cultural constraints. Such constraints reveal the functions of apparently irrational practices and help us to understand the possibilities and limits of attempts at social reform.

Using CA, Schegloff has shown that a great deal depends on the pace at which we proceed:

> the study of talk should be allowed to proceed under its own imperatives, with the hope that its results will provide more effective tools for the analysis of distributional, institutional and social structural problems *later on* than would be the case if the analysis of talk had, from the outset, to be made answerable to problems extrinsic to it. (Schegloff, 1991: 64; my emphasis)

Quite properly, this will mean delaying what I have called 'why' questions until we have asked the appropriate 'how' questions. But how, eventually, are we to make the link between the two?

A solution is suggested in Maynard's account of medical talk discussed above. Maynard shows how paediatricians giving diagnostic information may use a 'perspective display series' where they first invite the parents' views. He then moves on to the 'why?' question, relating the 'perspective display series' to the functions of avoiding open conflict over unfavourable diagnoses. In this way, the device serves to preserve social solidarity.

So Maynard's close focus on *how* the parties locally produce patterns of communication ends up by considering the 'functions' of the forms so discovered. The lesson is clear. We cannot do everything at the same time without muddying the water. For policy reasons, as well as from conventional social science concerns, we may well want to ask what we have called 'why' questions. There is no reason not to, providing that we have first closely described how the phenomenon at hand is locally produced. If not, we are limited to an explanation of something that we have simply defined by fiat.

This means that there is nothing wrong with the search for explanations, providing that this search is grounded in a close understanding of how the phenomena being explained are 'put together' at an interactional level. So wherever possible one should seek to obtain 'naturally occurring' data in order to obtain adequate understanding, leading to soundly based policy interventions.[9] We now consider the space for such interventions based upon the type of research discussed here.

Practical interventions and CA-based counselling research

My aim has been to demonstrate a way of working with data which seeks to preserve the local production of social phenomena. Take the issue of training counsellors. The implication is that effective training begins from a close analysis of the skills of counsellors and their clients revealed in careful research rather than from normative standards of good practice.

Consider Extracts 2.1 and 2.2 discussed earlier. We noted then that the information-driven agenda found in Extract 2.2 generated minimal patient uptake. Predictably, the use of hypothetical questions and summaries by the counsellor in Extract 2.1 produced considerable patient response.

Advice sequences like those found in Extract 2.2 are very common at three out of the five centres examined here. So we have to ask ourselves why counsellors should use a format which is likely to generate so little patient uptake. However, since my preference is not to criticize professionals but to understand the logic of their work, we need to look at the *functions* as well as the dysfunctions of this way of proceeding.

The first thing we might note is that topic follows topic with a remarkable degree of smoothness and at great speed. This might indicate one function of this style of counselling. With more conventional counselling, based on extended question–answer sequences like that seen in Extract 2.1, counselling interviews average between 40 and 45 minutes. This compares to the clinic from which Extract 2.2 is taken, where pre-test counselling interviews average between 10 and 15 minutes. Truncated, non-personalized advice sequences are usually far shorter – an important consideration for hard-pressed counsellors.

Second, we can observe that, in Extract 2.2, C avoids referring directly to P but uses the non-specific term 'someone'. As argued in Chapter 6 below, this may allow P to hear what C is saying as *information* rather than advice.

This has three neat functions for C. First, it allows her to manage possibly 'delicate' topics by formulating them as 'general' information matters not necessarily relevant to this particular patient. Second, unlike a question-driven style of counselling, which can involve very complicated strategies to encourage clients to talk about 'delicate' topics (see Peräkylä, 1995), in the information delivery mode very little client participation is needed for the introduction and management of delicate topics. This also means, thirdly, that counsellors need not treat P's minimal responses as indicating resistance as they would if C were offering personalized advice.

Lest readers throw up their hands at my apparent 'support' for what may appear to them to be, in normative terms, 'bad' counselling practice, let me speedily point out that I am more than aware of the possible 'dysfunctions' of the professional-centred style of counselling seen in Extract 2.2. Not only is there no exploration of the patient's perspective, but P's minimal responses mean that C never knows how far P is aligned to her information. This lack of patient uptake fails to create an environment in which people might re-examine their own sexual behaviour (as P does in Extract 2.1).

Equally, however, apparently 'good' counselling practice, based on extensive elicitation of clients' perspectives, is fraught with interactional traps (see Peräkylä, 1995). The point is not to adopt a normative position but to examine the gains and losses of any method.

Two possible solutions suggest themselves from the data analysed by this study (see Silverman et al., 1992a): avoiding necessarily 'delicate' and unstable advice sequences but encouraging patients to draw their own conclusions from a particular line of questioning (see Extract 5.6, p. 95); and, since both this method and step-by-step advice-giving take considerable time, finding ways of making more time available for more effective counselling.

The question of 'effective' counselling and 'effective' counsellors can only be addressed in the context of the management of the interactional and practical constraints on counselling practice. There are no simple normative solutions to these constraints – although my experience running workshops for such counsellors suggests the value of these kind of detailed transcripts in in-service training provision. We take up the practical issues this raises in a further discussion of 'policy' issues at the end of this book.

Conclusion

As I noted at the start of this chapter, I share the belief that there is no right or wrong method in science, any more than there is an essentially right or wrong method of counselling (see Feltham, 1995). At some level, everything depends on what you are trying to do.

My findings, discussed in this book, arose because of the research methods used. My use of CA led to a focus on the sequential organization of talk. It also created an embargo on appeals to what participants are thinking, and concentrated instead on the pursuit of what they are doing.

CA has been used for two reasons: because it is appropriate to an understanding of the complexity of our data, and because CA has demonstrably established a fruitful dialogue with practitioners in a range of work settings (see Drew and Heritage, 1992a). In this study, CA has encouraged us to look at the local functions of people's activities in a way which I believe has a direct bearing upon policy issues. I develop these points in the chapters that follow.

Notes

1 Of course, I realize that these problems are recognized by researchers who use such research instruments. In turn, they have ingenious methods for dealing with them.

2 This suggestion was made to me by a senior physician at an AIDS unit in Sweden.

3 Anssi Peräkylä has suggested that the problem caused by the 'window period' might possibly be overcome by assembling samples from each centre large enough to carry more or less equal numbers of people who carry the virus despite having tested seronegative.

4 Extract 2.2 is discussed at length in Chapter 5 (p. 113ff.).

5 Sacks, Schegloff and Jefferson (1974) offer an Appendix which provides a detailed description of the notation they use. The interested reader is recommended to study it. An alternative source is Atkinson and Heritage (1984).

6 I have discussed the positioning of interviewees' questions in an early paper on selection interviews (Silverman, 1973). However, as Peräkylä (personal correspondence) has pointed out, Sacks's chaining rule is too general a way to speak about the role of counsellors as questioners. In fact, counsellors maintain their role as questioners in subtle, locally variable ways, rather than primarily relying on a general rule (see Peräkylä, 1995).

7 See Heritage (1984) and Silverman (1993: 133–43) for further information.

8 The argument here might be that CA's focus on talk might throw out the baby with the bathwater. This clearly relates to the issue with which this chapter concludes: what practical impact can such research have on counselling practice?

9 We often falsely assume that there is inherent difficulty in obtaining naturally occurring data in many situations, e.g. 'family life' or 'sexuality'. However, this assumption trades off a commonsense perception that these are *unitary* phenomena whose meaning is constructed in a single site (e.g. households, bedrooms). But 'family life' is going on all around us – in courtrooms and social security offices as well as households (see Gubrium, 1992). Equally, 'sexuality' is hardly confined to the bedroom; discourses of sexuality are all around us (see Foucault, 1979).

PART TWO

COMMUNICATION IN HIV COUNSELLING

This chapter introduces the concept of 'communication formats' as a way of understanding professional–client talk in HIV counselling. It shows how such talk involves a movement between an Interview Format (based on questions and answers) and an Information Delivery Format (where the counsellor delivers information and the client offers response tokens).

3

Communication Formats in HIV Counselling

In this chapter, following Peräkylä and Silverman (1991a), I shall suggest that the flow of events in an HIV counselling session can be viewed as a chain of shifts between a small number of simple sets of locally managed conversational roles of questioner, answerer, speaker and recipient. Unlike ordinary conversation, in counselling only two of these cover most of the talking done: the counsellor and the patient are respectively aligned either as the questioner and the answerer, or as the speaker and the recipient. These persistent sets of roles can be called the *interview format* and the *information delivery format*.[1]

In the Interview Format (hereafter IV) the counsellor (hereafter C) and the patient (hereafter P) are aligned as questioner and answerer. Typical examples of the Interview Format are the following:

```
Extract 3.1 (UK3)
 1  C:      Has your pa:rtner ever used a condom with you?
 2          (1.0)
 3  P:      N:o
 4          (1.5)
 5  C:      Do you know what a condom looks like?
 6          (.5)
 7  P:      (I don't.)
 8          (.3)
 9  C:      (Did you-) (.3) have you perhaps- (1.0) the condom
10          shown to you at school?=Or:?
11  P:      No:
```

```
Extract 3.2 (UK4)
 1  C:      (. . .) What you think the wo:rst thing would- (.) be:
 2          (.5) knowing your result, (.) one way or the other,
 3          (1.6)
 4  P:      Erm::
 5          (1.2)
 6  P:      Well I mean obviously (.) (if it wasn't AIDS er)
 7          (1.8)
 8  C:      um
 9  P:      that would be great (.) or:
10          (.6)
```

```
11   P:        but if it was positive I (really) don't kno:w ho:w
12             (.3)
13   C:        um:
14             (.2)
15   P:        ((sniff, cough)) I would be able to deal with
16             this.=er::
17   C:        uhm: whad you thin:k (.2) the problems would be:
18             immediately on hearing it,
19             (.2)
20   C:        jst (.6) out of curiosity?
21             (3.8)
22   P:        I don't know (        )
```

The basic structure of IV appears to be a very simple chain of questions and answers. The participants often produce long sequences of interaction where Cs act exclusively as questioners and Ps correspondingly as answerers. The production of these appears unproblematic.

The persistence of such chains draws upon two conversational rules which have been laid bare in the early work of Sacks and his followers (see Chapter 2, pp. 29–30). First, until the P has provided an answer, the C cannot go on to ask a further question. This is because question–answer sequences are 'adjacency pairs', coupled activities in which the first part creates a strong moral expectation for the second to appear (Schegloff and Sacks, 1973).[2] Second, a completed answer (particularly in a two-party conversation) gives the floor back to the questioner, who thus is free to ask a further question (Sacks, 1974).

The conversational rules entailed in the question–answer chains do not, however, *determine* the actions of the participants. Each time after having received the P's answer, the C is free to stop asking questions; and the P equally free to add components of other kinds of turns to his/her answers (see Extracts 3.8 and 3.9, pp. 47, 50). The long sequences of questions and answers are then locally and collaboratively produced by the participants, who recurrently opt to confine themselves to the roles of a questioner and an answerer.

Questions and answers serve a variety of interactional purposes in the counselling sessions. In Extract 3.1 above, they were used to convey factual information from P to C; and in Extract 3.2, the C used the questions for enhancing exploration and expression of P's fears and beliefs. This has a bearing on the design of questions and answers: in Extract 3.1, they are unequivocal and short; and in Extract 3.2 longer and more vague (cf. Heritage, 1984: 180–90).

In information delivery (hereafter ID), the C has the role of the speaker and the P confines him/herself to recipiency. Apart from factual information, the Cs sometimes deliver advice to the Ps through this format. We see the asymmetric division of labour of the ID format clearly in the following excerpt, where the C tells the patient about the implications of a positive result.

Extract 3.3 (UK1)

```
 1  C:      now we're getting heterosexual (.)
 2          [transmission as well. .hh Uhm=
 3  P:      [Mm hm
 4  C:      =so obviously everyone really needs to careful. .hhh
 5          Now whe- when someone gets a positive test result
 6          er: then obviously they're going to ke- think very
 7          carefully about things. .hhhh Being HIV positive
 8          doesn't necessarily mean that that person is going
 9          to develop ai:ds (.) later on.
10          (.)
11  P:      Mm hm
12  C:      Some people seem to be able to sta:y (.) fit and
13          healthy, (.) although obviously they're carriers and
14          can still infect others. (.) .hhh We can't te:ll you
15          know who's going to become ill and who isn't.
16  P:      [Mm hm
17  C:      [.hhh But the advice we give really is commonsense
18          if you think about it. .hh What we try and do is
19          keep them as healthy as possible.=So it means .h a
20          well balanced diet, plenty of exercise,=a good
21          night's sleep each night,=and all the things that we
22          should do normally to keep us healthy.
23  P:      Mm hm
24  C:      .hhh .hhh Also of course they need to be into safer
25          se:x,=and that's really ((continues))
```

In ordinary conversations, if one party takes a long turn, stretching beyond the ordinary boundaries of turns of talk (called 'turn construction units' by Sacks et al., 1974), he or she usually engages in specific activities in order to hold the floor. For instance, a 'story preface' announces that the current speaker wants to produce an extended turn of talk. The co-participants, correspondingly, are expected to display their agreement in the production of such a turn by producing 'continuers'. These are small response tokens usually taking the form of 'hm-mm', 'yes', or the like which appear close to the potential slots of change in speakership. The continuers do the work of passing an opportunity to produce a full turn of talk, thus giving 'permission' for the current speaker to continue; through passing the occasions for recipient-initiated repairs, they also claim that the talk has been satisfactorily understood (Schegloff, 1981).

In counselling sessions, the production of multi-unit turn seems to be less problematic than in ordinary conversation. Although it may appear that the Cs could talk almost indefinitely, while the Ps remained silent, a closer examination, however, shows that a collaboration of both parties was needed to achieve such long turns.

In Extract 3.3 above, the C does not produce a proper equivalent of a 'story preface'. However, she begins the new topic (lines 5–7) with a general and open-ended gloss 'Now whe- when someone gets a positive test result er: then obviously they're going to ke- think very carefully about things'. This seems to be a particularly recipient-oriented utterance, which perhaps is designed to motivate the P to attend to the coming information. Neither does the P pass the opportunity to get the floor by producing continuers in every possible turn-completion point. Nevertheless, her continuers appear between two or three turn-completion points. This is a part of P's contribution to the maintenance of the ID format.

Apart from an open-ended, recipient-oriented gloss, two devices for retaining the floor in a multi-unit turn seem to recur in C's talk. One of them is numbering the items that are going to be produced:

```
        Extract 3.4 (UK1)
 1  C:      As far as sex is concerne:d, it means: keeping to
 2          the safer sex guidelines.
 3  P:      U[mh
 4  C:       [For two reasons.     .hh Firstly: (.5) to try and
 5          prevent them passing it on to anyone else:?=
 6  P:      =uh-hum
 7  C:      A:nd (.) and secondly: because really they can't
 8          afford to catch:: (you know) some of the other
 9          sexually transmitted diseases that are around.
10  P:      Yeah. (Why) (          [     )]
11  C:                             [A:nd ] (.2) and basically it
12          means either sticking to:: noninsertive sex, like
13          mutual masturbation? (.3) an::d (.3) massage.=That
14          kind of thing? .hh[hhhh Or=
15  P:                        [umh
16  C:      =else if they do::-
        ((Information delivery continues))
```

In Extract 3.4, the C embeds in her multi-unit turn a device for retaining the floor, the numbered list ('firstly' and 'secondly'). The numbering covers the information delivery until line 9. Correspondingly, the P seems to orient to the end of the list in line 10 by a response which seems to entail a move out from mere recipiency. The C, however, continues the information delivery, and as the P re-aligns himself as the recipient through his continuer in line 15, the format has been re-instituted.

An information check also serves as a method for retaining the floor during Information Delivery. We see this method used below in an extract from the same interview:

```
        Extract 3.5 (UK1)
 1  C:      .hhh How much do you know about the (.) test itself.
 2          (1.0)
 3  P:      Other than it's a blood test, I really don't know
```

```
4                    anything else:.
5      C:            Right. .hh (.2) What it is it's an- (.2) antibody
6                    test.
7      P:            Oh: (.2) right (ye).
8      C:            .hh Now from:: (.2) the time::? (.2) someone's
9                    infected,
                     ((information-delivery continues))
```

The beauty of this information check is that it sets up the ID format as implicitly requested by the P (who lacks the information). As the information delivery then begins (from line 5 onwards), the P responds accordingly. His turn in line 7 ('Oh: (.2) right (ye)') bears the typical characteristics of a 'change of state token' (Heritage, 1984), proposing that the preceding talk has been informative for the respondent.[3] The information check seems to have immediately motivated the P to display an especially active recipiency.

We can conclude that even though the ID format seems to be a very C-centred form of talk, nevertheless maintaining it and sometimes also setting it up seems to be a joint achievement of both participants. Whether or not the counsellors use specific devices like numbering and information checks, the patients regularly withhold their own turn initiations, confining themselves to the production of continuers and other response items.

Departures from the communication formats

Interview and Information Delivery are the stable and persistent formats in counselling sessions. In multiple ways, both Cs and Ps seem to orient collaboratively to these formats throughout the counselling sessions. However, the patients and the counsellors occasionally also step outside the stable formats. The possibility of this was hinted at in Extract 3.4 above, where the P's response to the completion of the C's list of items indicated more than mere recipiency. In that time, however, the slight misalignment didn't lead to a full departure from the format.

There are two main types of departure from recurrent communication formats: (1) questions intiated by the patient, and (2) conversational contributions from the patient. In the following, we shall examine how the participants collaboratively restore the stable formats after such departures.

The questions asked by the patient create a footing that is a mirror image of the interview format. Now their roles as questioner and answerer are reversed. This footing can be achieved in two ways: either the C offers the P an opportunity to ask questions, or the P volunteers one.

By offering a 'question time', the counsellor can provide the space for the patient's questions. In the majority of cases, the Ps respond to such offers by reporting that they have no questions; in Extract 3.6, however, one does emerge.

```
        Extract 3.6 (UK1)
  1   C:        er: Is there anything you want to ask?
  2             (0.2)
  3   C:        (  [                    )
  4   P:           [er: Well (it's just a- a theoretical question
  5             actually wu-) (0.2) straightforward kissing and things
  6             like that would [that
  7   C:                         [That's fi:ne.
  8   P:        That's [fine.
  9   C:               [Yea:h.
```

The offering of a question time in itself contributes to the constitution of P's questions as departures from ordinary communication formats. It marks P's questions as an exceptional phase in the consultation, thus orienting to and reproducing an expectation that outside the 'question time', questions usually do not appear. This marginalization of 'question time' is further confirmed through its location in the overall structure of the consultation: as a rule, it occurs in connection with the closing either of a topic or of the whole consultation.

While 'question time' preserves the core of the C's footing as the initiatory party of the interaction, the P's volunteered questions constitute a more serious break away from it. Now the P unilaterally initiates an action that projects the C's performance in the subsequent turn. However, the participants as a rule quickly allow the initiatory role to pass back to the counsellor. We see this in Extract 3.7.

```
        Extract 3.7 (UK4)
  1   C:        = infectious it's (.) it's not really a lot (  )
  2             because we still got to-
  3             (.5)
  4   P:        Y[es
  5   C:         [really a[ct as if they're infectious all =
  6   P:                  [sure
  7   C:        = the ti:me.
  8             (.5)
  9   P:        What kind of treatment do you give after (.2) afte-
 10             (.5) after you been diagnosed positive,
 11             (1.6)
 12   C:        It's mainly: emotional suppo:rt.
 13   P:        Uhu?
 14   C:        Erm::: (.2) we've got various support groups
 15             available if people want them,
 16             (.7)
 17             (and then there's) (.3) counselling.
 18   P:        uhu?=
 19   C:        = medically: (.5) we offer them regular
 20             check-ups: ((continues))
```

Extract 3.7 is a typical instance of a P's question as regards the length of the sequence. Usually, this alignment persists no longer than one or two question–answer adjacency pairs (cf. West, 1983). The brevity of the sequences, however, is not imposed upon the P by the C, but is accomplished collaboratively by both participants.

In Extract 3.7 above, both the adoption and abandonment of P's role as a questioner are jointly achieved. The P's questions are anticipated by her response tokens 'Yes' and 'sure' in lines 4 and 6. They are more 'active' response tokens than the ordinary continuers, which usually take the form of 'uhu' or 'uh-hum', or the like. 'Sure' in line 6 is also located elsewhere than in a potential slot of speakership. According to Jefferson (1984), these kind of 'active' response tokens may convey their producer's intention to gain speakership. C seems to analyse the response tokens this way, as she allows a gap to emerge in line 8. Using the space thus opened, in line 9, P enters with a question.

After the C has begun the answer to the question in line 12, P aligns as a recipient through the continuer 'Uhu?' (line 13).[4] In line 14, while continuing her answer, C hesitates and pauses ('Erm::: (.2)') at the beginning of her turn. This would have allowed the P to produce a further question should she have chosen to do so. P, however, remains aligned as the recipient; and correspondingly, C continues her turn. Along with this, Information Delivery is seamlessly re-instituted as the basic format.

Another form of departure from the recurring formats is a conversational contribution from the patient. This is the mirror image of Information Delivery: now the P is speaker and the C is recipient. Instances of this are even more rare than those of P's questions. Also these sequences tend to be very short-lived. Moreover, the participants regularly maintain at least a minimal orientation to the stable formats throughout the patient's conversational contribution, thus making it typically an ambiguous footing.

In Extract 3.8, P produces his reflections about the possible development of a cure for HIV:

```
        Extract 3.8 (UK4)
  1   C:      (. . .) But do you know how it's not transferred.
  2           (.5)
  3   P:      No idea.
  4           (.7)
  5   C:      I mean do you think perhaps you could possibly get
  6           it fro:m touching other people:
  7           or[:
  8   P:        [We:ll [a t-  a t-  a t-
  9   C:               [drinking out of the same cup.
 10   P:      at this moment in time the doctors are- are really
 11           er just ser- er fumbling aren't they really.=They
 12           come out with different things .h about H uh about
 13           the ai- the aid thi:ng. .hh er I-I think it'll be a
```

14		number- a number of years before they ever (.) ever
15		cure it.=It maybe a hundred years' ti:me or even
16		[more:.
17	C:	[Right.
18		(.8)
19	P:	er I don't think that they'll even do it-(.5) it
20		must take at least a- (it may be over) a hundred
21		years' time. But .h I don't think they'll actually
22		cure it.=They'll probably prolong people's li:fe
23		actually. .hh er (.4) In er some sort of way.
24	C:	.hhh Right.
25		(1.0)
26	C:	So we've said about that.=Also from m-mum (.) to
27		baby:, sometimes in the-
28		the [( ) at birth it could be=
29	P:	[Yeah:
30	C:	=transferred because ((information delivery
31		continues))

In Extract 3.8, the participants begin in an Interview Format; the C is engaged in pedagogical questioning about the transmission of the HIV virus. From line 8 onwards, however, the P gradually abandons the role of an answerer. Notably, however, throughout the P's turn of talk, an orientation to the interview format is maintained.

The P begins his turn in lines 8 and 10 as a response to C's question. The location of the turn, then, is that of a latter part of a question–answer adjacency pair. However, the propositional content of the P's turn is unrelated to the question: instead of reporting his own views (solicited by the C), the P describes doctors as 'fumbling'. The P, then, exploits the sequential location of an answer turn in IV format to produce a statement of his own.

Nonetheless, the tag-question 'aren't they really' after the first part of the P's turn (line 11) still displays an orientation to the initial pedagogical use of an interview format. So the P offers his views to the C to be confirmed. But after the tag-question, the P makes a hurried beginning into the next unit of his turn ('(. . .) aren't they really.=They come (. . .)'), thus not allowing a gap to emerge for C's confirmation. From line 13 onwards, the P introduces still more topical material of his own.

The C's response to this statement of the patient seems to be equivocal. On the one hand, through withholding the production of talk of her own, and by producing two response tokens ('Right' in lines 17 and 24), she aligns as a recipient of P's statement. On the other hand, the design of the response tokens makes them hearable as confirmations of P's views rather than as mere continuers. By designing her response in this way, she implicitly maintains her role as knowledgeable specialist rather than as mere co-conversationalist, thus extending the preceding footing where she did the pedagogical questioning.

C's alignment as a recipient of P's statement can then be said to be implicitly reluctant. However, she does not force the P to abandon his footing as the speaker. Most importantly, after both of her 'rights', she allows gaps to emerge (lines 18 and 25), thus giving the P an opportunity to continue. After the first gap, P produces further talk, and after the second, he fails to do that. Only thereafter, does C take the floor. Again, then, far from being imposed upon the P, information delivery is collaboratively re-instituted.

Having given examples of each format and departures from them, we are now in a position to summarize some of their features. The two stable formats have at least two features in common regarding the local identities they allocate to the participants. First, in both of them the C is in an *initiatory* role and the P in a *responsive* one (cf. Greatbatch, 1988). The Cs initiate the actions which project an adequate next action by the Ps.[5] This also entails control of the topical focusing and the opening and the closing of the consultation. Second, in both stable formats, the C is allocated a *knowledgeable* identity. In information delivery, this is realized in the production of specialist knowledge; and in interview, it means a warrant to ask questions and sometimes to evaluate the answers.[6]

The departures from the formats entail a shift in these identities. P's questions and conversational contributions shift the initiatory role to the patient; volunteered questions occur to a greater extent than those asked in a question time. P's questions nevertheless usually maintain the knowledge-ability of the C, unlike the P's unelicited conversational contribution, which can also undermine this.

Given this format structure, the remainder of this chapter is devoted to the address of two questions:

How are the formats deployed in practice, i.e. in what sequence and in what patterns?
What may explain the persistence of certain patterns?

In order to concretize the discussion, we take as examples two topics that are covered in most HIV counselling. One is sexual beliefs and practices, often related to discussion of less risky, or 'safer', sex. The other is the prospects for the future of the patient if he or she is seropositive. Following Miller and Bor (1988), I refer to this second topic as 'dreaded issues'.

The deployment of formats: sexuality

At the beginning of pre-test counselling in all centres, talk about sexual matters occurs by the P providing answers to questions asked by the C:

```
     Extract 3.9 (UK1)
1  C:      Right. hh .hhh (.) Erm: (0.5) You've come just for
2          an HIV te:[st.
3  P:               [uh-hum.
```

```
 4   C:      .hhh (.4) Can I just ask you briefly:: (.2) erm: one
 5           or two questions before we start. .hh Have you ever
 6           had a test before,
 7   P:      N:o.
 8   C:      No. .hhh Have you ever injected drugs:?
 9   P:      No.
10           (2.0)
11   C:      Have you ever had a homosexual relationship?
12           (.5)
13   P:      No.
14           (.5)
15   P:      And that's not really- (.5) (I mean) (.2) put me in
16           a high risk group h[as it.
17   C:                         [hnoh
18   C:      No it doesn't.
```

Extract 3.9 begins with the C setting up an Interview Format where the P delivers answers to a series of questions. However, the P's final answer tacks on a question which reverses the roles of questioner and answerer. So there is a temporary departure from the format – but a departure which maintains the knowledgeability of the counsellor.

What seems to be happening at the start of this extract is a communication pattern modelled on a medical history-taking. Although Cs are not specifically concerned with diagnosis, the use of an IV format at this stage is probably a useful way for the C to assess the P's sense of their risks and so to tailor the later discussion to the P's individual needs and fears.

After this initial use of an IV format, Cs differ widely in the communication format which they use to discuss sexual behaviour. In most centres, quite early in the consultation, Cs use another format to discuss safer sex: information delivery. We have seen an example of this in Extract 3.4, which is reproduced below.

```
     Extract 3.4 (UK1)
 1   C:      As far as sex is concerne:d, it means: keeping to the
 2           safer sex guidelines.
 3   P:      U[mh
 4   C:        [For two reasons.    .hh Firstly: (.5) to try and
 5           prevent them passing it on to anyone else:?=
 6   P:      =uh-hum
 7   C:      A:nd (.) and secondly: because really they can't
 8           afford to catch:: (you know) some of the other
 9           sexually transmitted diseases that are around.
10   P:      Yeah. (Why) (          [    )]
11   C:                            [A:nd ] (.2) and basically it
12           means either sticking to:: noninsertive sex, like
13           mutual masturbation? (.3) an::d (.3) massage.=That
14           kind of thing? .hh[hhhh Or=
```

```
15  P:                    [umh
16  C:        =else if they do::- (.3) you know carry on having
17            full sex: (.2) to use a condom,
18  P:        U[mh
19  C:         [preferably with a spermicidal back-up as well.
20  P:        (Umh)
```

Here the C delivers a package of information to the P about safer sex. At this stage of pre-test counselling, almost identical packages are used with other Ps attending this centre. This seems to happen because Cs do not pursue an interview format in order to establish each P's own beliefs and practices regarding 'safer sex'. By contrast, the information delivery format used at this early stage makes the P a passive recipient of generalized information. P shows his attendance to the format by a few monosyllabic response tokens (e.g. lines 3 and 6). However, the completion of the C's two-part list (line 9) may mean that ID format no longer applies. At this point, the P seems to attempt to gain a more initiatory footing (line 10) but the C persists in ID (line 11 ff.) and the P produces the appropriate response-tokens.

A second pattern involves the C staying in the IV format to discuss sexuality. An example of this is given in Extract 3.10.

```
      Extract 3.10 (UK4)
 1  C:        What do you understand about your own- (.5) risks
 2            for HIV=
 3  P:        =.hhh Well- (.2) hhh (.2) I suppo:se, (.2) I'm in
 4            (.3) one of the high risk categories,=because I've
 5            had a lot of partners. .hhh I don't know call a
 6            lot.=Certainly I've had over a hundred. :hhh Erm::
 7            (1.0) (        ) this is I think why- (.2) the
 8            doctor said it perhaps would be a good idea, .hh
 9            because of that.
10            (1.0)
11  P:        Because it does put me into a:- (.3) the high risk
12            category.
13            (.7)
14  C:        .hh Right. (.4) When you've had intercourse with
15            these partners, have you (.) used any kind of
16            protection at all?=
17  P:        =I have in the last two years. (.4) Erm: (1.2)
18            Certainly I haven't had unprotected sex:: for the
19            last (.) two years.
20  C:        So what have you been doing for the last two
21            ye:ars,=
22  P:        =Always used condoms.
23            (.6)
24  C:        Right. .hh Do you use anything
25            else (  [              ) use a cap as well?=
```

```
26   P:              [No
27   C:       =or (   ) use spermicide or?
28   P:       No.
29            (.2)
30   (?):     .hh
31   C:       (That can) sometimes that can increase the-
32   P:       Um[h
33   C:          [protection, because: as you know condoms aren't-
34   P:       Yeah
35   C:       necessarily hundred percent safe (   [       )
36   P:                                          ([Allright) (.2) I
37            accept that.
38            (.5)
39   P:       No.
40            (.6)
41   P:       [Just condoms.]
42   C:       [(              )] (From the point of) pregnancy:
43            (.4)
44   P:       Umh.
45            (.5)
46   P:       No as it happens my last two regular (.5)
47            girlfriends (1.0) erm: (.3) neither of them were on
48            the pill,
49            (1.5)
50   P:       Erm: (.4) but I'd (.2) I'd use-d a condom anyway.
51   C:       Yes sure right, the pill [(      ) wouldn't=
52   P:                                [Umh
53   C:       =protect you against HIV at all. .hhh=
54   P:       =No.
55   C:       Right. (.2) .hh What made you think abou:t- (.3)
56            starting to use a-a condom,=couple of years ago,
```

The extract begins in the IV format with a question that is asked at early stages of pre-test counselling in all centres participating in the study. However, in most centres Cs treat the P's answer about sense of 'risk' as relevant to history-taking and speedily move into information delivery. Here, on the other hand, the C stays in an IV format by asking the P to unpack his initial answers. A certain amount of information is conveyed by the C (about other forms of protection than condoms) but this is tailored to the P's answers and also serves to explain the rationale behind the C's questions. The extract concludes with the C using the IV format to encourage the P to talk about what has influenced his behaviour in regard to condom use.

Interestingly, in lines 36–38 and 46–50, the P responds to the C's information delivery with turns that are hearable as the rephrasing and expansion of his initial short answer (in line 28) to C's question about uses of additional means of protection. In other words, he maintains an orientation to the Interview format, while the C inserts information into the sequence.

These two patterns are depicted schematically in Figure 3.1.

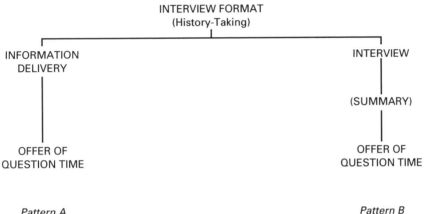

Figure 3.1   *Two ways of discussing sexuality*

It ought to be stressed that Figure 3.1 presents ideal-types of the patterns we have found at different centres. For instance, Extract 3.9 showed a P intiating a question during a history-taking interview sequence; equally, in Extract 3.10 beginning in line 31, the C switches out of an Interview format into information delivery only to return to an Interview format at the end of the extract. Put at its strongest, what we are talking about here is only what appears to be C's *preferred* formats for discussing sexuality. Another way of putting this is to say that we have identified different *home-base formats*.

The deployment of formats: dreaded issues

The introduction of 'dreaded issues' usually does not happen at the beginning of the session but only later on. There seem to be two distinctively different ways to initiate this topic. One is based on Information Delivery, and the other on interview. In the former type of introduction, the shift in footing may take place either *before* the topic shift (so that ID has been set up already when the 'dreaded issues' are introduced) or alternatively *simultaneously* with the topic shift. Extract 3.11 provides an example of the latter kind of introduction.

        Extract 3.11 (UK4)
    1   C: Erm: (.3) do: you know, (.6) er: Betty (.) if: any
    2   of your sexual pa:rtners have been bi:sexual,
    3   (1.0)

```
 4  P:      *No [no: I don't know*
 5  C:           [No
 6           (1.9)
 7  C:      Ri:ght.
 8           (1.1)
 9  C:      .hhhh
10           (1.0)
11  C:      We ha:ve
12           (1.2)
13  C:      a fe:w people: or a nucleus of people that we:
14           kn:ow: (.2) are carrying (.5) the HIV virus.
15           (.2)
16  C:      .hhhh we:'ve found antibodies (.2) in their blood,
17           (.4) now most of them are fit and well. (.6) And
18           they look like you and me: and the're about to:
19           their normal jo:b. (.2) ((continues))
```

At line 11 here we see a shift of topic as well as a shift of format. At the beginning of the extract, the participants are talking about the P's sexual history using the IV format; the end of it addresses 'dreaded issues' using the ID format.

The other recurrent type of introduction to 'dreaded issues' employs the IV format. Here, too, the format can be set up either simultaneously with the topic shift or before it. Extract 3.2 is one of the cases where setting up the IV and the topic shift coincide.

```
        Extract 3.2 (UK4) [E4.26] (Extension)
 1  C:      .hhh So I think that that (.4) that is changed
 2           slightly:,=and I- (.2) perhaps: (.3) give you the
 3           impression that (you) should have a test, (.) and
 4           I'm not (.) sure that that should be though advised.
 5           (.) Because I'm not sure (whether it's) right or
 6           wrong.=But I think just- (.2) so tha:t have that
 7           idea: (      ). .hhh What you think the wo:rst thing
 8           would- (.) be: (.5) knowing your result, (.) one way
 9           or the other,
10           (1.6)
11  P:      Erm::
12           (1.2)
13  P:      Well I mean obviously (.) (if it wasn't AIDS er-)
14           (1.8)
15  C:      *um*
16  P:      that would be great (.) or:
17           (.6)
18  P:      but if it was positive I (really) don't kno:w ho:w
19           (.3)
20  C:      um:
```

```
21                    (.2)
22    P:              ((sniff, cough)) I would be able to deal with
23                    this.=er::
20    C:              uhm: whad you thin:k (.2) the problems would be:
21                    immediately on hearing it,
22                    (.2)
23    C:              jst (.6) out of curiosity?
24                    (3.8)
25    P:              I don't know (        )
26                    (1.0)
27    P:              [how its gonna- (.8) affect my life?(.) or
28    C:              [*uhum*
29                    (.3)
30    C:              Ho- how do you 'ma:gine that does affect people's:
31                    live:s.=From what you know.
32                    (4.0)
33    P:              I suppose it (might) just make you
34                    (3.0)
35    P:              just be a little bit mo:re
36                    (.4)
37    P:              aware of
38                    (.8)
39    P:              .hhh dying an:d
40                    (1.0)
41    P:              the way of dying,=you know I mean
42                    (.6)
43    P:              how you die.
44                    (.3)
45    C:              Wh- whad it is abo:ut ho:w one dies that- (.6) that
46                    might be a problem,
47                    (.7)
48    P:              Just becomi:ng:: dependent on somebody::
49                    ((continues))
```

From line 7 onwards, we can observe a simultaneous change of format and initiation of new issues. Before that point, the C has been delivering information about the recent developments in medical care for HIV/AIDS. He concludes his ID with a formulation of his preceding talk, emphasizing that in spite of his optimism about medicine, he is not trying to persuade the patient into having a test. Thereafter we see the shift into IV format, and simultaneously an introduction of the issues about the frightening aspects of knowing one's result. C's questions challenge the P to unpack his initial answers; and soon the participants end up talking about death and dying.

The two different entrances into 'dreaded issues' usually do not lead into further shifts in formats. In other words, the whole sequence of 'dreaded issues' is often completed while staying in one format, either ID or IV. There are, however, typical 'appendices' to both of these formats: the sequence beginning with ID may be completed by an offer of question time, and the one beginning in IV may be completed by information delivery. These complementary formats typically appear at the end of the sequence.

In sum, then, an obvious preference for two alternative formats is clearly observable in counselling sessions. The participants use either information delivery or interview as their home-base formats. This distinction is most clearly observable in the initiation of the topic.

The functionality of each format

We have found that either the Interview or Information Delivery format works as the home base in HIV/AIDS counselling activities, at the expense of other forms of alignment. The final analytical task is to explain this: why do the participants end up preferring these particular formats?

The excerpts analysed above display the collaborative character of setting up and maintaining different formats. Even though departures from them are quite rare, these alternative forms of interaction cannot be said to be normatively sanctioned. Unlike formal institutional settings, no orientation to externally given social norms regarding proper C or P behaviour is visible (cf. Heritage and Greatbatch, 1991). The participants simply, locally and collaboratively, avoid certain forms of interaction and choose others.

In order to find an explanation for this, we have to turn to more traditional ethnographic concerns. Rather than offering new ethnographic research results, I will consider hypothetical explanations for the observations made in the sequential analysis presented above, using ethnographic as well as CA studies of medical settings.

As a rule, in professional–client exchanges, clients expect professionals to command a specialized body of knowledge and, based on experience of many 'cases', to have a clear sense of the purposes of the encounter. We should not be surprised, therefore, when we find that the two stable formats – through allocating the C the initiatory role and the knowledgeable identity – put the professional firmly in control (cf. Parsons, 1951; Jefferson and Lee, 1981).

Here we should be careful not to rush to the assumption that every case of professional control, all things being equal, is evidence of coercive professional imperialism (Waitzkin, 1979). Indeed, there is persuasive evidence that, where such professional control is absent, the net result is *not* client empowerment but client *confusion* (Hughes, 1982; Jefferson and Lee, 1981; Baldock and Prior, 1981).

However, we must not generalize about all cases of professional–client encounters. Looking only at health-care settings, we are likely to find variation in the predominant communication formats used. Where the client's problem is not known in advance, for instance, we are likely to find that the patient's questions dominate in the early stages of the consultation.

An example of this pattern would be a general practice interview. Conversely, where Ps are referred to hospital specialists with specific problems, we might expect the consultation to be more focused and the Interview format to be adopted at the start.

Of course, other factors are also relevant to which formats are favoured. We may take three examples from my own research (Silverman, 1987).

1 the stage of treatment (more experienced Ps initiate more questions);
2 the nature of the condition (for instance cosmetic surgery demands the use of formats giving the P an opportunity to speak);
3 the mode of payment for the service (fee-for-service medicine is, on the whole, far more favourable for P's questions and conversational contributions than state-provided medicine: see ibid.: 104–33).

Counselling around the antibody test in British National Health Service medicine fits all the criteria which encourage the predominant use of the professionally structured interview and information delivery formats. Ps testing for the first time are inexperienced, concerned about a condition that is unlikely to have manifested itself in any perceptible symptoms and reliant on whatever time the centre allocates for each consultation. Moreover, the agenda of professionals is more delimited than in many other medical or para-medical consultations. The C has a huge agenda of topics to cover (including the nature of HIV, what is safer sex, insurance, and who to tell) in order for the P to be able to give informed consent to the test (see Chapters 1 and 10).

All HIV counselling (including that with people who have tested positive) involves talking about sex, illness and death. Introducing and addressing such 'delicate' topics which are usually avoided or approached only very carefully (cf. Jefferson, 1985) seems to be easier if the C is in control of the agenda (see Chapter 4 below).

I suggest, therefore, that the character of HIV counselling as a focused conversation on mostly delicate topics explains why the two professionally structured formats predominate in our transcripts. Clearly, each, in its own way, is functional for the achievement of the task at hand.

These ethnographic observations are based on the British data. Different conditions seem to arise in US counselling: in particular, the common absence of one-to-one pre-test counselling and the presence of usually more highly informed client-populations. However, even in a US gay men's health clinic, the professionally structured ID and IV formats turn out to be the most stable.

One US interview from this clinic will have to serve to illustrate this point.[7] Extract 3.12 below is taken from a post-test counselling interview:

```
Extract 3.12 (US1)
1  C:     Okay. So you probably know that there are a few
2         things that er: (0.2) we need to go over here
3         obviously I want to (0.2) give you your test results
```

```
 4           [and then
 5  P:       [O k a : y.
 6  C:       talk about what those results (.) mean for you:.
 7  P:       Okay.
 8  C:       Individually and (0.2) answer any questions.
 9  P:       Okay.
10  C:       That you might have so: (0.5) where would you like
11           to begi:n.
12  P:       .hhhh U::hm hhhhhuh .hhh well I was negative last
13           time. I'm hoping I'm still negative. U:hm (.) as I
14           don't believe I've (0.3) done anything (0.4) that
15           would put me at risk in the last year,
16           [.hhhh My main concern has bee:n I read so many=
17  C:       [Mm hm
18  P:       =different thi:ngs,=some people say it can be eight
19           to ten year:s before it shows u:p and things like
20           that and of course eight to ten years ago: (0.4) you
21           know things were different. [You know=
22  C:                                   [Mm hm
23  P:       =the last few year:s .hhh 'a' I have not had any
24           relationships a:nd 'b': (0.7) er: (.) anything that
25           I have done has been safe.
26  C:       Mm hm=
27  P:       =So: (   [   )
28  C:                [Mm hm
29  C:       So as far as the past couple of years are
30           [concerned you feel like you've been at minimal=
31  P:       [Oh yeah.
32  C:       =risk [and-
33  P:             [Minimal risk. [Yeah absolutely=
```

At first sight, Extract 3.12 may look different from our earlier extracts taken from British pre-test counselling. In particular, we might note how C offers P an opportunity to set his own agenda at lines 10–11 which P uses to introduce several new topics. However, like 'question time', as already noted, this agenda offer preserves the core of C's footing as the initiatory party. First, note how the offer is preceded by C's statement of his own agenda.[8] Second, while mentioning his 'hopes' about his test result (lines 12–13), P does not directly ask for his result to be given immediately.

The closest that P gets to asking for his test result is when, after completing his review of his past sexual behaviour, he says 'So:' (line 27) which might be heard as implicative of the telling of some upshot by C. Now, in fact, C does not deliver P's test result but returns to an IV format to ask a question about P's account of his past behaviour. We thus have here precisely the features found in the British data, with both parties constituting C as holding the initiatory position.

Conclusion

In a paradoxical way, then, our observations about the recurrent patterns of talk in counselling sessions tell us about the *flexibility* of the conversational machinery. Given certain circumstances, the conversationalists can shape their interaction to follow patterns that are remarkably more uniform than those found in casual conversation. This uniformity is reached using the same tools as applied in the ordinary conversation. Moreover, the uniformity of the interaction can take distinctly different shapes: in some clinics the counselling practices favour one format, and in others, another format.

The particular character of 'counselling' as an institutionalized speech event entails much more than the specific application of the turn-taking machinery examined in this chapter. Most notably, acting as a 'counsellor' or as a 'patient' seems to be related to the organization of talk about 'delicate matters' (see Chapter 4). However, the consistent use of the stable communication formats appears to be a central precondition for achieving these more specific 'counselling' tasks.

The fact that either format may be used as a home base suggests that we need to examine the more specific functions each serves. The interview format has the major advantage that, because of the nature of question–answer adjacency pairs, Ps are required to speak. This is particularly important concerning topics like safer sex or the medical aspects of HIV and the HIV test. As all research shows (see Nelkin, 1987; Aggleton, 1989), the lack of impact of information alone on behavioural change suggests that to rely solely upon the use of an information delivery format for the discussion of safer sex is probably inadequate. Regarding talk about 'dreaded issues', the benefit of the interview format is that it gives the P an opportunity to express his or her own concerns and fears about the future.

In comparison with the interview, the information delivery format is far less complicated for the C. Although multi-unit turns of information delivery are a joint achievement, the contribution required from the P is of a smaller scale than in an Interview Format. This has two advantages for the hard-pressed C: the C can deliver pre-designed information packages without much reflection, and a similar range of issues can be covered in a shorter period of time.

However, much depends on the sequence in which formats are placed. In our material, Cs using the interview format to discuss safer sex do quite often also offer Ps their own views on the topic. But that happens only after a long sequence of questions and answers and is grounded on the P's own account of what they are thinking and doing. This suggests that favouring an interview format is not incompatible with giving the P the latest expert information – indeed it is highly compatible with delivering that information in a way specifically designed for its recipient, following a long question–answer sequence in the interview format.

This illustrates how we can readily move from analytic to practical concerns. The concept of communication format has allowed us to understand better the turn-taking procedures in a non-formal institutional setting. By so doing, it offers the possibility of responding to calls for an evaluation of counselling (see Carballo and Miller, 1989; Bor, 1989; Peterman and Curran, 1986; Green, 1989) in a conceptually based and rigorous manner.[9]

Using transcripts of actual counselling interviews, we have been able to describe how talk moves between formats and to suggest some tentative explanations of the stability and functionality of two home-base formats. By analysing comparative material from different centres and countries, such research hopefully can contribute to a soundly based evaluation of professional practice.

Notes

1 The notion of communication format represents one aspect of what Goffman (1974, 1981) called footing: 'A change in footing implies a change in the alignment we take up to ourselves and the others present expressed in the way we manage the production or reception of an utterance' (Goffman, 1981: 128).

2 I exclude the issue of 'insertion sequences': see Goffman, 1981; Merritt, 1976.

3 The pause between 'Oh:' and 'right' could perhaps also convey understanding difficulties. That interpretation, however, seems not to be the one that C makes of P's response.

4 The rising intonation at the end of 'uhu?' could perhaps encourage the analyst and the other interactant to treat it as a question token rather than a mere continuer. This patient, however, used the same token with the same intonation throughout the interview; mostly in contexts where it was obviously no more than a continuer.

5 C's initiatory footing is strongest in the Interview format, where C's questions project P's answers. In information delivery, C's assertions project recipient activity from the P, entailing a somewhat weaker initiatory position of the C. Similarly, P's initiatory footing is stronger in unelicited questions than in P's conversational contributions.

6 Asking questions, e.g. in the context of a diagnostic interview, of course also entails lack of knowledge: the P knows his/her sexual history, and information is transferred to the C. But C's questions nevertheless are *questions asked by a specialist*. A long sequence of questions creates and maintains an expectation of 'a reason for' the questions, which is something the C *knows*. Moreover, the C's knowledgeability as a questioner is displayed through the lack of 'change of state tokens' (Heritage, 1984) when receiving the answers (see Extracts 3.1 and 3.2).

7 This extract is discussed, in relation to different issues, in Chapter 5 below.

8 The preface to the agenda offer here may create confusion about what kind of P reply is appropriate.

9 Successful workshops using these materials have been held with AIDS counsellors from England, the USA and Trinidad and Tobago. The close attention to the analysis of transcripts of actual counselling episodes was found to offer insights largely unavailable in normative models of counselling.

PART THREE
DELICATE DISCUSSIONS

In Part 3, we look at the way in which HIV counsellors and their clients treat certain matters as 'delicate'. We see that the marking and management of such matters can be viewed less as a matter of individual 'embarrassment' and more as a co-operative, social organized accomplishment. Chapter 4 applies this perspective to the elicitation of clients' sexual histories, while in Chapter 5 we focus on the causes and consequences of delaying the delivery of the HIV test result. Both chapters show how cautiousness is a major feature of HIV counselling.

4

The Construction of 'Delicate' Objects in Counselling

> although lots of people figure that experience is a great thing . . . they are
> extraordinarily carefully regulated sorts of things. The occasions of entitlement to
> have them are carefully regulated and then the experience you are entitled to have
> on an occasion you are entitled to have one is further carefully regulated. (Sacks,
> 1992: 248)

Sex and death are culturally constituted as central human experiences. Yet, despite Sacks's observations, the descriptive apparatus through which we understand them has been more the topic of fiction writers than of scientific work (for recent exceptions see Foucault, 1979 and Prior, 1987). Perhaps the romantic impulse which threatens to engulf certain parts of the human sciences (see Silverman, 1989c; Strong and Dingwall, 1989) makes us reluctant to treat them as simply language-games among others.

Yet the legal requirement that HIV testing should be preceded by counselling guarantees, tragically, that 'sex' and the prospect of death should become topicalized in large numbers of professional–client exchanges which, if the patient is seropositive, are likely to be lifelong.[1] A social force, even prior to HIV, counselling now offers more people than ever the opportunity to 'learn what we are like, what our experience is, how things are with us' (Taylor, 1986: 78).

It is now a commonplace that the HIV pandemic will not be resisted simply by giving people better information. For, as all studies of communication have shown, many other conditions have to be satisfied before knowledge leads to behaviour change (see Nelkin, 1987; Aggleton, 1989). In the context of HIV, we may assume that part of the difficulty resides in broaching the topic of safer sex with partners (for interviews on this topic with drug users see McKeganey, forthcoming).

Yet we lack knowledge of how people talk about their sexual behaviour in naturally occurring situations. In this context, Coxon's conclusion to a recent article on what he calls 'sexual research' is remarkably optimistic:

> The enormous growth in studies of sexual behaviour at an international and
> national level under the impact of Aids has . . . had the unanticipated and
> welcome result that scientific, intellectual and practical understanding of sexuality
> has now been immeasurably improved. (Coxon, 1989: 24)

Certainly, we have epidemiological work, together with the British survey of people's sexual behaviour (thanks to a private charity) (Wellings et al., 1990). There is also Coxon's own pioneering study of sexual vocabularies, obtained by asking a cohort of gay men to keep sexual diaries. But where are the studies of such vocabularies as they are deployed in naturally occurring situations? It is difficult to argue that keeping a diary on one's sexual behaviour is a routine activity for many people.

To the objection that such studies are impossible without prying or engaging in other improper behaviour (perhaps placing a tape-recorder under a bed), we can answer: why accept the essentialist assumption that sexuality occurs only between sexual partners? Increasingly, ethnographers are resisting the naive suggestion that phenomena like 'the family' or 'science' are only (or most 'authentically') constituted in single sites, such as households or laboratories (Gubrium, 1989; Silverman, 1993). Why should not the same be true about 'sexuality' or, indeed, 'death'?[2]

The discussion of sexual matters may sometimes be marked as a 'delicate' matter. In part, this may relate to the social context in which this topic arises. For instance, where parties are routinely or professionally concerned with matters related to sexuality or death (e.g. in case conferences of surgeons treating transexual people or discussion between workers in funeral parlours), one need not expect to find delicacy markers.

However, such speculation is fruitless. In particular, it would limit us to a social psychology of how people respond to 'embarrassing' situations which would have to take it on trust that this is how the participants are orienting to the context. As it turns out, what is a 'delicate' matter is something that is locally produced and managed as participants themselves assemble some context for their talk.

The production of 'delicate' matters

The management of 'embarrassing' or 'delicate' situations is addressed both in the theoretical gaze of books of etiquette and in the practical organization of everyday life. For instance, in the context of doctors' conduct of physical examinations of their patients, both parties organize the marking and management of potentially 'delicate' items. In general practice consultations, Heath (1988) has shown how patients position themselves and organize their gaze to mark their disattendance to the parts of their body being examined.

However, Heath's analysis does not depend on an assumption that certain situations are intrinsically 'embarrassing' (or 'delicate'). Instead, Heath shows how we can analyse the co-operative marking and management of 'delicate' objects without attributing psychological states, like 'embarrassment', to the individuals concerned.

Research on the local organization of 'delicacy' reveals that it may be functional to proceed 'cautiously'. For instance, Maynard (1991) has noted that conversationalists may seek to elicit an opinion from someone else before making their own statement. Maynard gives an example I first mentioned in Chapter 2:

Extract 4.1 (Maynard, 1991: 459)
1 Bob: Have you ever heard anything about wire wheels?
2 Al: They can be a real pain. They you know they go outta
3   line and--
4 Bob: Yeah the-- if ya get a flat you hafta take it to a
5   special place ta get the flat repaired.
6 Al: Uh-- why's that?

Maynard concludes that the PDS has a special function in circumstances requiring *caution*. In ordinary conversations, this may explain why it is seen most frequently in conversations between strangers or acquaintances where the person about to deliver an opinion is unlikely to know about the other person's views.[3]

As Bergmann (1992) suggests, psychiatric intake interviews may also be a site where we can expect expressive caution, foreshadowing 'delicate' matters. Bergmann notes that a recurrent feature of such interviews is that patients are not directly interrogated. Instead, the psychiatrist proceeds by proffering information he has received or impressions he has reached and the patient responds *without having been asked a question*. For instance:

Extract 4.2 (Bergmann, 1992)
1 D: Doctor Hollman told me something like you were running
2   across the street (not so completely dressed) or
3   something like that,
4 P: (h)yes: that's:-I am a child of God;=
5   =I am his child

In Extract 4.2, notice how D's assertions are very unspecific. By saying 'not so completely dressed' rather than 'naked', Bergmann notes that D makes use of the rhetorical form of 'litotes'. Litotes allows one to speak without specifying what one is talking about. It also serves as an invitation to name or further specify the referred-to object without the doctor having to say why he has topicalized it.

We can see the function of litotes more clearly if we note that 'not so completely dressed' is downgraded twice through D's use of 'something like'. Litotes and down grades imply what Bergmann calls 'caution' and 'discretion'. Such caution functions to mark an upcoming 'delicate' object.[4] Like Heath, Bergmann refuses to accept that we should assume that certain topics are intrinsically 'delicate' or 'embarrassing'. As Bergmann remarks:

> By describing something with caution and discretion, this 'something' is turned into a matter which is in need of being formulated cautiously and discreetly. Viewed sociologically, there is not first an embarrassing, delicate, morally dubious event . . . instead, the delicate . . . character of an event is constituted by the very act of talking about it cautiously and discreetly. (1992: 154).

The management of delicacy is not confined to medical encounters. For instance, Clayman (1992) characterizes TV news interviewing as a site for much 'expressive caution', given that news interviewers are supposed to be neutral or objective.

Clayman investigates how interviewers shift footing when they come on to relatively controversial opinion statements. Look at the interviewer's utterance in Extract 4.3, line 4 below:

Extract 4.3 (Clayman, 1992) [*Meet the Press*] (IV=Interviewer)
1   IV: Senator, (0.5) uh: President Reagan's elected
2   thirteen months ago: an enormous landslide.
3   (0.8)
4   IV: It is s::aid that his programs are in trouble

In lines 1–2, a footing is constructed whereby IV is the author of a factual statement . However, at line 4, the footing shifts to what 'it is said'. As Clayman suggests, such a formulation indicates that IV is no longer the author of the assertion. This serves to mark the item as possibly 'controversial' and to preserve IV's position of 'neutrality' towards such matters. Once more, expressive caution is being used to mark and manage 'delicate' items.

Expressive caution in HIV counselling

Counselling around the antibody test routinely involves Ps being asked to describe their reasons for wanting a test. We present below extracts from several transcripts where C asks such a question. Although these transcripts derive from recordings at three different testing centres (two in England and one in the USA), our analysis will show that certain phenomena are massively recurrent in how Ps answer this question. Let us examine Extract 4.4 below:

Extract 4.4 (US1)
1   C: erm: what made you decide to come in then [softer]
2   to be tested?
3   (1.0)
4   P: er: well I (1.2) actually I'd been thinking about
5   doing it for some ti:me er:: (0.5) I had (.) I was
6   in a relationship about er six or eight months ago
7   (0.7) which lasted (1.0) well it ended six or eight
8   months ago it lasted for about three years and er
9   (1.0) er we had engaged in some unsafe sex
10   activities and er I later found that er my partner
11   had been having (.) sex with other people

P begins his answer in a flow of perturbed speech (a hesitation and a 1.2 second pause, followed by a repair). Again, when P begins to describe a relationship in line 5, he hesitates ('er::'), pauses and then repairs ('I had (.) I was in a relationship').

P here attends to the issue of the length of time he had given to thinking about having an HIV test. Two functions seem to be served by introducing this topic. First, it may put P in a favourable light since 'thinking about doing [things] for some time' may be hearable as an activity which suggests the category 'responsible person'. Second, it avoids P getting straight into the issue of his risky activities. This expressive caution is underlined since P's initial utterance ('er: well I (1.2) actually') *might* have led to an immediate disclosure of his sexual activities but is forestalled by its repair.

Such caution allows P to set up a 'good news' sequence prior to what may be the delivery of delayed (and hence dispreferred, that is, problematic in one way or another) 'bad news'. Already hearable as a 'responsible person', P initially uses description of others, with whom he participated in sexual activities, which imply a long-term involvement ('a relationship' and, at the end, 'my partner' – also delivered after a hesitation).

Extract 4.4 shows that the phenomenon of delay extends to descriptions of activities as well as relationships. Observe P's hesitations and pause which make his activity-description of 'unsafe sexual activities' and the micro-pause in 'having (.) sex with other people' hearable as dispreferred.

Notice also that P's failure to specify the people involved or the nature of their activities may invite C to treat his description as an 'indefinite' reference and to request that he should specify it further. Should C request such specification, then C shares the responsibility for any potentially delicate items that P delivers.

So, by postponing specification, until requested by C, patients neatly find a solution to two interactional problems. First, they avoid the potentially morally dubious activity of volunteering details of sexual activities. Second, not knowing what is appropriate in such a consultation, they give the professional an option about whether specification is in order.

The apparatus of description

The extracts above contain a more general message: participants as well as sociological analysts skilfully manage their descriptions of events. As Harvey Sacks noted, this raises some vital methodological questions for ethnographers and anyone else attempting to construct sociology as an 'observational' discipline. Sacks puts the issue succinctly:

> Suppose you're an anthropologist or sociologist standing somewhere. You see somebody do some action, and you see it to be some activity. How can you go about formulating who it is that did it, for the purposes of your report? Can you use at least what you might take to be the most conservative formulation – his name? Knowing, of course, that any category you choose would have the[se] kinds of systematic problems: how would you go about selecting a given category from the set that would equally well characterise or identify that person at hand? (1992, Vol. 1: 467–8).

Sacks shows how you cannot resolve such problems simply 'by taking the best possible notes at the time and making your decisions afterwards' (ibid.: 468). Instead, our aim should be to try to understand when and how members do descriptions, seeking thereby to describe the apparatus through which members' descriptions are properly produced.

Consider this description in which the identities of the parties are concealed:

The X cried. The Y picked it up.

Why is it that we are likely to hear the X as, say, a baby but not a teacher? Furthermore, given that we hear X as a baby, why are we tempted to hear Y as an adult (possibly as the baby's mother)?

In this chapter, I draw upon some of the concepts that Sacks uses to answer such questions. For simplicity, I will only refer to two such concepts:

Membership categorization devices (MCDs)

Each identity is heard as a category from some collection of categories which Sacks calls a membership categorization device. For instance, in the example above, we hear 'mother' as a category from the collection 'family'. The implication is that to choose one category from an MCD excludes someone being identified with some other category from the same device.

Category-bound activities (CBAs)

Many kinds of activity are commonsensically associated with certain membership categories. So, by identifying a person's activity (say, 'crying'), we provide for what their social identity is likely to be (in this case a 'baby'). Moreover, we can establish negative moral assessments of people by describing their behaviour in terms of performing or avoiding activities inappropriate to their social identity. For instance, it may be acceptable for a parent to 'punish' a child, but it will be unacceptable for a child to 'punish' a parent. Notice that, in both cases, 'punish' serves as a powerful picture of an activity which could be described in innumerable ways. Categories can usually be read off the activities in which people engage. Thus, to hear a report of someone crying *may* be heard as the activity of a baby. Similarly, a person who properly picks a baby up *may* be hearable as a 'mother'. Moreover, if both baby and mother are mentioned, we will try to hear them as a 'team' – so that, if the mother picks up the baby, we will hear the mother as not any mother but as the mother of this baby.

Using Sacks's (1972) account of how descriptions are organized, we can show how the marking of potentially delicate items carries strong implications about the moral status of clients. Following Heath's (1988) work on 'embarrassment' in the context of doctors' conduct of physical examinations of their patients, we have also demonstrated how, having marked an item as delicate, both parties co-operatively restore a life-as-normal framework.

Expressive caution in one counselling interview

Let us try to demonstrate these processes using an extended example taken from a pre-test counselling interview in a British testing centre. The extract begins about three minutes after the start of the consultation.

```
     Extract 4.5 (UK1)
 1   C:     Let's finish this HIV thing. .hhhhh So (.) do you
 2          understand about the antibodies.=
 3   P:     =Yes I [do:.
 4   C:            [Ri:ght. .hh So: .h how lo:ng is it since you
 5          think (.) you might have been at ri:sk (.) of being
 6          infected with HIV.
 7   P:     Well uh- (0.4) uhuh to tell you the truth it's only
 8          l- like er Friday I had a phone call from a .h ex-
 9          girlfriend- my boyfriend's ex-girlfriend .hh to say
10          that uh:m (0.5) she'd been to the VD clinic (0.2)
11          and uhm she thought that I should go:, (0.2) bu:t
12          (.) (since) then I've never worried. It was only (.)
13          after the phone-ca:ll.
14   C:     Oh ri:ght.=
15   P:     =That I thought that well I'd better go check it
16          o(h)u(h)t. .hhhh You kno:[w.
17   C:                              [So: the thing is you see
18          w- wh- what abou:t contacts before your present
19          boyfriend if I might ask about (tha:[:t).
20   P:                                        [Well I had (.)
21          since my: divorce in eighty-two (.) I've only had
22          two relationships.
23   C:     Right.
24   P:     And uh:m (0.2) one lasted for eight years and one
25          lasted for three year:s.
26   C:     Uh huh
27   P:     So I don't- I haven't worried
28   C:     No sure.
29   P:     you know because uh- those are the only two me:n.
30          Bu:t (.) on saying tha::t (0.2) my latest boyfriend
31          (.) is the only one that I've well had to worry
32          about because of the phone-ca:ll.
33          I'v[e never worried before.
34   C:        [(Yea:h).
35   C:     How long have you been with your latest boyfriend.
```

```
36   P:        Three months.
37   C:        Three months.
38   P:        Yea:h.
39   C:        Right. .hhhhh So: (.) we are only just really on the
40             time limit for this HIV for your present boyfriend
41             [then aren't u- aren't we.
42   P:        [Yea:h.
43   P:        [Mm hm
```

Extract 4.5 begins just as C has completed a long sequence of information about the nature of an HIV test (data not shown). By line 7 of this extract, however, P is into a much longer turn at talk. This is tied into a question asked by C which sets off the long question–answer chain shown in this extract.

Let us look first at how P sets up her reply to C's question beginning at line 7 compared to her answer at line 3. P was quickly into her earlier answer – indeed the transcript indicates the absence of even the slightest pause between the answer and the preceding question. Here, by contrast, there is considerable hesitation before P gets into her answer.

At line 3, P can latch her 'yes' immediately to the completion of C's turn because this is the candidate answer hearable from the question's juxtapositioning with the agenda statement. This is not to say that P could *not* have said that she didn't understand about antibodies, merely that what is, in this context, a problematic answer would normally be marked. However, in lines 7–8, P precisely does mark her answer as problematic through considerable expressive caution which includes two hesitations (uh, uhuh), a pause, two downgrades (well, only), a repair (I like er) and a preface (to tell you the truth). P's use of 'only' to describe how long she has been worried suggests that she is setting up her answer as delicate because she hears C's question as implying that most people will spend a lot of time deliberating before coming for an HIV test.

However, I am more concerned here with such expressive caution in the description of sexual activities. Note, once again, that I do not begin from the assumption that sexual matters and the like are intrinsically 'delicate' because of cultural taboos. Any such assumption is defeasible since we can visualize sequential features and other local circumstances where such taboos do not operate (see Extract 4.8, p. 77). Instead, I am concerned with how expressive caution works in the *local* production of delicacy.

Let us begin by looking further at P's utterance in line 7 'to tell you the truth'. As we will see, the story that P tells between lines 7 and 13 involves a highly organized set of disclosures which delay certain items. Before making a set of observations, I will reproduce this passage below:

```
     Extract 4.5 (part of)
7    P:        Well uh- (0.4) uhuh to tell you the truth it's only
8              l- like er Friday I had a phone call from a .h ex-
9              girlfriend- my boyfriend's ex-girlfriend .hh to say
```

10		that uh:m (0.5) she'd been to the VD clinic (0.2)
11		and uhm she thought that I should go:, (0.2) bu:t
12		(.) (since) then I've never worried. It was only (.)
13		after the phone-ca:ll.
14	C:	Oh ri:ght.=
15	P:	=That I thought that well I'd better go check it
16		o(h)u(h)t. .hhhh You kno:[w.

The story begins with the report of a phone call. Straight off we can remark that phone calls are a routine part of ordinary modern existence. This sets up a nice contrast with C's question about the relatively extraordinary topic of thinking about one's risk of being infected with HIV. How do we account for this contrast? We can find a parallel in the reports of witnesses to the assassination of President Kennedy who typically prefaced their accounts by referring to their original thoughts that perhaps what they had heard were the sounds of an ordinary event, such as a car backfiring. As Sacks has observed:

> there is a preference for descriptions which start off by exploring routine, normal or non-problematic explanations of unexpected events: members are 'engaged in finding out only how it is that what is going on is usual'. (Sacks, 1984: 419)

After the phone call is reported in speech which exhibits none of the perturbations present in the beginning of the turn, P moves once again into a very turbulent delivery pattern from the end of line 8 to the end of line 10. Before she says 'ex-girlfriend', P takes an inbreath and then after a short pause she repairs her description into 'my boyfriend's ex-girlfriend'. Clearly, expressive caution is being displayed here. What work is being done in the production of such perturbations? First, in naming an associate (here boyfriend's ex-girlfriend), one implies a description of oneself – in this case the standardized relational pair (SRP) (Sacks, 1972) of boy-friend:girlfriend. Because of this self-involvement, descriptions of certain types of associates may be foreshadowed as delicate matters. By referring to the ex-girlfriend of your boyfriend, you describe yourself as having a boyfriend who has had at least one earlier partner. Now the fact of having a relationship with someone who has had at least another partner may not be extraordinary. However, *reporting* such a fact may be heard as a category-bound activity with potentially delicate implications (casting doubt on whether this present relationship may be temporary, etc.). Indeed, P's use of 'ex' in the description 'ex-girlfriend' suggests that we are to hear her boyfriend as engaged in serial monogamy (i.e. as not promiscuous) which creates, by implication, the SRP of 'faithful partners'. This may have something to do with her repair from her original formulation of 'a .h ex-girlfriend'.

The hesitation and repair prior to this report thus constitute a nice solution to the problems of delicacy which may arise in describing one's sexual partners – proceed with expressive caution by delaying such descriptions. Moreover, such caution is not just self-interested. It shows a fine attention to what a recipient may want to hear. By producing a minimal amount of potentially delicate items at a first turn after a question, one leaves it up to the recipient to decide whether to treat it as a gloss which needs unpacking, for example via a probe or a demand for specification. Such requests provide a favourable environment for disclosing items marked as delicate because such items can now be produced as demanded by C rather than as volunteered by P.

Further turbulences (a hesitation and a half-second pause) occur in P's delivery of the item 'she'd been to the VD clinic' (line 10). Here we are concerned with a description of an activity rather than an associate. As Sacks (ibid.) also notes, activities are category-bound because they imply the kind of persons who might engage in them, e.g. 'crying' may be heard as being done by a baby. However, while a baby crying may be heard as 'normal', this is unlikely to be the case with going 'to the VD clinic'. P's expressive caution in the delivery of this item nicely marks the delicate implications of having a boyfriend who has had an affair with someone who has gone to a VD clinic. The delay also marks out the speaker as someone-who-does-not-normally-talk-about-people-going-to-VD-clinics. Throughout, P's own visit for an HIV test (in what may be described as 'a VD clinic' is produced as something that arises from someone else's suggestion (her boyfriend's ex-girlfriend) and from someone else's actions (her boyfriend who presumably had infected the ex-girlfriend).

Now P produces her reasons for seeking a test in terms of her caller's wishes ('she thought that I should go') (line 11) and her own sense of the situation ('I thought that well I'd better go check it o(h)u(h)t') (lines 15–16). Note the appeal to doing what someone else thinks best and to the responsibility of 'checking out' things. Both delay the description of one's own sexual activities while trading off life-as-usual situations which serve to downgrade the unusual and delicate business of seeking an HIV test. Now P's rapid visit for an HIV test is reconstituted as depicting a responsible person (who realizes she must rapidly 'check it out') rather than someone who has not reflected sufficiently (recognized in her earlier 'it's only l- like er Friday').

In the passage above, we have seen how both parties steer away from problematic explanations of such an unexpected event as seeking an HIV test. As Sacks (1984: 419) puts it, members are 'engaged in finding out only how it is that what is going on is usual'. But the co-operative accomplishment of expressive caution sits uneasily with the prescribed tasks of HIV counselling which require that clients address their risks in specific terms (see Peräkylä and Bor, 1990).

While Ps' initial descriptions can appear perfectly adequate at the time, Cs' follow-up questions and/or requests for specification redefine Ps' answers. These answers are then transformed into indefinite references requiring further specification.

Bearing in mind the expressive caution about delicate items, two questions remain: (1) how do Cs set up their requests for specification?;

and (2) how do Ps expand (what are now received as) insufficiently precise references? The next nine lines of the extract bear upon these questions:

Extract 4.5 (part of)

```
17   C:                                    [So: the thing is you see
18         w- wh- what abou:t contacts before your present
19         boyfriend if I might ask about (tha:[:t).
20   P:                                    [Well I had (.)
21         since my: divorce in eighty-two (.) I've only had
22         two relationships.
23   C:    Right.
24   P:    And uh:m (0.2) one lasted for eight years and one
25         lasted for three year:s.
```

C's 'so' (line 17) locates her upcoming question as the natural upshot of P's account, while her reference to P's boyfriend (line 19) nicely ties her question to P's own description. Moreover, C's initial question: 'how lo:ng is it since you think (.) you might have been at ri:sk' has already provided for the possibility that P may have been at risk longer than she suspects and thus warrants the line of questioning beginning here.

Before introducing her own term 'contacts', C marks its potentially delicate character by a set of perturbations ('w- wh- what abou:t contacts'). Having 'contacts', while the standard term used by professionals in STD clinics, can be heard by clients as an activity bound to the category of 'promiscuous person'. Indeed, we shall see that this is a deviant case since elsewhere both parties recurrently strive to locate patients' sexual activities in the context of long-term relationships.

As Schegloff (1980) points out, various types of action projection can serve to mark out and request formal permission for potentially delicate or risqué actions. So here C adds a little rider to her question ('if I might ask about (tha:[:t).'). Although, unlike question projections, this request comes after, rather than before, the question, it serves the same function of marking out that C understands that this may be heard as a delicate topic.

Here, then, C has skilfully prepared the ground for exploring a potentially delicate topic. In doing so, she has provided some kind of a favourable environment in which P can specify her indefinite reference.

Faced with C's request for specification, P does tell more in relatively undisturbed speech. But note two things. First, she converts the C's professional item 'contacts' into 'relationships'. This transforms the relational pairs involved: compare the description of sexual partners as contacts (for sexually transmitted disases) to ones involved in relationships (implying that the sexual activity is necessarily contexted in 'commitments' and other non-sexual matters).

Second, note that the P prefaces her response by 'since my: divorce'. This does a lot of interesting work:

– it gives us a favourable context to read her upcoming MCD 'relationships' (by implying that prior to her divorce she was only involved in one relationship);
– it makes several relationships permissible to a 'single' woman (but only one after the other, as she later makes clear). Even though the years do not add up (eight plus three years from 1982 takes us to 1991 and the interview takes place in 1989), we hear her as engaged in consecutive monogamy – just as in her earlier description of her boyfriend's 'ex-girlfriend'.

As C's disturbed delivery of the term 'contacts' showed, professionals display caution in organizing questions about potentially delicate matters. In turn, one of the strategies available to clients is to portray themselves in a favourable light – as in P's appeal to a pattern of serial monogamy. However, we should not emphasize the separate strategies of each party since the identification and management of delicacy tends to be a co-operative matter. This is nicely shown as the interview continues:

```
       Extract 4.6 (UK1) [Extract 4.5 continued]
44  C:     [.hhh Uhm .hhh d'you know if any of your: your er
45         partners have been drug users.=Intra[venous drug=
46  P:                                          [No:.
47  C:     =[users is our main [uhm you- you've never used=
48  P:      [They haven't.     [Mm
49  C:     =needles for yourself [(either.=No). .hh I ask=
50  P:                           [No:
51  C:     =everybody those questions.=I haven't saved them
52         [up for you. .hhhh Obviously when we're talking=
53  P:     [(That's okay yeah).
54  C:     =about HIV .hhhh uhm (.) the intravenous drug using
55         population are a population that are at ri:sk.
56  P:     Yea[:h.
57  C:        [Because (.) if they share needles (.) then
58         they're sharing (.) infection with the blood on the
59         needles obvious[ly.
60  P:                    [Mm h[m
61  C:                         [.hhhhhh Uhm (0.5) d'you know if
62         any of your partners have been bisexual.
63  P:     No they haven't.=
```

The task of pre-test counselling involves asking clients to assess the nature of their risk of having been exposed to HIV. In this passage, both parties have to cope with the implications of discussing potentially delicate aspects of the status of P's sexual contacts.

The extract is closely analysed below to show how delicacy is nicely marked and managed. C prefaces her question at line 44 by 'd'you know'.

We can see the power of this preface by imagining an alternative way of posing the question:

*C: Have any of your partners been drug users

Putting the question this way would imply that P is the kind of person who *knowingly* might associate with drug users. So this form of the question can be a category-bound activity, where its recipient is to be heard in the category of a-person-who-might-consort-with-drug-users. The C's preface is a neat device to overcome this hearing. It allows P, if necessary, to reveal that she had subsequently discovered that a partner was a drug user, without any kind of implication that she would knowingly associate with that category of person.

In line 45, C uses the category 'partner'. Note the expressive caution ('er') that precedes it. Massively recurrent in these materials are such delays in the first delivery (by both professionals and clients) of descriptive categories relating to sexual associates and activities. However, note that the category 'partner' may be less damaging to the propriety of P's behaviour than 'contact' – C's earlier term. Although both relate to sexual activity, the SRP 'partner–partner' is less implicative of promiscuity than the pair 'contact–contact'. Again, both professionals and clients in these sessions strive to present client behaviour in the best possible light.

Note how, in line 50, P overlaps with C's talk in order to produce a reply at the first available turn-transition point. In this way, non-delicate matters are marked by unqualified delivery at the first opportunity.

Equally, at lines 46–8, P marks her answer ('no . . . they haven't') as preferred by producing it early and without qualification, overlapping with C's elaboration of her question. Moreover, at line 46, P does not embed her 'no' in C's 'd'you know' format. Thereby, she elides the possibility that she could be the sort of person who did not fully 'know' all her partners.

Again, see how, in lines 47–9, C redesigns her next question. This may be in order to re-orient towards P's presentation of herself, dropping the 'd'you know' format and offering a negative answer as the preferred one.

More plausibly, C is now asking about P herself, not some other about whom her knowledge might be incomplete. (For a treatment of how we talk about our own and other's experiences, see Peräkylä and Silverman, 1991b.)

C's justification of her line of questioning ('Intra[venous drug users is our main; I ask everybody those questions.=I haven't saved them up for you') works as a retrospective justification for asking such a question. It serves neatly to counter the category-bound implications of the activity of asking someone if they have had sex with drug users. Without the elaboration, the implication might be that C had reason to suspect that P might be the sort of person who would engage in such an activity. The elaboration, however, seems to be about to make clear that the question has not been generated by anything that P has said or done – other than presenting herself at a clinic in which 'intravenous drug users is our main' (client population?). This is underlined by C's observation 'I haven't saved them up for you'.

P's agreement tokens on line 53 ('that's okay yeah') show her acceptance of C's elaboration and thus mark her continued recipiency for this line of questioning. This allows C to tag on a further question (about 'bisexual partners') whose delicacy is nicely marked and managed by the same 'd'you know' format as used on line 44.

Extracts 4.5 and 4.6 have allowed us to distinguish a number of practices involved in the local production and management of 'delicate' items by counsellors (C) and their patients (P). These are set out in Table 4.1.

Table 4.1   *Delicacy, description and expressive caution: some findings*

---

1. Cs and Ps use 'expressive caution' to mark potentially delicate objects: i.e. they delay their delivery, engage in various speech perturbations, and use elaborations and story-prefaces to mark and manage delicate items.
2. Ps produce a minimal amount of potentially delicate items at a first turn after a question, leaving it up to the recipient to decide whether to treat it as a gloss which needs unpacking.
3. Cs provide a favourable environment for disclosing delicate information by using perspective display sequences, downgrades, ambiguous and indirect questions and prospective and retrospective justifications for questions and requests for specification.
4. Cs and Ps show a preference for descriptions which start off by exploring routine, normal or non-problematic explanations of unexpected events.
5. Cs and Ps endeavour to put Ps in a 'positive' light, e.g. by countering implications of P promiscuity.

However, as I have argued elsewhere (Silverman, 1993), we must guard against the ease with which we can select instances from qualitative data which confirm an initial hypothesis. One check on such anecdotal use of data is deviant-case analysis.

Inspection of 50 transcripts from our corpus of almost 200 consultations has so far revealed three apparently deviant cases. Space allows us only to deal with one of them. Extract 4.7 is unique in our corpus of data in that a patient seems to produce straight off a description which implies that he engages in casual sex:

```
     Extract 4.7 (US1)
1    P:        Well I've- I've (0.5) I have been out with a (0.7)
2              er: hhh (1.7) you know I have paid for sex you know
3              o[ff- off streetwalker[s I think I =
4    C:         [Mm hm            [Uh huh
5    P:        =might have got it (that way because)
```

Note how P produces the category-bound activity 'paid for sex' and the MCD 'streetwalkers' in his first turn. However, a closer reading of this extract shows that 'streetwalker' is *not* P's first description of his partner. Notice that P begins with this description: 'I have been out with a (0.7) er:'. Although this first description is not completed, it may appeal to an activity very different to that of 'paying for sex'. After all, 'being out with [someone]' is a description which can be heard as bound to the 'life-as-usual' activity of 'dating'. Like the standard examples, then, Extract 4.7 shows how objects can be marked as potentially delicate by being offered as disturbed *second* descriptions.

Nonetheless, when a speaker does use a description which does not respect this preference, (s)he marks it.[5] In Extract 4.7, note the turbulent delivery before the MCD 'streetwalker' is produced – the aborted initial delivery (after a repair and two pauses), the further turbulences before the activity-description ('I have paid for sex') and the repair immediately before 'streetwalkers'. These multiple speech perturbations mark the account as particularly extra-ordinary and delicate.

The local production of delicate matters

We have demonstrated how counsellors and patients organize their talk in ways which mark and manage potentially delicate items. However, as already noted, a sociology of embarrassment can only fail if it depends on the analyst's assumption that certain situations are intrinsically 'embarrassing' (or 'delicate'). This means that we are limited to a social psychology of how people respond to 'embarrassing' situations but have to take it on trust that this is how the participants are orienting to the context. So, by affirming Ps' non-promiscuity (item 5 on Table 4.1, p. 76), professionals and clients are not simply reproducing some general rule of good behaviour. Because neither party is a 'cultural dope' (Garfinkel, 1967), what is proper behaviour is always a local matter – locally produced and sustained. So at times non-promiscuity can be heard as being made accountable.

Extract 4.8 begins with C asking a female patient about her present partner:

```
      Extract 4.8 (UK1)
1     C:                    [How long have you been with him?
2     P:        Six months.
3     C:        Six months. (0.3) When were you last with anyone
4               before that?
5     P:        About thr(h)ee years. .hhh=
6     C:        About three yea[rs.
7     P:--->                   [hhh I'm a Catholic.=heh
8               he[h .hhhhh
9     C:          [Ri:ght.
```

In Extract 4.8, P's laughter token at line 5 ('thr(h)ee years') may point to something remarkable about her account of her 'long' period of celibacy. Moreover, when, at her next turn, C repeats P's utterance ('about three years') (lines 5–6), this can be heard to make it accountable. Not having a sexual partner for three years at a stretch now may appear to be inappropriate to the category-bound activity of seeking an HIV test. Note how P does indeed now offer an account, appealing to a religious MCD (arrowed). Now when P makes a joke, C doesn't join in.[6]

Not sexuality but morality

Ironically, as always, interactional solutions are solutions to the very problems that members locally produce for themselves.[7] This means that both problems and solutions arise in the sequential organization of talk. It also means that much more is potentially at stake in these interviews than mere issues of sexual behaviour. As it turns out, such behaviour is only relevant in the context of an indefinite series of other matters that may be held to pertain to the moral standing of clients and their partners. I will demonstrate this point through a turn-by-turn analysis of one further long extract set out below.

Extract 4.9 is taken from the very beginning of a pre-HIV test counselling interview held at the sexually transmitted disease department of a hospital in a provincial British city:

```
       Extract 4.9 (UK3)
  1  C:      righty ho (0.2) could you tell us (.) why you've
  2          come for an HIV test today=
  3  P:      =well basically (.) because I'm: worried that I
  4          might have AIDS (0.2) er: (0.2) when my girlfriend
  5          (.) like she was on holiday in: (.) [X]* (0.2) in
  6          April with her friend
  7  C:      mm hm
  8  P:      I didn't go because I was busy (1.0) er:: (0.6) she
  9          came back but she was away for three weeks she came
 10          back (0.6) er: April (    ) May (.) April (.) May
 11          June July August September October November (0.8)
 12          and it's now November she's just told me (.) that
 13          she had sex with (.) a [Xian]* when she was out there
 14          well not actually had sex with but this she said
 15          that this guy (0.2) this is what she told me this
 16          guy had (.) forced herself (.) hisself upon her you
 17          know (0.6) er:: [further details of what happened]
 18  P:      so: that's what I'm worried about
 19          (0.8)
 20  C:      [mm
 21  P:      [and it's been unprotected sex as well
 22  C:      right: so obviously someone had forced (0.2) himself
 23          on her=
 24  P:      =yeah=
 25  C:      =hh there was: nothing she could do
 26  P:      mm hm
```

```
27  C:      (   ) hh
28  P:      but apparently that's what they're like out there:
29          you know
30          (0.6)
31  C:      mm
32  P:      so:: (0.6) that's what the score is (0.4) that's
33          what I'm worried about
```

* I have deleted the country referred to in line 5 and the nationality in line 13 in order
  to preserve P's anonymity.

In Extract 4.9, as in the other extracts, category-bound activities and membership categorization devices are used to confirm each other. So being 'worried' about 'AIDS' (lines 3–4) is appropriate to the implied category 'patient' who has 'come for an HIV test today'. Moreover, descriptions construct a profoundly *moral* universe of 'reasonable' activities conducted and perceived by 'reasonable' people. So, for instance, coming today for an HIV test is not only an 'appropriate' activity if you are 'worried', it is also a sensible and reasonable activity, serving to protect yourself (against further 'worry') and the community (because it shows you are aware of the dangers of receiving and transmitting the HIV virus).

Since HIV is hearable as a sexually transmitted disease, answering why one wants an HIV test often involves references to relationships with others. As Sacks tells us, how one describes a related other and their activities is deeply morally implicative of oneself and one's own activities. Let us now look at how this moral universe is constructed as P tells his story.

'My girlfriend' (line 4) tells us that P is heterosexual or at least bisexual. Moreover, by choosing 'girlfriend' rather than 'girl', 'woman', etc., P implies that, at least in this case, he is someone who has a 'relationship' rather than other alternatives (a 'one-night stand', commercial sex, etc.).

'She was on holiday' (line 5) is a CBA tied to the category 'holidaymaker' but also associated with other activities such as holiday 'romances', holiday 'flings'. Because we know that holidays are a time when moral inhibitions may be temporarily lifted, the upcoming description of potentially 'promiscuous' behaviour is potentially downgraded or at least made comprehensible.

'With her friend' (line 6) tells us that she had not gone away on her own, where going away on your own *may* be heard as implying a problem with a relationship, although it does leave a question hanging about why P had not accompanied his girlfriend. 'Her friend' does not tell us the gender of the 'friend'. However, we know that, if that gender had been male, it would have massive implications for the story that is being told and, therefore, P would have been obliged to tell us. Given that he doesn't, we must assume that 'her friend' is female. Moreover, we can also assume, for the same reason, that it is not a sexual relationship.

'I didn't go because I was busy' (line 8) attends to the question that is hanging about why P didn't accompany his girlfriend, given that 'going on holiday together' is a CBA appropriate to the SRP girlfriend/boyfriend. Here P shows that he analyses these inferences in exactly this way. First, he underlines what we had inferred in his original description: 'I didn't go'. Second, he shows that this 'not going' is accountable and provides its warrant: 'because I was busy'.

'She's just told me (.) that she had s̲e̲x̲ with (.) a [Xian] when she was out there' (line 13) consists of a series of highly implicative CBAs. Having 'sex' with a third party is category-bound to the category 'being unfaithful'. Although the earlier CBA being 'on holiday' (confirmed by the place-locater 'when she was out there') may make this description understand-able, it may not make it excusable. As we shall see, first P and then C engage in considerable interpretive work to preserve the moral status of P's girlfriend.

However, the 'telling' of a story which reflects badly on oneself can itself be a praiseworthy activity.[8] Moreover, given that we are not told that the 'girlfriend' was not forced to tell her story or 'found out', we must assume that her admission was voluntary – itself a praiseworthy activity as we learn from the sentencing policy of most criminal courts.

One aspect of the content of this description, namely having 'sex with a [Xian]', where an Xian may be known to be category-bound to the description 'possible HIV carrier' and the CBA 'risky activity' neatly provides the warrant for P wanting an HIV test.

The account also creates a standardized relational pair of news-teller/news-receiver. This SRP has an implication for P's own moral status. Because he has only 'just' (line 12) heard about his girlfriend's implied risky activity (and hence his own risk), the delay between his being at risk and coming for a test is explained and, indeed, his immediate appearance at the clinic is implicitly 'praiseworthy'.

'Well not actually had sex with' (line 14): here the damaging CBA 'having sex (with a third party)' is immediately repaired by B. Thus we have to suspend the category-bound implication 'unfaithful girlfriend'. But this repaired description is ambiguous. For instance, are we to hear 'not actually sex' as a physical or social description of the activity?[9]

'She said that this guy (0.2) this is what she told me this guy had (.) forced herself (.) hisself upon her you know' (lines 14–17). It is clear from his next utterance that P is attending to this ambiguity as something in need of further explication. If 'he forced . . . hisself upon her', then we are given a CBA implying the categories rapist/victim where 'victim' implies the activity of not giving consent. So P reworks his original category 'having sex', with its damaging implications, by positing the absence of consent and thus a withdrawal of the warrant of the charge 'unfaithful girlfriend'. Later, in a different portion of the transcript, he attends to the physical nature of the act to warrant his description of 'not actually having sex'.

There is a further nice feature embedded in P's description. It arises in its preface: 'she said that this guy (0.2) this is what she told me'. P's story of these events is thus doubly embedded (both in 'she said' and in 'this is what she told me'). How does 'this is what she told me' serve to repair 'she said'?

We can unpick the nature of this repair by recognizing that when somebody offers an account the upshot of which puts them in an unfavourable light, we may suspect that they have organized their description in order to put themselves in a more favourable light. So, if P had simply reported what his 'girlfriend' had said about this incident, then, although he would be implying that he was a 'trusting partner', he could be seen as 'too trusting', i.e. as a dope.

Now we see that 'this is what she told me' makes him into an astute witness by drawing attention to the potential credibility problem about his girlfriend's account. As one of the people involved in a British sex scandal of the 1960s said about the story of another participant: 'He would say that, wouldn't he'? However, note that, unlike this comment, P is *not* directly stating that his girlfriend is to be disbelieved. Rather her story is offered just as that – as her *story* without the implication that P knows it to be true or false.

The beauty of P's repair into 'this is what she told me' is that it puts him in a favourable light (as an astute observer), while not making a direct charge against his girlfriend's veracity (an activity category-bound to the description 'disloyal partner'). This allows a hearer of his story to believe or disbelieve his girlfriend's account and allows him to go along with either conclusion. And this is precisely what happens.

'So obviously someone had forced (0.2) himself on her' (lines 22–3): note how, in this formulation of the upshot of P's account, C elects to believe his girlfriend's reported account. C's use of 'obviously' makes such belief apparently natural and inevitable. Yet how can this be? After all, P has distanced himself from the story by his repair into 'this is what she told me'.

We can resolve this problem by considering the interactional consequences of a recipient of P's story doubting his girlfriend's account. This would transform P's general doubt about such accounts into a specific charge against someone whom C didn't know. Moreover, it would not be a charge against any stranger but a stranger with close ties to the story-teller. Were C to disbelieve P's girlfriend's reported account, then this would make the friend into a recognizably disreputable character and, by implication, cast doubt on P (as someone-involved-with-a-disreputable character). None of this would be desirable if the interview is to proceed. There are strong interactional grounds here for hearers of P's story to suspend disbelief.[10]

From now on, this version of P's girlfriend as both the innocent victim and the teller of truthful stories is co-operatively developed. At line 24, P supports C's version at the earliest opportunity, despite his previous attempt to distance himself from it.

Consider the implications of P contesting C's account. First, he would be doubting the upshot-formulation of an impartial hearer. Second, he would have to move from the sensible doubt about the testimony of any interested party to making a specific charge against his girlfriend's veracity and faithfulness. Immediate agreement thus serves as a CBA which allows him to be described as 'loyal'. As C embroiders her account, 'there was nothing she could do' (line 25), P continues not to contest it, offering a response-token at line 26.

'But apparently that's what they're like out there' (line 28): now, when C has apparently passed her turn, P himself continues the embroidery, finding a reason to explain why an [Xian] might have 'forced himself' on a woman.

However, remarks like this *can* be heard not simply as explanations of particular conduct but as an activity which is category-bound to the category 'racist'. Notice now that, while C does offer a response-token (line 31), it is delayed. Of course, response-tokens like 'mm' are hearable as anything from indications of co-presence, coupled with a passing of one's turn, to agreement. However, if C's 'mm' is hearable as an agreement, given the preference for agreement, its delay is highly implicative of (suppressed) disagreement. And, of course, there is evidence that P hears it this way too – notice his exit from the topic via a summary statement (32–3).

Our analysis of this extract has revealed that hearably 'delicate' matters extend far beyond the sphere of sexual behaviour. Rather, as Sacks has suggested, the description of *any* matter involves both speakers and hearers in a profoundly moral universe in which they can be held to account for a huge number of inferences of their viewings and hearings.

We have seen how both parties attend to such matters as explaining particular courses of action, the warrant for believing other people's stories and taking action on hearing such stories. As speakers modify and embellish each other's accounts, the moral universe they inhabit is both locally and sequentially established.

A final extract from the same counselling interview shows how patient and counsellor constitute this universe in relation to the organization and management of a 'complainable' matter.

```
        Extract 4.10 (UK3) (continuation)
141  C:      um:: (0.8) was yer partner tested at all:
142  P:      tt she hasn't been tested no: that's what I I'm
143          really angry about yer know she never told me about
144          it
145  C:      yes
146  P:      until (0.6) not long ago (0.4) well just the other
147          day (0.8) hh and she never told anybody else about
148          it she didn't [go
149  C:                    [yeah
150  P:      and get herself tested as soon as she
151          [came back you know
152  C:      [hm
153  C:      yeah: so she's [borne
154  P:                     [so
155  C:      quite a heavy burden [in her
```

156	P:	[yeah
157	C:	hea[rt
158	P:	[she has aye
159	C:	[( )
160	P:	[like she's been : (.) li (.) getting a bit (.)
161		depressed and stuff like that yer know

C's initial question (line 141) allows P to set up a series of complaints where being 'really angry' (line 143) is category-bound to the category 'someone who has a complaint' rather than, say, 'someone who is just in an angry mood'. In particular, P has three related complaints about his girlfriend (now defined as 'yer partner' by C):

She didn't have a test.
She didn't tell P about 'it'.
She didn't tell anyone else about 'it'.

Using the MCD apparatus, we can see how P (and C) might analyse these three issues to constitute them as complainable matters:

She didn't have a test: having an HIV test is hearable as an activity category-bound to people in the category 'someone who perceives themselves at risk'. If you can categorize yourself this way, then not testing is hearable as 'irresponsible', particularly in regard to the other party in the SRP 'partner–partner' (or 'girlfriend–boyfriend').

She didn't tell P about 'it': since 'truthfulness' is not always to be recommended, telling 'partners' about an affair may be read as the activity of either an 'honest' person or a 'naive' person. However, where that affair may have put the partner at medical risk, 'honesty' may be held to be required. Hence not telling P about 'it' constitutes a 'complainable' matter.

She didn't tell anyone else about 'it': 'honesty' with partners about 'infidelity' may be presumed to be a 'difficult' matter. In such circumstances, people might, in the first instance, be expected to 'confide in' or 'ask advice from' others, where such confidences might lead to telling one's partner. However, since P's girlfriend did not even take this action, P has another complainable matter.

Given that P has established his multiple complaints, what becomes of them? I take it that hearers of complaints have several options. One can deal with a complaint by telling one's own story about how a similar complainable matter arose in one's own life. However, as Sacks (1992) points out, while such 'second stories' work very well among friends, they are neither expected nor even welcome in the context of a professional–client encounter.

One option that remains for professional hearers of complaints is to offer advice about how the complaint may be remedied. However, C has already made it clear to P (untranscribed) that the purpose of the interview is simply to ensure that P's consent to an HIV test is 'informed consent'.

In this context, C elects to focus on the purported *consequences* for P's 'partner' of taking the actions she has (i.e. 'so she's borne quite a heavy burden in her heart', line 153 ff.). This gloss on P's account has two neat interactional consequences. First, it will not lead to a long discussion about the facts of the case as would a direct challenge to the legitimacy of P's complaint. Second, it encourages P to focus on rebuilding his 'partnership' by formulating his partner's behaviour as that of a moral-person-who-has-made-one-slip.

In this light, P's partner becomes reconstituted as a moral actor precisely because she can experience 'heartache' after acting in a way that she knows to be wrong. Moreover, as before, as C offers such a reading, P confirms it in overlapping talk (lines 156 and 158) and in a summary statement (line 160) which supports C's interpretation with his own experience. To challenge such a reading, after C has offered her gloss, would now transform P into the 'disloyal' partner. So the 'upshot' of P's complaint is discovered in the way it is received.

Summary

Throughout these extracts, we have seen how both speakers fashion their account in a way which attends to the implications of their descriptions. Those implications derive from the machinery of interaction: i.e. *both* that of the apparatus of description (notably in the form of category-bound activities) and the sequential organization of turn-taking. Through this apparatus and this organization, people co-operatively organize and discover anew what it is that they must have meant.

This serves to underline rather than evade the locally organized employment of such an apparatus. As we saw in Extract 4.8, while we might assume that presenting oneself as reasonably non-promiscuous might be a shared norm in professional–client interactions, local considerations cause some variance. Therefore, while it is tempting to appeal to apparently self-evident norms of interaction, close investigation of such local practices reveals that people are far from being 'judgmental dopes'. Consequently, the appealing prospect of a sociology of the moral order must begin by clearly delineating the local production of the phenomenon itself.

Practical implications: description and empathy

What are the implications of our research for counselling practice? I will briefly touch on one implication – the relation between my analysis of how counsellors (and their clients) co-operatively produce and manage 'delicacy' and professional accounts of 'empathy'.

'Empathy' between professional and client is a central concern of counselling texts. Carl Rogers (1975:4) has offered a highly respected definition:

> [empathy] means entering the private perceptual world of the other and becoming thoroughly at home in it. It involves being sensitive, moment to moment, to the changing felt meanings which flow in the other person. . . . To be with another in this way means that, for the time being, you lay aside the views and values you hold for yourself in order to enter another's world without prejudice.

A technique held to embody this empathy is for counsellors to use their turns at talk to offer regular *paraphrases* of clients' utterances (Rogers, 1975; Nelson-Jones, 1988). In Extract 4.11 below, in lines 22 and 23, we see a paraphrasing sequence:

```
      Extract 4.11(UK1)
11  C:      umm er why did you want to have the test done?
12  P:      oh well (1.0) err I've just moved in with my current
13          (0.3) girlfriend
14  C:      mm hm
15  P:      and err (0.5) before we actually start (2.0) full
16          sexual relationship we thought it was best if we
17          both (1.0) screened just to be just to be on the
18          safe side it's not as if both of us have been (0.3)
19          sleeping around for the last few years but just
20          [to be
21  C:      [right
22  P:      it's just to put our minds at rest=
23  C:      =just to be safe
24  P:      it I mean it's unlikely that there again there is
25          that chance of
26  C:      right
27  P:      that chance exists
```

Here, after C's paraphrase, P does indeed continue his turn at talk that looked as if it might have come to an end at line 22. This seems to follow what counselling texts suggest about the possible functionality of C's paraphrasing or repeating P's terms.

Moreover such texts seem to be in line with recent theoretical work in linguistics. For instance, Tannen (1987) has noted the commonsense assumption that repetition in conversation is dysfunctional. However, she suggests that this assumption depends upon an erroneous picture theory of language which holds that, since repetition does not appear to convey information, it is superfluous and an instance of bad communication. On the contrary, Tannen argues that repetition of another's words is functional because

> Repeating the words, phrases or sentences of other speakers (a) accomplishes a conversation, (b) shows one's response to another's utterance, (c) shows acceptance of others' utterances and their participation, and (d) gives evidence of

one's own participation. It provides a resource to keep talk going – where talk itself is a show of involvement, of willingness to interact. (Tannen, 1987: 584)[11]

Despite Tannen's persuasive arguments, we should be cautious about assigning a universal functionality to any conversational device. We have already examined one data-extract which can be used to show the potential unintended consequences (if not dysfunctions) of such repetition:

```
      Extract 4.8 (UK1)
1     C:                        [How long have you been with him?
2     P:         Six months.
3     C:         Six months. (0.3) When were you last with anyone
4                before that?
5     P:         About thr(h)ee years. .hhh=
6     C:         About three yea[rs.
7     P:--->                     [hhh I'm a Catholic.=heh
8                he[h .hhhhh
9     C:            [Ri:ght.
```

In Extract 4.8, as we saw on p. 77, somewhat remarkably, P provides an account of her *non*-promiscuity (line 7). Now, if we look at the prior organization of the talk, we can see that C is indeed repeating P's answers at two different places (lines 3 and 6). Why might this repetition create an environment in which P might feel it necessary to produce such an account?

It seems that repetition of another's utterance may be heard as two different activities: (1) 'I hear what you say' and (2) 'Please warrant what you say'. Only activity (1) fits the textbooks' account of repetition as empathetic. Activity (2) may produce warrants (as in Extract 4.8) which are hearable as defensive reactions not predicted by the textbooks.

This example give us an interesting contrast with most accounts of empathy. Exemplified by Rogers's definition above (but also see Nelson-Jones, 1982: 212–14), they imply a view of communication as a public process building a bridge between two *private* consciousnesses. This leads to research which treats different verbal and non-verbal modes of action as indications of the underlying characteristics of empathic orientation between the participants (see Ellickson, 1983; Maurer and Tindall, 1983; Barkham and Shapiro, 1986).

The problem with these studies is their unacknowledged leap from public to private, and vice versa.[12] Contrary to these approaches (and to common sense), the above analysis suggests an approach to empathy less as the psychological propensity to attune to the private meanings of the client and more as the social ability to pick up the behavioural cues present in what clients are saying and doing. The core of this process is not the interplay of two private selves, but the interplay of actions making use of publicly available apparatuses of description.

It is evident that, in this perspective, there are no *a priori* right or wrong ways of responding to clients. What works has to be interactionally devised on each occasion. This suggests a revision of the conceptions we have about counselling (and indeed any profession involved in communicating with clients). The skills of the counsellors we have examined in these excerpts are not primarily based on owning a special (professional) body of knowledge. Instead, such skills depend upon an apparatus of description that is publicly available to everyone – including clients, as the extracts above have graphically shown.

The distinctive character of counselling arises in the systematic deployment of this apparatus in encouraging the client to talk.[13]

Notes

1. This chapter concerns itself with how 'risk behaviour' is discussed in HIV counselling. For extended discussion of how 'death' is discussed as a 'dreaded issue' in family-therapy-based counselling see Peräkylä, 1993 and 1995.

2. For example, Prior's (1987) inventive ethnography shows how 'death' is differently constituted in the mortuary, the Coroner's Court, the official records office, the funeral parlour and the death announcements in newspapers.

3. In the paediatric setting discussed, the functions of the PDS are obvious:

By adducing a display of their recipients' knowledge or beliefs, clinicians can potentially deliver the news in a hospitable conversational environment, confirm the parents' understanding, coimplicate their perspective in the news delivery, and thereby present assessments in a publicly affirmative and nonconflicting manner. (Maynard, 1991: 484)

4. Bergmann notes that one function of such 'indirectness' is that it allows D to catch P 'lying'. Having elicited P's version, D can produce further information which undercuts P's account.

5. When people straight off produce a non-routine description, they mark it' (Jefferson, 1985: 450).

6. For C to join in P's laughter at this point might imply that C was laughing at P's religion. In these consultations, Ps' preferences, whether sexual or religious, are not routinely heard by Cs as a laughing matter.

7. This, of course, is part of the phenomenon of 'reflexivity' (Garfinkel, 1967). For an example of institutional talk which exemplifies the local production and management of 'problems' see Lynch's (1985) discussion of how laboratory workers assemble slides of data.

8. As Cuff (1980) remarks, delivering news about a hearably 'bad' feature of oneself may serve as a pre-emptive strike by showing that, at least, the teller is aware of her culpability. Note, for instance, how it is always newsworthy when criminals show 'no remorse'. I have also discussed this kind of news delivery in the case of the woman who describes herself to the doctor treating her adolescent daughter as 'the neurotic mother' (Silverman, 1987: Ch.10).

9. Anssi Peräkylä (personal communication) has suggested that the ambiguity created by P's repair nicely serves to present the reported events in a way which constitutes their 'real nature' as unclear to the teller. When wedded to P's use of 'this is what she told me', there is perhaps then a double layer of cautiousness about P's account.

10. Given that C's job is to assess the degree of risk involved in P's sexual relations, the 'truth' of his girlfriend's sexual episode is not primarily relevant for C's task at hand. Hence C opts for the interactionally least complicated 'hearing' of P's ambiguous description. Another consideration relates to the rule of 'politeness is all' observed by Strong (1979a) in a study of paediatric clinics. By not openly casting doubt on their patients' stories, however absurd or morally damaging, the interaction is maintained on a smooth basis.

11. Although Tannen does not discuss the functions of repetition or mirroring of body language, this would be wholly consonant with her analysis. Indeed, this is taken up by some counselling psychologists (see Maurer and Tindall, 1983). In his work on videotapes of HIV

counselling, Peräkylä (1995) shows how body movements accomplish various interactional tasks, including the display of 'delicacy'. This is consistent with Heath's trail-blazing work on the local and context-bound positioning of both P and C body-movement, particularly in relation to the organization of 'embarrassment' (Heath, 1988).

12. An important opening has been made by Barrett-Leonard (1981), who wants to treat empathy as an interactional process, rather than as a quality of individuals or relations. But he also shares the above-mentioned model of communication in which communication is between two private selves, mediated through the public sphere.

13. I am most grateful to Anssi Peräkylä for this way of formulating the practical import of our research.

5

Offering the Agenda to the Patient: Delays in Delivering Test Results in post-HIV Test Counselling Interviews

To anyone familiar with the experience of testing for HIV, one might expect the test result to be the first topic discussed in post-test counselling. Pre-test counselling routinely covers how patients might respond to a positive test result (Bor et al., 1992). The interview usually concludes by discussing when, and in what circumstances, the test result will be available. Indeed, the only question that many patients ask during the pre-test counselling interview relates to such practicalities (see Chapter 6).

Above all, counsellors assume that the wait for the test result is likely to generate stress for the patient. Hence counsellors are encouraged 'to explore the extent of the patient's social support . . . during the potentially stressful time between having the test and awaiting its result' (Bor et al., 1992: 68). In order to reduce this presumed stress, many private clinics and one London NHS hospital now offer the test result on the same day as blood is taken – although even the reduced waiting period (around six hours) is topicalized as 'stressful' in the hospital's pre-test counselling.[1]

In this context, it is hardly surprising that HIV counselling texts take for granted that the test result should be the first item on the agenda of post-test counselling. For instance, a 'checklist of points to be covered in post-test counselling' begins: '1. Give the result' (Miller and Bor, 1988). The reasoning behind this priority is explained in a later text prepared by the same authors. The test result, they write, 'is best given as soon as possible in order to use the time available to discuss the patient's concerns and to give information' (Bor et al., 1992: 69).

However, it should be pointed out that these texts draw upon the British experience where pre-test HIV counselling is more or less universal (Bond, 1990). In other countries, where pre-test counselling is infrequent or sporadic, the post-test interview may be the first time that counsellor and client meet.

In the course of inspecting a corpus of post-HIV test counselling interviews at a gay men's health clinic in a large US city (US1), differences were noted in the positioning of the telling of the HIV test result. In a minority of these interviews, the test result was not given in the counsellor's first or even second turn and, in two cases, the test result did not appear until several minutes into the interview.

Without any pre-test counselling, we might speculate that such delay in giving the test result may be due to counsellors seeking to establish their patient's perspective prior to their delivery of this crucial information. As a textbook suggests: 'Questions are the main catalyst for patient change and healing and they provide patients with opportunities to make further changes in their lives' (Bor et al., 1992: 15).

This orientation indicates that the delay in giving test results may be caused by counsellors first offering their patients an opportunity to think through how they might react to different results in the way they do in pre-test counselling. If so, then our puzzle is solved.

However, there are two reasons to suspect such a simple solution: one empirical and one analytic reason. First, it turns out that, in our corpus of post-test counselling data, the interviews with the longest delay in delivering the test results are not structured around such hypothetical questions designed to tease out the patients' orientations but arise instead after counsellors offer to turn the agenda over to their patients.

Second, conversation analysis's own theory of action requires us to inspect the local, turn-by-turn organization of any sequence of talk without making prior assumptions about the relevance of our intuitive knowledge of its apparent social context, including participants' own stated theories (see Schegloff, 1991). This means, at the very least, that explanatory 'why' questions should be delayed until we have established 'how' contexts of talk are assembled locally by the participants (Silverman and Gubrium, 1994).

The rest of this chapter will begin with analytical issues, only returning to the implications for counselling practice in the concluding observations. The logic of this approach means that we have, for the moment, to abandon our intuitive surprise or even anger at the absence of the test result statement in a counsellor's first turn.[2]

Instead, we will treat the delivery of this statement as the outcome of *some* procedures used by *both* parties and seek to investigate precisely what these procedures are.

Data

Thirteen post-test counselling interviews were analysed at this US gay men's health clinic. Each was the first one-to-one meeting between counsellor and patient. Prior to this meeting, each patient had participated in a group question-and-answer session about the HIV test, filled out a questionnaire with personal details of their concerns, and had blood taken. Each patient was asked to provide a set of numbers deriving from their birthdate which were then used to set up a 'code' for their blood sample (and hence for their own test result).

Discarding one interview where recording had not begun at the start, inspection of these interviews revealed two different ways in which test results were announced. In eight cases, the counsellor (C) stated the test result within the first minute or two, without any request for the result from the patient (P). In these cases, one or two questions from C were always followed by the test result. For instance:

Extract 5.1 (US1) {positive result}

```
 1  C:      Just to make sure that (0.7) I've got the s- right
 2          number (.) could you just tell me your number one
 3          last time to make sure[:.
 4  P:                            [W: nine ni:ne (.) one eight
 5          six nine.=
 6  C:      =Okay. .hhh U:hm (.) you were (.) tested how long
 7          ago:? Was er was it a Saturday.
 8  P:      Yeah. Frida:y. No Wednesday.
 9  C:      The Wednesday session ok[ay.
10  P:                              [Yeah.
11  C:      How have your anxieties been waiting for this re-
12          these results.=It's been almost a week now.
13  P:      er: (0.2) Not too ba:d. hhh=
14  C:      =Okay kind of (okay)
15          (1.2)
16  P:      I haven't really thought about it. I- because
17          Friday when I was supposed to come (0.2) I had to
18          cancel, (                    ).
19          (0.5)
20  C:      So it's not been something too oppressing for
21          you.=
22  P:      =(No) (   ).
23  C:>     Okay. .hhh Why don't we go ahead and talk about
24          what your results are okay?
25  P:      Uh huh
26  C:      .hh Your results came back as positive.
27  P:      Mm
28          (3.6)
```

In Extract 5.1, several questions are asked by C before the test result is delivered. C's first question (lines 1–3) requests P's code number to ensure that, in the context of anonymous testing, the test result is correctly matched.

Then, after a question about the day when P tested (lines 6–7), C asks two questions about P's 'anxieties . . . waiting for these results'. Now P's positive result is announced, prefaced by a brief agenda statement (arrowed) which, despite its question form, is treated by P as an announcement rather than an offer.

Now, on the basis of Extract 5.1, it might be thought that this early statement of the test result might be a feature of the telling of positive results. In fact, six out of the eight 'early' tellings turn out to involve negative results. Extract 5.2 is an example:

Extract 5.2 (US1) {negative result}

```
 1  C:       You've tested before:.
 2  P:       Mm [hm
 3  C:          [Two weeks ag[o.
 4  P:                        [About- about three weeks ago
 5           yea:h.
 6  C:       Three weeks ago. And your results at that point
 7           were .hh [positive.
 8  P:               [Positive.
 9  C:       Oka:y. .hhhh So [you're-
10  P:                       [Well he- he insists that it can't
11           be po:sitive. So we came together: on Wednesda:y
12           (0.5) and I talked to counsellors here and (that's
13           right) (.) talked to Willie I don't know if you
14           kno- he's a part-ti:me
15  C:       I don't know (about it).
16  P:       You don't. (0.4) And he says it might be a false
17           po:sitive and my room-mate insists that it was a
18           false positive.=It can't [be:.
19  C:                                [Your room-mate slash
20           lover.
21  P:       Yeah.
22  C        (Slash ex-lo[ver)
23  P:                   [Lover. Now he's my an ex-lover.
24  C:       Okay.
25  (?):     .hhh hhh
26  C:>      Okay well let's get to your resu:lts. Straight
27           o:ff. (0.2) er:: (0.6) Your number: once again is,
28  P:       J nine nine eight O seven seven seven.
29           (3.1)
30  C:       .hhh Okay. According to this .hh you are negative.
31           (0.7)
```

As in Extract 5.1, questions from C reveal P's expectations about the result. We then get a similar agenda statement leading to the announcement of the test result, which this time is negative.[3]

In all these eight cases, 'early' tellings follow C's request to Ps' to reveal their expectations and concerns. Ps' answers to such questions are strongly implicative of the telling of the test result in C's next turn.

However, in the remaining four interviews, conducted by a single, different counsellor, there are no initial questions to patients about their concerns. Instead, we find the counsellor providing an agenda for the interview and then offering a choice to the patient about what topic to pursue. Extract 5.3 is such an example where the agenda statement begins around line 5 and the offer on line 14:

Extract 5.3 (US1) {negative result}
```
1   C:       So you'be been i:n (0.2) t[o the
2   P:                               [I came in about a year
3            ago.=([And I        Yeah).
4   C:               [Okay.
5   C:       Okay. So you probably know that there are a few
6            things that er: (0.2) we need to go over here
7            obviously I want to (0.2) give you your test
8            results [and then
9   P:               [O k a : y.
10  C:       talk about what those results (.) mean for you:.
11  P:       Okay.
12  C:       Individually and (0.2) answer any questions.
13  P:       Okay.
14  C:       That you might have so: (0.5) where would you like
15           to begi:n.
```

As we shall see, this form of C's post-agenda statement turn (lines 14–15) is treated by all Ps as implying an offer rather than an announcement. In this chapter, I will focus on these four interviews where the agenda statement and offer replaces the initial question about Ps' concerns. Obviously, these interviews are practically interesting in terms of how a normatively encouraged strategy of client-centredness (expressed in allowing the patient to nominate the agenda) can actually create confusion. However, my initial focus will be on analytic issues which bear quite strongly on such practical matters.

Agendas and early tellings

How does an agenda-offer shape the subsequent emergence of the topic of the HIV test result? CA's insistence on focusing on the turn-by-turn organization of talk precludes the mistake of assuming that particular conversational gambits (like agenda statements followed by agenda-offers) have any single outcome (like delay in telling the test result). Indeed, two of the four 'agenda' interviews exhibit tellings of the test result positioned immediately after P replies to the offer.

Let us inspect these two interviews to see how far Ps' response to such an offer may be strongly implicative of such an 'early' telling.

Extract 5.4 (US1) {negative result}
```
1   C:       Have you been into the clinic (.) to be tested
2            before.=
3   P:       =No not here.=
4   C:       =Okay this is your first time here,=
5   P:       =Mm
6   C:       .hhhh Oka:y u:hm (0.2) and I'll tell you we have a
7            few things that er:: we need to do:, in our time
```

```
 8              together (          ) (.) give you the results,
 9   P:         Mm hm
10   C:         of the te:st er: (0.2) and talk about what the
11              test results (0.3) mean for you: er individually,
12              (0.2) and answer any questions
13   P:         (          )
14   C:         that you might ha:ve.
15              (1.1)
16   C:         So where would you like to begi:n?
17   P:         The results (heh huh) .hhhhh [hh hh hh
18   C:                                      [O k a : y. Your test
19              came back negative,
20   P:         Okay.
21              (1.2)
```

In Extract 5.4, P treats the choice offered to him by C (line 16) as a choice between the courses of action set out by C's three-part list (lines 8–14). He nominates hearing 'the results' as his choice (line 17) and gets his results in C's very next turn.

The other agenda-choice followed by an early telling is to be found in Extract 5.5 below:

```
     Extract 5.5 (US1) {negative result}
 1   C:    Can you read me back your registration number
 2         Yourself. [(To make sure that)-
 3   P:              [T zero one twenty eight fifty four.
 4   C:    Okay.
 5         (1.1)
 6   C:    Have you been into this centre to be tested
 7         before?
 8   P:    No.
 9   C:    This is your first time. Oka:y. (0.2) There are a
10         few things that (0.4) er: we need to do: during
11         this (.) time together.=One, I obviously want to
12         (.) give you your test result[s and (0.5) two=
13   P:                                  [hhhh
14   C:    =talk about what those test results mean for you
15         [uh
16   P:    [Uh huh=
17   C:    =individually and
18         (.)
19   P:    Uh hu[h
20   C:         [(then) to answer any questions
21   P:    Uh huh
22   C:    that you have.
23         (1.0)
24   C:    So where would you like to begin.=
```

```
25  P:        hhhhuh I don't care. .hhhh
26            (.)
27  (?):      (      )
28            (0.4)
29  P:        I just want to get- find out what's happening
30            really.
31  C:        Okay. (.) Your test result came back negative.
32  P:        hhhh
33            (0.7)
34  P:        That's good. hhhuh
```

In Extract 5.5, after C's offer on line 24, P initially says that he doesn't care (line 25). After a breath, two pauses and an untranscribable utterance, P respecifies his answer but in very general terms (lines 29–30). Nonetheless, P's answer – 'I just want to get- find out what's happening really.' is presumably treated by C as strongly implicative of a telling of the test result and this result is delivered in the very next turn (line 31).

Extracts 5.4 and 5.5 reveal two ways to turn the agenda-offer into an early telling of the test result: actually asking for the result (Extract 5.4) or refusing the offer followed by a request which is strongly implicative of the telling of the test result as an activity in the next position.

So far, then, the two alternative ways of beginning the post-test interview seem to produce the same outcome. Whether counsellors begin with a question about P's concerns (Extracts 5.1–5.3) or an agenda followed by an agenda-offer (Extracts 5.4–5.5), the test result appears once patients have responded.

However, in two of the four interviews that commence with agenda-offers, the test result is delayed. Let us explore the conversational mechanisms through which the agenda-offer can lead to a delay in telling the test result as well as the devices through which, after this delay, the result is eventually told. In this way, we will be in a better position to understand the interactional dilemmas that the apparently 'patient-centred' agenda-offer can produce.

Agendas and delayed tellings

Extract 5.6 is an example of an agenda-offer leading to a delayed telling. After checking P's registration number, C appears to look at P's completed questionnaire and observes that P has tested at this clinic (and been counselled) before:

```
        Extract 5.6 (US1)
1  C:        So you'be been i:n (0.2) t[o the
2  P:                                  [I came in about a year
3            ago.=([And I            Yeah).
4  C:                [Okay.
```

5	C:	Okay. So you probably know that there are a few
6		things that er: (0.2) we need to go over here
7		obviously I want to (0.2) give you your test
8		results [and then
9	P:	[O k a : y.
10	C:	talk about what those results (.) mean for <u>you</u>:.
11	P:	Okay.
12	C:	Individually and (0.2) answer any questions.
13	P:	Okay.
14	C:	That you might have so: (0.5) where would you like
15		to begi:n.
16	P:	.hhhh U::hm hhhhhuh .hhh <u>well</u> I was negative last
17		time.

P's acknowledgment that he 'came in a year ago' (lines 2–3) leads into C's agenda statement in another three-part list (lines 5–14) followed by an offer to P to choose the initial topic: 'where would you like to begi:n.' (14–15) as in Extracts 5.4 and 5.5.

What can we observe about P's uptake of these activities? First, observe that, at line 16, there is considerable turbulence as P begins his answer (a hesitation surrounded by three breaths). This turbulence was also found in the same position in Extract 5.5 and, arguably, was also suggested by P's laughter in this position in Extract 5.4.

Now such turbulence can be monitored in several ways, for instance as foreshadowing some delicate object (Silverman and Peräkylä, 1990). Another possibility is that the turbulence may be heard to indicate some uncertainty as to the shape of the turn design – for instance, although an answer will complete the adjacency pair, what kind of answer is appropriate?

Look at how C appears to have prioritized his agenda by indicating a preferred sequence in his three-part list. Note how the list is organized:

Extract 5.6 (US1) [shortened]

7	C:	obviously I want to (0.2) give you your test
8		results [and then
9	P:	[O k a : y.
10	C:	talk about what those results (.) mean for <u>you</u>:.
11	P:	Okay.
12	C:	Individually and (0.2) answer any questions.
13	P:	Okay.
14	C:	That you might have so: (0.5) where would you like
15		to begi:n.

The first part of the list is the only part to be prefaced by 'obviously' – presumably an appeal to what C and P can be assumed to know in common about an 'obvious' purpose of post-test counselling, i.e. giving the test result. More importantly, C himself seems to prioritize this item by chaining the other two items to the first by 'and then' (line 8). In this way, C implies a preferred temporal order of activities.

In the light of C's indication of a preferred order, beginning with the giving of 'your test results', P may be in some difficulty in selecting a preference when C asks him subsequently 'where would you like to begi:n' (lines 14–15). Of course, C could be heard to be displaying his agenda (in its preferred sequence) and then asking P to nominate his own. However, there are strong theoretical and empirical grounds to suggest that clients will usually be very cautious about introducing their own agendas once professionals have nominated their preferred agenda or course of action.[4]

If valid, this argument would suggest that the turbulence at the beginning of P's answer at line 16 can be heard to indicate *both* cautiousness foreshadowing a delicate object and uncertainty about the shape of the design of his turn.

The same point could also be made about Extracts 5.4 and 5.5, where, as already noted, turbulence follows an agenda-sequence which is either very similarly put together to Extract 5.6 (Extract 5.4) or almost identical to it (Extract 5.5 contains, in the same order, the 'obviously', 'then' and 'so' to which we have been referring). In these earlier extracts, however, the patients' replies deploy mechanisms which are strongly implicative of an early result-telling, unlike Extract 5.6.

As with Extract 5.6, such mechanisms are also absent from Extract 5.7. However, unlike Extracts 5.4–5.6, P's initial response to the agenda-offer (line 13 onward) shows no turbulence.

Extract 5.7 (US1) {negative test result}

1	C:	Oka:y. So you probably know there are a couple of
2		things that (0.2) we need to go over here: [uh:m
3	P:	[Mm hm
4		(0.2)
5	C:	(I would sooner) (.) communicate the (0.2) test
6		results to you and (.) interpret (.) what your
7		test results mean (.) for you individually and (.)
8		answer any questions (0.2) [that you have
9	P:	[( )
10	P:	( )
11		(0.2)
12	C:	So where would you like to begin.
13	P:	Okay u:hm: (0.7) .hhh first of all I guess er I've
14		been reading in the paper about the Eliza test and
15		that they have found traces of HIV (0.2) er:
16		through more sophisticated testing methods where
17		they like culture the blood for six months and
18		stuff like that. .hh And I was wondering if you
19		have any recent statistics on .hh what they- the
20		use of the er Eliza test as a predictor: or as a

21   (.) an indicator (0.3) er like if you get a
22   negative result (.) can you be fairly certain
23   it's- it's an accurate result?

As with Extract 5.4, in Extract 5.7, C's agenda-offer (line 12) is treated at face value and a topic is nominated by P. However, unlike Extract 5.4, where C nominated his test result as next topic, here P uses the agenda-offer to ask a question about the accuracy of the testing regime (lines 13–23). As we shall see later, this question sets in train a series of topics which further delay the delivery of the test result.[5]

Agenda-offers/responses and institutional caution

The cautiousness with which Ps respond to the agenda-offer in Extracts 5.6 and 5.7 may relate to something more general about counselling than the potential for uncertainty created by C's own preceding three-part agenda list. Peräkylä has argued that such caution may stem from the relatively opaque meaning of 'counselling' to the general public. As he comments:

> We – as ordinary members of Western societies – do not know what happens in counselling with the same precision as we know what is going on in a doctor's surgery or in a lecture hall. For the clients, then, what the general goals of a counselling session are may be more or less *opaque*. (Peräkylä, 1995: 98).

Peräkylä suggests that among the possible consequences of this opacity are that clients 'may be inclined to confine themselves to *responsive* actions' (ibid.: 99). More specifically, in terms of this chapter, Peräkylä argues that 'clients may want to avoid *agenda-setting* moves because they do not know what the agenda is supposed to be' (ibid.).

Even when, as here, the client is asked to nominate his agenda, Peräkylä's argument ties the responses we have found to client caution in an opaque setting. This seems most clear in the two cases where Ps do not nominate the test result as where they would like C to begin. However, elements of caution are also found even where Ps get their test result in C's next turn. We see this most directly in Extract 5.5 (lines 25–30) when P takes a breath and then says 'I don't care' and then only refers to finding out 'what's happening'. But, even in Extract 5.4, where P immediately asks for 'the results' (line 17), he follows this up with laughter, as if this might be an odd thing for him to be doing.

Such caution is not confined to clients. In any professional–client interview which includes the disclosure of some finding, possibly involving 'bad news' to the client, the professional may elect to proceed cautiously. As Maynard (1991) and Bergmann (1992) have shown, professionals use certain devices to align their clients to such news. These devices (perspective display, third-party tellings and litotes) all involve delay in telling the news in order to obtain such alignment.

The single positive test result in our data-set perfectly fits such an analysis. In Extract 5.1, as we have seen, C delays delivering a positive test result by asking a question about P's anxieties, as follows:

```
Extract 5.1 (US1) {positive result}
11  C:      How have your anxieties been waiting for this re-
12          these results.=It's been almost a week now.
13  P:      er: (0.2) Not too ba:d. hhh=
14  C:      =Okay kind of (okay)
15          (1.2)
16  P:      I haven't really thought about it. I- because
17          Friday when I was supposed to come (0.2) I had to
18          cancel, (                    ).
19          (0.5)
20  C:      So it's not been something too oppressing for
21          you.=
22  P:      =(No) (    ).
23  C:>     Okay. .hhh Why don't we go ahead and talk about
24          what your results are okay?
```

Here C's question (lines 11–12) may serve to align P to his upcoming positive test result. Presumably, if P had replied that he indeed had been very anxious, then C would have been able to fit the delivery of the test result to a client who was already potentially aligned to it (because of his 'anxiety'). However, this perspective display sequence does not reveal an 'anxious' client and, consequently, C is forced to deliver the test result without the alignment his question was seeking.

Along these lines, it could be argued that our four agenda-offer interviews are further attempts at alignment where the mechanism used is not a question about a client's 'feelings' but an open-ended question about the client's agenda. In this respect, the counsellor concerned is displaying the same kind of 'caution' as C in Extract 5.1.

However, Maynard specifically discusses the use of the PDS in contexts where the professional is attempting to align the client to 'bad' news. By contrast, in all four cases of the agenda-offer discussed here, a negative test result is awaiting disclosure.

Two aspects of such agenda-offers will be explored shortly. First, how the client can hear such cautiousness as implying an upcoming positive test result (see pp. 104–05). Second, the practical issue of the possible misplacing of such professional caution in environments where the news that is about to be delivered is likely to be 'good'.[6]

In the next section, I will pursue these issues by examining the environments in which test results are eventually delivered when Ps respond to agenda-offers either by a question (Extract 5.7) or a statement (Extract 5.6) neither of which demands an immediate result-telling.

Further delays in tellings

As it turns out, after an agenda-offer, if the offer is not declined (as in
Extract 5.5) or accepted, with a request for the test result (Extract 5.4), then
it can be a tortuous business to find an environment in which the test result is
delivered. In this regard, let us examine the future course of Extracts 5.6 and
5.7 which derive from interviews in which tests results are not told after P's
first turn.

This is how Extract 5.6 continues:

```
       Extract 5.8 (US1) (Extract 5.6 continued)
16   P:        .hhhh U::hm hhhhhuh .hhh well I was negative last
17             time. I'm hoping I'm still negative. U:hm (.) as I
18             don't believe I've (0.3) done anything (0.4) that
19             would put me at risk in the last year,
```

At first sight, in this continuation, P selects an answer which is strongly
implicative of a result-telling:

```
16   P:        .hhhh U::hm hhhhhuh .hhh well I was negative last
17             time. I'm hoping I'm still negative.
```

P's 'hope' seems to invite C's correction or confirmation in the context of a
result-telling. It is worth comparing a similar statement found in Extract 5.5
which does elicit a C turn involving a result-telling:

```
29   P:        I just want to get- find out what's happening
30             really.
31   C:        Okay. (.) Your test result came back negative.
```

Here P's statement, although it does not mention a possible test result is
equally strongly implicative of a result-telling where 'what's happening' is
likely to be heard as 'what's happening regarding my HIV status'. However,
in Extract 5.5, P's use of 'just' serves to indicate that this is the *only* issue he
wants to raise and so may serve to generate the actual result-telling in the
next line. Moreover, in Extract 5.8, P continues without a break to talk
about a fresh topic. Without the kind of turn-transition point found in
Extract 5.5, C would be heard to be interrupting P if he were to deliver the
test result at this point.

P's account of his presumed lack of exposure to risk 'in the last year' leads
up to a statement of his 'main concern':

```
       Extract 5.9 (US1) (Extract 5.6 continued)
20   P:        [.hhhh My main concern has bee:n I read so many=
21   C:        [Mm hm
22   P:        =different thi:ngs,=some people say it can be
23             eight to ten year:s before it shows u:p and things
24             like that and of course eight to ten years ago:
25             (0.4) you know things were different. [You know=
26   C:                                               [Mm hm
```

```
27   P:        =the last few year:s .hhh 'a' I have not had any
28             relationships a:nd 'b': (0.7) er: (.) anything
29             that I have done has been safe.
30   C:        Mm hm=
31   P:        =So: (  [    )
32   C:                [Mm hm
33   C:        So as far as the past couple of years are
34             [concerned you feel like you've been at minimal=
35   P:        [Oh yeah.
```

On line 31, P starts to complete his long turn with a drawn-out utterance ('so:') which can be heard as strongly invitational to the delivery of some upshot-statement by C in the next turn. In the context of P's reference to his lack of 'relationships' and his 'safe' behaviour, that upshot might well be P's test result. Yet, although C does indeed take a turn here (line 33), he does not deliver P's test result but proffers a candidate-summary of P's sense of risk.

What seems to be happening here is that P has raised many more possible next topics than simply his test results. In particular, his references to his sense of risk are open to confirmation and/or clarification, while his mention of what he 'reads' about what 'shows up' in tests invites confirmation or correction. Both topics are indeed subsequently taken up by C through a statement about the validity of HIV tests after different periods of risk exposure (data not shown) and by questions about various risky behaviours.

In pursuing these topics raised by P by candidate-summaries (Extract 5.9, lines 33–4), by requests for specification and by information delivery, C is fulfilling many of the activities ordinarily associated with counselling. P's response to C's initial agenda-offer 'kicks in', as it were, the routine counselling practices described in Chapter 3. The practical issue, already signposted, is simply how appropriate these activities are *prior to* the delivery of the test result.

The test result is finally delivered by C in the course of this sequence:

```
        Extract 5.10 (US1) (Extract 5.6 continued)
107   P:          [But uhm (0.3) a:nd (     )- no I've not been with
108               anyone for=
109   C:          =Mm hm
110               (0.6)
111   P:          I guess er:: (0.3) this time last year so (you
112               know) if it's still negative then I'm oka:y.
113   C:          Your test result came back negative.
```

The extract above is instructive about the possible local environments in which test results can eventually get delivered when not provided early by a counsellor. On line 107, P is completing an answer to a question from C about 'high risk' behaviours. In principle, that answer, like others before, might allow C to ask still further questions or to deliver more information (other than P's test result). But note that P concludes his answer with:

P: so (you know) if it's still negative then I'm oka:y.

This utterance is hearable as a proposed upshot of P's answer which shows understanding of what C has recently said about the validity of HIV tests, i.e. that a negative test result will be valid if P has not engaged in any risky behaviours in the last six months. Its beauty in relation to obtaining the test result is that, since both parties know that only C has the test result, it is strongly implicative that C, in his next turn, should confirm whether indeed P is 'okay'. And this is precisely what C does.[7]

In the other interview where the test result is delayed, it will be recalled that P uses the agenda-offer to ask about the general validity of test results. The conclusion of C's answer is set out below:

       Extract 5.11 (US1) (Extract 5.7 continued)
53   C: But er: it's over ninety-nine per cent accurate.
54   With the: (0.5) with the negative results there's
55   a very low (.) rate of false negatives.
56   (0.5)
57   P: Okay. Okay that's reassuring.
58   C: Mm hm
59   P: er: I guess that was my main que:stion. er[:
60   C: [Okay.
61   P: The reason I came in here was because (0.2) I have
62   ha:d- I ha:d a lot of high risk activity up
63   through ninety eighty-five.
64   C: Mm hm

P's marked acknowledgment to C's answer ('Okay. Okay that's reassuring.', line 57) serves to close that topic. Additionally, P's gloss on his activity ('I guess that was my main que:stion.', line 59) also seems to complete the sequence begun by C's earlier agenda-offer. With both topic and sequence apparently closed, this might seem to be an appropriate environment for C to take a turn in which P's test result might be delivered. But C simply uses his turn to provide a response-token ('Okay') and P continues with another topic on line 61.

How might C have inspected P's utterance at line 59: 'er: I guess that was my main que:stion. er[:' as not being an appropriate point to tell the test result? First, P's extended 'er:' at the end of his utterance can be heard as hesitation prior to the speaker raising a further topic. Second, note that P defines his activity as his *main* question. Unlike Extract 5.5, where a patient uses the term 'just' ('I just want to get- find out what's happening'), 'main' can imply imply that P may be about to nominate, within this turn, further questions – albeit of a more minor nature.

P now continues his turn with a statement of his reasons for testing:

```
      Extract 5.12 (US1) (Extract 5.7 continued)
61  P:          The reason I came in here was because (0.2) I have
62              ha:d- I ha:d a lot of high risk activity up
63              through ninety eighty-five.
64  C:          Mm hm
65  P:          A:nd you kno:w (.) .hh I've had some health
66              problems and my doctor (0.2) said that there are
67              some people that don't convert or don't (.)
68              produce antibodies for up to like thirty-six or
69              forty-eight months. [And so he thought he=
70  C:          [Mm:
71  P:          =thought I should come in and have another test.
72  C:          Mm hm
73  P:          Just to: (0.6) make sure:.
74  C:          Mm hm
75  P:          So:
76  C:          But within the last year: (0.3) er [you don't=
77  P:                                            [No I've-
78  C:          =consider (0.2) [your behaviours have been risky.
```

Exactly as in Extract 5.6, this patient completes his long turn with a drawn-out utterance ('so:', line 75) which can be heard as strongly invitational to the delivery of some upshot-statement by C in the next turn. Once again, this time in the context of P's reference to his doctor's recommendation that he should 'have another test . . . just to make sure', that upshot might well be P's test result.

As with the interview from which Extract 5.6 was taken, P has raised other possible next topics than simply his test results. In particular, his reference to his 'high risk activity' is open to clarification by C using his next turn to question P rather than to deliver the test result. And this is exactly what happens next, as from line 76 onwards C asks P about his past behaviours.

Once again, as in the other delayed telling, the topics raised by P 'kick in' standard counselling activities. In this manner, C now asks a question about P's understanding of the lack of likelihood of being exposed to the HIV virus if he had stuck to 'safe' behaviour:

```
      Extract 5.13 (US1) (Extract 5.7 continued)
86  C:          .hh You understand it's a real: small percentage
87              of people (.) who take that time to sero-convert.
88  P:          Yeah that's what he told me tha:t. [And that=
89  C:                                             [Yeah.
90  P:          =he's- he said in view of (0.4) the medical
91              history and- and some of the (.) things that were
92              er: going o:n (.) as early as four years ago that-
93              that I should go in there [just to make sure.
94  C:                                    [Sure.
95  C:          Sure:. Mm
```

96		(0.2)
97	C:	Typically six weeks to six months is the (0.2)
98		time frame than will en̲compass (.) ninety-five per
99		cent of the (.) the people who are going to sero-
100		conver:t.

P's answer to C's knowledge question (lines 86–7) turns the topic round to what P's doctor told him (lines 88–93). P ends his turn by referring to his doctor's instruction: 'that I should go in there [just to make sure.'

This can be heard as invitational to an immediate test result disclosure in two ways. First, it offers a topic directly relevant to P's test result, i.e. 'making sure' that P is HIV negative. Second, as a 'third-party telling' (Bergmann, 1992), P's utterance can be heard as strongly implicative that the second party will reveal more about the topic.[8]

As it turns out, C responds to both these invitations *without* introducing P's test result as next topic. Instead, C topicalizes the period taken to seroconvert rather than the test result itself, thereby responding to P's third-party telling by implicitly criticizing P's doctor's advice about the need to test (lines 97–100).

Immediately after this, P makes another attempt to close his response to C's initial request to him to nominate the agenda:

Extract 5.14 (US1) (Extract 5.7 continued)

101	P:	Okay.
102		(1.3)
103	P:	All right.
104		(0.6)
105	P:	I think that pretty well covers what I need to
106		know.
107	C:	Oka:y.

As the extract above shows, however, P's closing invitation elicits merely a response-token from C ('Oka:y', line 107). Once again, perhaps, there is an ambiguity present in P's choice of adverbs since 'pretty well' might just indicate a further upcoming topic in a way that 'entirely' would not.[9]

Now P hears C's passive response-token as an invitation to take another turn. In this turn, P introduces the topic of 'support groups' for 'HIV positive people':

Extract 5.15 (US1) (Extract 5.7 continued)

107	C:	Oka:y.
108	P:	I know that there's- I go to AA so I have er
109		support groups if I need them a:nd I know where
110		there are (.) HIV positive meetings,
111	C:	Mm hm
112	P:	er: and I uh- guess you guys have a list if
113		there's (.) you know a need for it so
114	C:	Mm hm

115	P:	and you have counselling services here.
116	C:	Yeah we do:. For people who test positive.

At first sight, P's introduction of this topic is surprising in the light of C's immediately preceding observation that low-risk activity is unlikely to lead to being HIV positive. Yet here (lines 108–115) he raises a topic and asks two questions (lines 112–115) category-bound to the MCD patient-likely-to-be-HIV-positive.

We can explain this incongruity by attending to how P might analyse C's failure to deliver his test result (a task itself category-bound to the activity of a post-test counselling interview) either at the commencement of the interview or, as we have seen, after *four* P turns which might be heard to be implicative of such a telling.

Given that we all know that bad news is properly delayed or even organized so as to be guessed by its recipient (Sacks, 1992), I suggest that P can monitor C's non-telling of P's test result as possibly implicative that there is indeed such 'bad news' to tell in his case. The non-telling thus works as the kind of activity that Maynard (1996) has described as 'stalling' where avoiding disclosure of some information can lead to a misinterpretation by its recipient.

Such a misinterpretation is readily shown in P's references to 'support groups' and 'counselling services' which show that he is getting C's presumed drift – albeit, as it turns out, mistakenly. Moreover, P is by now actively co-operating in the delivery of the 'bad' news by creating a nice environment for such a delivery because P has shown himself prepared for it.

Of course, as it now turns out, P's test result is HIV negative so, rather than help C's delivery of the test result, P's observation and question have put C into an interactional fix.

Notice how C now extricates himself from this fix by immediately making it clear (line 116) in his answer to P's question that such services are available: 'For people who test positive.' When this answer is receipted by P who then fails to take another turn, C now offers P's test result to him:

Extract 5.16 (US1) (Extract 5.7 continued)

116	C:	Yeah we do:. For people who test positive.
117	P:	Okay.
118	C:	Mm
119		(1.0)
120	C:	Would you like to know your test resu[lt?
121	P:	[Yes. hheh
122		hhuh
123	C:	Your test came back negative.
124	P:	Okay.
125	P:	Thank you:. hhhhuhh=
126	C:	=Sure:.
127		(.)
128	C:	[[(Yeah)).
129	P:	[[That's a relief. hh

Ironically, then, C's eventual disclosure of P's test result seems to be produced here as a solution to the interactional fix that his prior non-tellings have produced. In this sense, P's assertion of 'relief' (line 129), following a deep breath (125), may be as much an interactional product as part of the predictable 'anxiety' about the result after an HIV test.

Let me conclude this chapter by a summary of the main points that have come out of this analysis, followed by a brief discussion of the practical implications.

Summary

Three major points have emerged from this discussion of a small number of post-test counselling interviews. First, following Peräkylä (1995), 'cautiousness' is seen, once more, to be a major feature of HIV counselling. This is true of the activities of both counsellors and clients. Thus these counsellors seek to align their clients to the disclosure of their test result, while clients, to whom the character of counselling is presumably 'opaque', often demur at taking any action which might demand an immediate telling of their test result (or indeed, many other activities, like directly demanding clarification of the validity of HIV tests) even when, as here, given agenda-offers. However, these agenda-offers, unlike the alignment strategies discussed by Maynard (1991) and Bergmann (1992), are being used in an environment where the upcoming diagnosis is likely to be heard as 'good'.

Second, we have seen how, when clients respond to agenda-offers by introducing topics other than the test result (e.g. volunteering statements about themselves or asking, usually indirectly, about the validity of the HIV test), they seem to 'kick in' standard counselling responses (e.g. information and requests for specification). While such responses are consonant with normative standards of good counselling practice, they are, once again, produced in an environment in which their positioning (prior to the telling of the test result) may be problematic.

Finally, we have demonstrated that, for at least one client, this delay in telling is problematic. As Extract 5.7 (and its continuations) showed, this client analysed the delay in the delivery of his test result as implying that C was about to deliver a 'positive' result – by referring to 'support groups' for HIV-positive people.

This apparent lack of fit between a delayed delivery of the test result and its content (i.e. as HIV negative) leads directly into some fairly clear practical implications.

Practical implications

I can best discuss these practical issues by quoting at length from a volunteer counsellor's response to a first draft of this chapter (Sheon, personal communication). Nicolas Sheon mentions how counsellors attempt to reinforce health education messages after delivering negative test results. However, he notes that this is not easy to accomplish:

> since many clients are tense and ready to bolt out the door as soon as they hear the result, and, even if they don't leave straight away, they are not really mentally present. Because it is a challenge to keep a client for a post-test, *it is sometimes tempting to use the delay of the result as a way to get the client to talk*. (my emphasis)

Sheon provides a convincing practical reason why the counsellor in Extracts 5.4–5.7 may not immediately offer a negative test result. However, he also argues that

> discussion of risk without reference to the result is not productive . . . [now] there is no convenient place to disclose because the client is freaking out and blabbering on and on about prognosis and referrals for positives. (ibid.)

Should the post-test counselling interview have got to this stage, Sheon argues that the only way out is 'to interrupt the client and say something like: "Well we could go on and on talking about this but it's only relevant if you are in fact positive. So why don't we get to the result?"' (ibid.).

In fact, Sheon's invented example is actually quite close to how our counsellor in Extracts 5.15 and 5.16 is led to deliver the negative test result when P wrongly draws the implication that he is seropositive. Instead of getting into that position, Sheon argues that it is more satisfactory simply to ask: 'Do you have any questions or would you like to get right to the result?' Following this disclosure, health promotion issues can properly be addressed by now asking: 'What originally brought you in for the test?' Overall, he writes: 'the strategy of the good counsellor is to siphon off this tension as quickly as possible because the longer you delay disclosure, the tension mounts exponentially and counselling becomes impossible' (ibid.).

Sheon's comments develop the point about early disclosure found in HIV counselling texts like that of Bor, Miller and Goldman (1992). So, at this point, non-sociological readers may be asking themselves: why spend so much time in analysing the apparently quirky communication methods of a single counsellor?

My answer is twofold. First, this counsellor is not really so quirky. In responding to the (pre-test results) utterances of his clients in the way that he does, he is recognizably doing counselling in the way that we have seen other counsellors fulfil their role (namely, asking questions and delivering information). Moreover, in making his agenda-offer, he is seeking to align himself to his client, using a tactic from a range used by apparently 'listening' or 'non-directive' professionals.

Second, this is not to deny that, in post-test counselling, the agenda-offer, positioned *before* the telling of the result, can create problems for both clients and counsellors. What is at issue here is simply the *timing* of a tactic which, when placed elsewhere, may be helpful to all parties. The importance of this example is simply to remind ourselves that mechanical application of communication 'techniques', without regard to their local relevance, can create confusion rather than mutual understanding.[10]

Notes

1. This observation is based on fieldnotes taken when the author was allowed to sit in at this hospital (but not tape-record) in the early 1990s.

2. On reading this chapter, one volunteer counsellor commented: 'It is not inconceivable that, in some cases only, delay of the result is prompted by a sadistic urge on the part of the counsellor who disapproves of the client's behaviours and wants to teach them a lesson so that they realize that they "got lucky this time"' (Nicolas Sheon, personal communication).

3. Note the hedging around the nature of the test result in Extract 5.2. Unlike Extract 5.1, the test result itself is prefaced by C saying: 'according to this'. This hedging may reflect the uncertainty generated by the unusual 'false positive' result last time.

4. Parsons (1951) has laid the basis for the theoretical claim that the doctor–patient relationship is based on the patient deferring to the doctor's expertise. Parsons's claim is supported empirically by Strong's (1979a) observation of paediatric encounters. Further support is provided by my own study of a cardiology clinic where the doctor's statement of his preferred decision ('what I propose to do at this stage') was never opposed by the patient or the patient's family (Silverman, 1981, 1987).

5. Using CA methods, we cannot answer why these two patients (in Extracts 5.6 and 5.7) do not directly ask for their test results when two other patients (in Extracts 5.4 and 5.5) more or less directly do this. It might only be noted that, in Extracts 5.6 and 5.7 but not Extracts 5.4 and 5.5, C refers to an earlier HIV test taken by the patient. It is possible, then, that this reference makes a second test immediately accountable. This interpretation is supported by the fact that, in Extracts 5.6 and 5.7, both patients, while denying any recent 'unsafe' behaviour, refer to their uncertainties about the length of the 'window period' in which HIV test results become valid. In this way, they make their repeat test accountable.

6. We have to be careful, however, about assuming that all patients desire 'negative' results. As one counselling text suggests: 'Some people are relieved by a positive test result as they can now understand their symptoms and no longer have anxiety about the diagnosis' (Bor et al., 1992: 70).

7. Of course, C is not mechanically constrained by P's implicit request for an upshot-confirmation. For instance, he could have topicalized P's sense of being 'okay'.

8. Bergmann discusses third-party tellings by professionals in his data on psychiatric interviews. Interestingly, this example shows that third-party tellings can be used, with the same function (of achieving further information) by clients.

9. We might speculate, in Basil Bernstein's (1971) terms, that P's attention to nuance, typical of Bernstein's 'elaborated code', has communicational dysfunctions as well as its more obvious functions.

10. This point is made very clearly by Maynard (1996). To some extent, this bears on the argument about the limits of 'patient-centred' medicine that I have developed elsewhere (Silverman, 1987). For instance, in a paediatric cleft-palate clinic, I noted how a similar, apparently patient-centred, tactic (the question 'how do you feel about your looks?') could create demonstrable confusion when addressed to an adolescent.

PART FOUR
ADVICE-GIVING

A central feature of most pre-HIV test counselling interviews is the provision of advice by counsellors to clients. This advice deals with such matters as 'safer sex', who to tell, when to have a repeat test and so on. But there is considerable variation between centres both in how early in the interview the advice is delivered and how far it is targeted at issues raised by the client.

In these three chapters I use transcripts of HIV counselling data to focus on the precise mechanics of advice-giving and advice reception. In Chapter 6, I set out the basic features of the phenomenon using data-extracts from three British centres. Chapter 7 then looks at how client resistance to advice is marked and managed in counselling interviews taken from one British centre (UK2). Finally, in Chapter 8, I use data from a US(US2) centre to deal more precisely with one way of managing advice-giving which allows multiple responses. Throughout, I will be concerned with how advice in counselling can be locally processed to promote its acceptance.

6

Advice-Giving and Advice Reception

Why advice?

Drawing upon the definition proposed by Heritage and Sefi (1992), I identify as advice those sequences in which the professional 'describes, recommends or forwards a preferred course of action' to the client, or in which 'she approves or supports a past course of action or present state of affairs' (1992: 368). Therefore, like Heritage and Sefi, I am interested in activities that have a normative dimension rather than information requests or deliveries (although, as Heritage and Sefi point out, what is taken to be information or advice is a locally managed matter).

As already noted in Chapter 1, 'counselling' is usually defined by practitioners in a way which distinguishes it from 'advice-giving'. Yet many counselling interviews which take place before and after the HIV-antibody test involve the delivery of advice in one form or another. Often this advice concerns safer sex, as in the extracts below:

        Extract 6.1 (UK4)
1   C: Uh:m: (1.7) I- I think perhaps just to be clear now
2   our suggestion would be that if you're going to
3   continue to have a sexual relationship and there's
4   no reason why you shouldn't [.hhhh then=
5   P: [Mm hm
6   C: =at this stage you: (0.2) should try to keep it as
7   safe as possible for a variety of reasons.

        Extract 6.2 (UK3)
1   C: this is why we say hh if you don't know the person
2   that you're with (0.6) and you're going to have sex
3   with them hh it's important that you tell them to
4   (0.3) use a condom (0.8)

In these three chapters, I will look closely at how such advice is delivered. We might immediately note, for instance, that in Extract 6.1 C says 'our suggestion would be' (line 2) but in Extract 6.2 the advice is packaged as 'this is why we say' (line 1). Chapter 8 will focus on the local impact of such nuances in the design of advice.

However, is there any reason why counsellors working outside the HIV area should be interested in advice-giving when advice is not part of their professionally defined mandate? I believe there are two answers to this question which may satisfy such doubts.

First, clients' reception of advice is affected by the conversational environment in which the advice is actually delivered. As it turns out, for instance, in Extract 6.2, unlike Extract 6.1, the advice is delivered without any prior questioning of the client about the topic. Attempts to elicit clients' perspectives prior to the delivery of advice (which advice can therefore be recipient designed) is strongly correlated with marked acknowledgments of that advice by clients. Conversely, clients typically offer minimal acknowledgments to advice which arrives 'out of the blue' without any attempt to elicit their perspective or concerns.

This finding is not only intuitively predictable but also fits the client-centredness implied in most accounts of counselling.[1] So the first reason why an analysis of advice-giving and advice reception may be of interest to counsellors is that it raises relevant general issues about how clients may be involved in the counselling interview.

The second reason why non-HIV counsellors might be interested in advice-giving is that 'advice' may not be as separate from counselling as we might suppose. As Feltham (1995: 18–19) points out, there are a number of ways in which advice-giving might arise in counselling. First, he suggests, abstaining from advice-giving may be unethical in certain situations, for instance where the client is 'vulnerable or confused'. Second, Feltham argues that 'covert advice-giving' is implicitly involved in certain styles of counselling.[2]

Of course, once we move out of the debate about what is 'counselling', it is beyond dispute that advice-giving is a major activity in many professional–client interviews, extending beyond HIV counselling to include medical and legal consultations. For those working in the health field, if we can identify effective forms of advice-giving we can make a direct contribution to the understanding of health promotion in face-to-face communication.

The topic of advice also fits neatly with earlier chapters which identified phenomena providing an important context for the analysis of advice sequences. As shown in Chapter 3, HIV counsellors use one of two kinds of communication format as their 'home base': an Interview format (in which Cs ask questions and Ps give answers) and an information delivery format (in which Cs deliver information and Ps are silent apart from small acknowledgment tokens). Other forms of communication (for instance Ps asking questions or delivering information) turned out to be less common and more unstable. The reception of advice is considerably influenced by which format is used by the counsellor immediately before the advice is delivered. This has important implications both for our analysis and for its import for practice.

Furthermore, as Chapter 4 shows, HIV counselling often involves multiple topics which both counsellors and clients mark (and manage) as 'delicate'. Clearly, the nature of such delicate topics may make advice-giving and reception particularly problematic. We will later develop this issue but it is worth bearing in mind as the reader peruses the extracts of advice-giving contained in this chapter.

Advice-giving: four forms

HIV test counselling is unlike many other forms of counselling in which clients may be expected to present with perceived problems. In all the centres represented here, counselling is something that simply comes with getting an HIV test rather than 'help' requested by a client.

Predictably, then, we find that nearly all advice sequences are initiated by the counsellor (see Table 6.1, p. 126). However, this uniformity masks four different forms in which advice may be delivered:

1   non-personalized advice within an Information Delivery Format;
2   personalized advice following an Interview Format;
3   hybrid or combined sequences;
4   client-inferred advice within an Interview Format.

We analyse an example of each form of advice-giving below using extracts from pre-test counselling interviews.

Non-personalized advice: information delivery

Extract 6.3 below is taken from an interview with a female. Up to this point, she has only been briefly questioned about her exposure to risk. This extract occurs in the middle of a long sequence of information delivery about various issues involved in having an HIV test:

```
      Extract 6.3 (UK1)
 1   C:      .hhhh Now when someo:ne er is tested (.) and they
 2           ha:ve a negative test result .hh it's obviously
 3           ideal uh:m that(.) they then look after themselves
 4           to prevent [any further risk of=
 5   P:                 [Mm hm
 6   C:      =infection. .hhhh I mean obviously this is only
 7           possible up to a point because if .hhh you get into
 8           a sort of serious relationship with someone that's
 9           long ter:m .hh you can't obviously continue to use
10           condoms forever. .hh Uh:m and a point has to come
11           where you make a sort of decision (0.4) uh:m if you
12           are settling down about families and things that you
13           know (0.6) you'd- not to continue safer sex.
14           [.hhhh Uh:m but obviously: (1.0) you=
15   P:      [Mm:
16   C:      =nee:d to be (.) uh:m (.) take precautions uhm (0.3)
17           and keep to the safer practices .hhh if: obviously
18           you want to prevent infection in the future.
```

19	P:	[Mm hm
20	C:	[.hhhh The problem at the moment is we've got it
21		here in ((names City)) in particular (.) right across
22		the boar:d you know from all walks of life.
23	P:	Mm hm
24	C:	Uh::m from you know (.) the sort of established high
25		r- risk groups (.) now we're getting heterosexual
26		(.) [transmission as well. .hh Uhm=
27	P:	[Mm hm
28	C:	=so obviously everyone really needs to careful. .hhh
29		Now whe- when someone gets a positive test result
30		er: then obviously they're going to ke- think very
31		carefully about things. .hhhh Being HIV positive
32		doesn't necessarily mean that that person is going
33		to develop AI:DS (.) later on.
34		(.)
35	P:	Mm hm

We can make three observations about this extract. First, C delivers advice without having elicited from P a perceived problem. Reasons of space do not allow us to include what immediately precedes this extract but it concerns another topic (the meaning of a positive test result) and no attempt is made to question P about her possible response to this topic, i.e. how she might change her behaviour after a negative test result. Moreover, within this extract, C introduces fresh topics (what to do in a 'serious' relationship in lines 6–13; the spread of HIV in the city, lines 20–2) without attempting to elicit P's own perspectives.

Second, at the start of this extract, C does not personalize her advice. Instead of using a personal pronoun or the patient's name, she refers to 'someone' and 'they' (lines 1–4). This allows P to hear the 'you' used several times in lines 7–13 as 'people in general' rather than P herself. Such a hearing is underlined by C's subsequent piece of advice (line 28) which is framed in terms of 'everyone'. Advice sequences like these are very common at three out of the five centres we have examined.

Third, predictably, P only produces variations on 'mm hmm' in response to C's advice. While these may indicate that P is listening, they do not show P uptake and might be taken as a sign of passive resistance to the advice (see Heritage and Sefi, 1992). Indeed, it is noteworthy that even these 'mms' are absent at the points where C might most clearly be heard to deliver advice about safer sex (as opposed to information). Thus, at the end of line 28, as C completes her advice, P remains silent.

At this point, readers may be tempted to respond critically to an extract in which the client's perspective is not obtained and in which, predictably, minimal uptake of advice is achieved. However, since our preference was not to criticize professionals but to understand the logic of their work, we need to look at the *functions* as well as the dysfunctions of this way of proceeding. A part of the answer to this question lies in the *dysfunctions* of more recipient-designed advice. Throughout our corpus of interviews, counsellors exit quickly from *personalized* advice when patients offer only minimal responses like 'mm mms' (see Chapter 7). It seems that, if someone is giving you personalized advice, if you don't show more uptake than 'mm mm', this will be problematic to the advice-giver. Conversely, if you are merely giving somebody general information, then occasional 'mm mms' are all that is required for the speaker to continue in this format. Moreover, truncated, non-personalized advice sequences are also usually far shorter – an important consideration for hard-pressed counsellors. Finally, predictably, information-oriented counselling produces very little conflict. So, in Extract 6.3, P's 'mms' are not heard by C to indicate *active* resistance. Indeed, topic follows topic with a remarkable degree of smoothness and at great speed.

As we move on to an example of personalized advice, we will see that the sequence takes far longer (hence the extended data-extract provided below).

Personalized advice: interview format

Extract 6.4 below is taken from a centre which routinely videotapes its counselling interviews (a matter referred to by P in lines 6–7 below). It involves the pre-test counselling of a gay man whose partner has just tested positive. Extract 6.4 occurs nearly at the beginning of the interview at which point, unlike Extract 6.3, no information had yet been delivered by the counsellor:

```
        Extract 6.4 (UK4)
 1  C:    Mm hm .hhh What sort of sexual relationship are you
 2        having at the moment with him.
 3        (0.6)
 4  P:    With X.
 5  C:    Mm hm
 6  P:    er::: (1.7) We:ll (0.6) hhh God how to go into this
 7        on camera: I don't know. .hhhh er:: (2.6) Let me
 8        just say I'm on bottom he's on to:p, (0.7) er::
 9        There was a period at the very beginni:ng (0.5) er::
10        (0.5) where a condom was not- ((Clears throat))
11        excuse me was not used. (0.6)
12        er:[::
13  C:       [Are you using condoms now?=[Or er-
14  P:                                   [uh We::ll (0.4)
15        yeah. Mm (1.0) er::: (.) There is: (.) still some
16        oral se:x, (0.6) er:: not passing any fluids alo:ng
17        but they say: (0.4) that yes you do pass fluid
18        along. (0.4) So I'm still kind of nervous about
```

19		that.=However: .hhhh (0.2) er:uh::hhh (0.8) I:- I
20		<u>don</u>'t know:: (0.5) what I don't know .hh is er::
21		(0.2) how: I would have contracted it to him.
22	C:	Mm:=
23	P:	=er::: (0.7) I have not (1.1) er:: (1.0) had anal
24		intercourse with hi:m.
25		(0.8)
26	C:	Okay.
27	P:	er::: (0.5) He ha:<u>s</u>
28	C:	Mm
29	P:	er:: (0.5) performed oral sex on me:
30		(.)
31	C:	M[m:
32	P:	[without a condo:m, (.) but I've not ejaculated
33		into his mouth.
34	C:	Mm
35	P:	er:: But (.) like they say you do (.) (lose <u>some</u>
36		though).
37	C:	Mm
38		(.)
39	P:	er::
40		(.)
41	C:	Yeah. .h I th<u>ink</u> (.) P how we understand things is
42		that it doesn't matter so much who's top or who's or
43		who's bottom, [uh:m although it- it may have=
44	P:	[Sure.
45	C:	=<u>some</u> influence.
46	P:	Mm hm=
47	C:	=And that is that (.) the virus can travel both
48		wa:ys. [It's actually like in hetero<u>s</u>exual sex=
49	P:	[Sure.
50	C:	=as we:ll.
51	P:	Mm [hm
52	C:	[But (.) m-men are (.) as (.) at much
53		risk (0.2) as women are:.
54	P:	Mm [hm
55	C:	[And the other way <u>r</u>ound.
56	P:	Okay:.=
57	C:	=Uh::m: (0.5) Although i- it's probably more
58		ef<u>fi</u>cient in- in one directio:n [uh:m simply=
59	P:	[Yeah.
60	C:	=because (.) there is more of it obviously in
61		<u>s</u>eme:n.
62	P:	Mm hm:
63	C:	Uh:m: (1.7) I- I think perhaps just to be clear now
64		our suggestion would be that if you're going to

```
65              continue to have a sexual relationship and there's
66              no reason why you shouldn't [.hhhh then=
67   P:                                    [Mm hm
68   C:         =at this stage you: (0.2) should try to keep it as
69              safe as possible for a [variety of reasons. Some=
70   P:                                [Yeah.
71   C:         =people think that well .h assume we both have HIV
72              .h (0.2) it doesn't really matter then because we
73              can't infect one another with aids [with HIV=
74   P:                                            [Mm hm:
75   C:         =aga:in, well y'know that is so but there is a
76              problem with that thinking.=And that is .hhh if you
77              have unsafe sex (0.5) uh:m: (0.3) you- you ca:n get
78              a higher level of the virus in you,=you can be
79              reinoculated [with it. [(        )-
80   P:                      [Okay:    [(Okay that)
81              (sounds-)[(Sure).
```

In Extract 6.4, unlike Extract 6.3, C begins the topic of sexual behaviour by asking a question of P rather than delivering advice. The question receives an answer which starts out (lines 3–7) by nicely reproducing the features of delay and generality that are recurrent in these interviews, irrespective of the sexual orientation of the patient (see Chapter 4).

Note now that, at line 13, C asks P to specify further the part of his answer that indicated a problem ('not using a condom'). Only after P has gone into a detailed specification of what he and his partner are doing, does C start to deliver information in line 41, based on the problem raised by P. This information-giving is preparatory to personalized advice-giving which begins on line 63 and is given most directly in lines 68–9.

Overall, this sequence bears a strong resemblance to the perspective display sequence discussed in Chapter 2. Like Maynard's (1991) paediatric interviews, the professional's advice (or diagnosis statement in Maynard's case) is delayed until after the client's perspective has been obtained. This allows the counsellor (or doctor) to tailor the advice (or diagnosis) to what the client has revealed.

Despite C's successful elicitation of P's current activities, P initially only gives the minimal kinds of response found in Extract 6.3 (e.g. 'sure' at line 44 and 'mm hm' at line 46). Now, however, C gives the reason for his advice, which takes up P's reference to not using a condom during oral sex, in terms of the dangers of unsafe sex even between two positive partners (lines 75–9). Following this recipient-designed advice, P now offers an early, overlapping strong uptake – [Okay: [(Okay that)(sounds-)[(Sure) (lines 80–1).

Extracts 6.3 and 6.4 present very clear differences. Extract 6.3 shows non-personalized information-giving not based on problems raised by a client. Conversely, Extract 6.4 shows how the Interview Format may be used to generate problems from the client for which personalized advice can be offered.[3]

Hybrid or combined sequences

Extracts 6.3 and 6.4 provide a very stark contrast between two different ways of setting up an advice sequence. As we have seen, in Extract 6.3 non-personalized advice is delivered in the context of an Information Delivery format. Conversely, in Extract 6.4, an Interview format preceded the delivery of personalized advice.

However, it should not be assumed that advice can only be offered in an environment provided by just one of these formats. Extract 6.5 below is an example of how counsellors can move between the two formats around a piece of advice.

The extract begins as C uses an information sequence about how HIV-positive people can 'stay well' (line 4) to lead up to a piece of advice about condom use to P, a young woman (whom we shall call Sarah) who has just left school:

Extract 6.5 (UK3)

```
 1   C:    so you know it's not hh dead set on ten years hh now
 2           there are other people who could be HIV positive but
 3           not actually develop AIDS as such hh so they could
 4           be (.) carriers they could (.) stay well hh but pass
 5           the virus to people that they have sex with hh this
 6           is why we say hh if you don't know the person that
 7           you're with (0.6) and you're going to have sex with
 8           them hh it's important that you tell them to (0.3)
 9           use a condom.
10          (0.8)
11   C:    or to practise safe sex that's what using a condom
12          means.
13          (1.5)
14   C:    okay?
15          (0.3)
16   P:    uhum
17          (2.4)
18   C:    has your pa:rtner ever used a condom with you?
19          (1.0)
20   P:    n:o
21          (1.5)
22   C:    do yer know what a condom looks like?
23          (0.5)
24   P:    (I don't)
25          (0.3)
26   C:    (Did you-) (0.3) have you perhaps- (1.0) a condom
```

```
27              shown to you (.) at school?= or:?
28   P:         no:
29   C:         yer didn't all right, =okay hhh
30              (2.0)
31   C:         is there anything that yer worried about in terms of
32              yer test if it's done today? (.) would you like the
33              test first of all to be done today?
34              (0.8)
32   P:         yeah
33   C:         yer would (1.0) ri::ght hh (.) if we do the test
34              today
```
(information follows on how the results of test are given)

Here, in lines 1–9, C offers an advice package which, as in Extract 6.3, has not been based on a prior specification of P's problem. However, P does not speak during the 0.8 second pause at line 10 which constitutes a possible turn-completion point.

Without any uptake to her advice, C now respecifies it, redefining condom use in terms of 'safe sex' (lines 11–12). When, at line 13, she still gets no acknowledgment of any kind, she pursues one (line 14) and finally gets a minimal acknowledgment at line 16.

C now moves into an Interview format based on questions about P's knowledge of condoms (lines 18, 22 and 26–7) which produce material that underlines the lack of likelihood that P will have understood C's earlier advice. Now C swiftly exits from the whole topic at line 31.

The movement from Information Delivery to this Interview format shows why we have treated Extract 6.5 as an example of a hybrid or combined sequence. However, Extract 6.4 also has a hybrid element in that, like Extract 6.5, it combines these two formats. In a sense, Extract 6.5 is a mirror image of Extract 6.4, in that it ends in an Interview format, while Extract 6.4 begins in an Interview format and only moves into Information Delivery once P's perspective has been elicited.

These two extracts (and their impact upon client uptake of advice) may be represented in the following way:

Extract 6.4: IV format > ID format > Uptake of advice
Extract 6.5: ID format > No uptake of advice > IV format

Extract 6.5 shows the potential instability of advice-giving when patients produce material that suggests the irrelevance of the advice to them. Since professionals presumably desire clients to take up their advice, the lack of such uptake would appear to indicate bad methods of communication. However, it is no part of our argument to suggest that these counsellors are short-sighted in avoiding recipient-designed advice based upon asking questions before delivering the advice. I do not want to suggest that these professionals do not know what they are doing (even if they cannot be aware of all the consequences of their actions).

We can start to look at this by examining the potential *dysfunctions* of more recipient-designed advice based on careful questioning. Throughout our corpus of examples, counsellors exit quickly from recipient-designed advice when patients offer only minimal response tokens or when they display overt resistance. A fascinating example of such resistance is found in two of our Trinidad extracts where patients overtly resist question–answer sequences about 'safer sex' by asserting that the counsellor should not be asking about their behaviour and knowledge but, as the expert, should be telling them directly (see Youssef and Silverman, 1992).

In this context, we can begin to see the function of how C constructs her advice in this extract. On the surface, it may appear strange that the advice is given (lines 5–9) in an apparently 'depersonalized' way. Instead of saying something like:

 * I suggest to you, Sarah, that you use a condom with
   your boyfriend

C, in fact, introduces her advice as follows:

 C: this is why we say hh if you don't know the person
    that you're with

Notice the alternative readings that C thereby creates for who is to be regarded as the sender and receiver of the advice: who is 'we'?; is 'you' Sarah or just anybody?; who is 'the person'? These different readings create the possibility that the client can opt either to hear what is being said as advice directed at her or as simply information-about-the-kinds-of-things-we-tell-people-in-this-clinic. In the latter case, all that is required for a smooth topic-continuation or topic-completion is for the client to produce a minimal response-token (like 'mm') which signals that the client hears what is being said but passes her turn (see Chapter 8).

The only problem for the counsellor here is that this client does not provide such a 'mm' at two successive possible turn-transition points (lines 10 and 13). Although we saw a similar absence of the minimal 'mm' in Extract 6.3 (end of line 28), in that extract, P had been providing these minimal response-tokens at earlier turns.

It is worth noting, at this point, that our discussion has left two matters hanging. First, conceived in practical terms, how *effective* is a client uptake limited to the occasional 'mm'? Second, we have barely sketched in the skilful use of the ambiguity between advice and information sequences identified here. This second issue is, we believe, sufficiently important to be considered at length elsewhere (see Chapter 8). The first issue will be considered in later sections of this chapter concerned with advice reception and practical implications in regard to advice-giving.

Before this, we turn to our fourth form of advice-giving.

Client-inferred advice: interview format

Extract 6.6 is an example of how a client can construct her own 'advice' from a question–answer sequence. On the surface it appears to be the very opposite of Extract 6.3 which, as we saw, was formatted as Information Delivery. However, it shares two features with Extract 6.3. First, both have few hybrid elements, being based on either Information Delivery (Extract 6.3) or an Interview format (Extract 6.6). Second, as argued in Chapter 3, both formats are relatively stable, allowing many topics to be aired with very little turbulence.

In Extract 6.6, the client is another young woman. The extract occurs about thirty minutes into a consultation almost entirely based on C asking questions of P. This underlines the length of time that counselling based on the Interview format can take.

The extract begins with C requesting specification of P's previous response (data not shown) where she has indicated that she is no longer using condoms with her steady boyfriend. Throughout, the symbol > indicates a passage that is important to our subsequent discussion.

        Extract 6.6 (UK4)
  1 C: Well it's- so why did you decide then to stop using
  2   condoms er I mean er presumably you could have used
  3   both the pill and condoms. (.) Why did you actually
  4   decide to stop using condoms?
  5   (0.2)
  6 C: D'you think.
  7   (0.7)
  8 P: hhhh I don't really like using condoms. hheh I don't
  9   think anybody does. .hh (0.7) But I mean if I found
 10   out (0.3) that I was HIV (.) negative (1.2) I: hhhh
 11   I would with- with er: h my boyfriend now I would
 12   start using them.=But If I: (0.2) broke up and
 13   started seeing someone else I would (0.6) make sure
 14   that I did. .hhh hhh=
 15 C:>   =Ri:ght. (0.2) Do you think you're: (1.2) that you
 16   feel happy then about (.) not using condoms with
 17   him, (0.2) uhm d'you- d'you think that there
 18   wouldn't be any risk. For example that he could not
 19   be with any other partner (.) so you wouldn't have
 20   to (0.5) ([   )
 21 P: [I don't think he's sleeping
 22   with anybody el[se.
 23 C: [I was thinking I mean say you were
 24   negative at the moment but he's positive.
 25 P: Mm

26   (0.5)
27   C: And you decide to carry on and not using condoms,
28   (1.1)
29   P: Yeah:?
30   (0.6)
31   C: I'm wondering what you think i- d'you think it's
32   worthwhile taking that risk.
33   (0.8)
34   P: .h[hh
35   C: [Or: d'you [think it's not.=
36   P: [We:ll
37   P: =I've only go:t (.) I- I don't think I- I'm going to
38   start (.) I've got to finish this packet and then
39   I've got another packet to finish of the pill. (.)
40   Then after that I'm not taking any more:.
41   (0.9)
42   C: .hh Right sorr[y but I meant about condoms.
43   P: [hhh
44   (.)
45   P: Yeah. (.) So [(you know) when I'm not taking it=
46   C: [I see.
47   P: =a- when I'm not taking the pill any more: I will
48   use condoms.
49   C:>   .hh Right. I mean what if- what if (.) say you got
50   infected then in the next month while you'll still
51   taking the pi:lls (0.5) [and let's just say=
52   P: [Yeah (   )
53   C: =he's positive (.) and you became infected (0.5)
54   what d'you think (.) if you could have (0.3) had
55   that experience agai:n how- how might things be
56   different do you think.
57   P:>   I would have u:sed .hh (0.2) used them.

Just before this extract begins, the counsellor has elicited a statement from
the patient that she has stopped using condoms with her present boyfriend.
Given this problem-indicative response, C follows it up, using an elaborated
PDS sequence, by asking P to specify her answer (lines 1–6).

P's specification is addressed to the future circumstances in which she
would use condoms even though she does not like them (lines 8–14). At this
point, instead of offering advice, C uses a leading question (lines 15–20,
marked >) which asks P to think about the risks of her present behaviour.

When P's answers to this and further questions still do not elicit from P a
commitment to change her behaviour at once, C changes tack. At lines
49–56 (>), C invites P to imagine a possible future in which she had been
infected because her boyfriend had been HIV positive. P now says she would
use condoms.

This sequence shows how hypothetical questions may encourage a client to hear a piece of advice which is never made explicit by the counsellor (see Bor et al., 1992). It may fruitfully be compared with Extract 6.3 where the same topic of condom use is addressed explicitly by C with a perspective display delayed until after the advice has been delivered.[4]

Having elicited the hypothetical commitment from P about condom use, C now asks about what other forms of protection she might use (lines 61–3 > in Extract 6.7).

```
        Extract 6.7 (Extract 6.6 continued)
57  P:>     I would have u:sed .hh (0.2) used them.
58          (1.6)
59  C:      .hhh
60          (0.8)
61  C:>     D'you know about anything else that you can use as
62          we:ll (0.2) as condoms to protect yourself or your
63          partners
64  P:      No I don't.
65  C:      .hhh
66          (0.6)
67  C:      I mean condoms are a good thing because they
68          obviously are a barrier.=They actua[lly
69  P:                                         [Yeah:.
70          (0.2)
71  C:      form a barrier between you and the partner. And as
72          we said (0.2) HIV's in .hh in sem[en vaginal=
73  P:                                       [hhhh
74  C:      =secretions and (        ). .hhh But that's the
75          reason for using them whether it's vaginal
76          intercourse anal intercourse ma̲ybe even oral se(h)x.
77  P:      Yeah:.=
78  C:      eh- eh- You know there's (.) potentially .hhhh (.)
79          uh- a possibility of .hhh transmission of body
80          flui:ds. .hhh Bu̲t (.) we know condoms aren't a
81          hundred percent safe.=They slip off,=they rip. (0.3)
82          have you a̲ny idea what you could use as we:ll?
83          [That might help (.) back up the- .hh=
84  P:>     [A diaphragm?
85  C:      =certainly. .hh Tha̲t's a uh:m particularly the
86          cervix can be a fragile
87          (1.0)
88  P:      Ye[ah:.
89  C:        [orga:n that can: tear: .hh [and- and]=
90  P:                                    [So- so a]=
91  C:      =[(be an open side).
92  P:      =[diaphragm
```

93   P:>   is actually a- a way of protecting yourself (is)
94   (what you're [saying).

When P says she doesn't know how else she might protect herself (line 64), C does not deliver the necessary information. Instead C continues the topic within an Interview format until P herself produces the item (84>). Beautifully, then (at 90, 93–4 >), P produces the advice as a summary of the argument present in C's questions and statements, acknowledged by C from line 95 onwards (not reproduced).

Note two nice features of this sequence. First, considered in practical terms, an advice summary by a patient is one of the strongest acknowledgments of a professional's advice that one sees. Second, this summary is produced in a local context where the counsellor has not actually delivered any direct advice, other than underlining some of what his patient has said.

Extract 6.7 thus shows how considerable uptake may be achieved by an Interview format without any explicit advice. However, in common with many consultations at this clinic, this interview lasts about 45 minutes. Staff at other centres might argue that this is an impracticable way to use their time and resources.

Some general features of advice reception

Having touched upon the link between advice-giving and advice reception, it is now time to focus more directly on this link. In doing so, we will briefly deal with previous social science research on this matter before detailing what our own research has discovered based on the analysis of a sample of 50 extracts of advice-giving.

Earlier research suggests that advice reception is strongly tied to how the advice is organized. As Jefferson and Lee (1981:408) argue:

> acceptance or rejection may be in great part an interactional matter, produced by reference to the current talk, more or less independent of intention to use it, or actual subsequent use.

Jefferson and Lee are mainly concerned with fragments of ordinary conversation where 'troubles' are told. They note that, in a troubles-telling, a teller properly receives and accepts 'emotional reciprocity' as much as advice. This means that in such everyday talk, advice can be rejected because advice recipients are reluctant to abandon their interactional rights as troubles-tellers (ibid.: 410). Conversely, in a service encounter, between a professional and client, they argue that advice reception is less problematic because 'an advice-seeker properly receives and accepts advice' (ibid.: 421).

However, service encounters vary. HIV counselling lacks both a formal turn-taking system or a clear agenda (see Chapter 3). In this respect, it is like the interactions between British health visitors and first-time mothers described by Heritage and Sefi (1992) where the participants seem to negotiate their way in a 'bottom up' fashion towards a sense of what the interaction will be about.

Moreover, in neither health visiting nor HIV test counselling is the professional's advice necessarily sought by the client. In situations like these, the role of the professional involves mainly gatekeeping or surveillance. When advice-giving has not been specifically requested by the client, it may be difficult to set up advice sequences.

Despite the differences, already noted, between our data and Jefferson and Lee's, we can learn from their discussion of the appropriate position for advice in a troubles-telling. Advice, they argue, is most likely to be well received

> in a Work-Up initiated by the troubles-teller, and emerging as the logical outcome of a diagnosis offered by the troubles-recipient and concurred in by the troubles-teller; i.e. the advice is sequentially appropriate and the talk is interactionally 'synchronous'. (1981: 408)

This means that, where these features are absent, i.e. advice is delivered 'prematurely', we are likely to find the advice rejected or, as in the case of Extract 6.6, minimally acknowledged.

Heritage and Sefi's data on advice reception in health visiting is in line with Jefferson and Lee's prediction. Unlike many other counselling situations, where the client comes with a presenting problem, most advice sequences in health visiting were initiated by the professional without any prior enquiry by the client. Health visitor (HV) initiated advice took four forms:

1 Stepwise entry in the sequence below:
  a HV enquiry
  b problem-indicative response by client
  c request for specification by HV ('a focusing enquiry')
  d a specification by the client
  e advice-giving
2 The same sequence but with no request for specification because the client volunteers how she dealt with the problem
3 No client statement of how she dealt with the problem and no HV request for specification (thus stages c and d are omitted)
4 HV-initiated advice without the client giving a problem-indicative response (i.e. stage a is followed directly by stage e).

The majority of advice initiations analysed by Heritage and Sefi were of the form 4 type. Indeed, in many cases, even the HV's enquiry was not problem oriented but was more concerned to topicalize the issue for which advice was subsequently delivered.

The reception of advice by mothers took three forms:

1 a marked acknowledgment (e.g. 'oh right' or repeats of key components of the advice); Heritage and Sefi say such utterances acknowledge the informativeness and appropriateness of the advice.

2   an unmarked acknowledgment (e.g. 'mm', 'yeah', 'right'-without an
    'oh'). These are minimal response tokens which, Heritage and Sefi
    argue, have a primarily continuative function; they do *not* (a) acknow-
    ledge the advice-giving as newsworthy to the recipient or (b) constitute
    an undertaking to follow the advice and (c) can be heard as a form of
    resistance in themselves because, implicitly, such responses are refusing
    to treat the talk as advice.
3   assertions of knowledge or competence by the mother. These indicate
    that the advice is redundant – hence they also may be taken as resistance.

Heritage and Sefi's study shows that mothers minimize the extent to which
they acknowledge that the advice of health visitors has been 'informative'
(e.g. they found only one example of a 'newsworthiness' token: ('Oh').
Generally mothers rarely acknowledge their previous ignorance nor do they
treat the HVs' talk as advice. Overwhelmingly, their most frequent response
is an 'unmarked acknowledgment' via response-tokens ('mm hm','yes',
'that's right') which do not constitute an undertaking to follow the advice
offered.

However, where HVs used a stepwise entry into advice-giving (form 1
above) they encountered less resistance and more uptake, displayed by
mothers' use of marked acknowledgments. Here the HV's request for her
client to specify a problem means that the advice can be recipient-designed,
non-adversarial and need not attribute blame. When discussed in this way,
the potential need for advice can emerge as the joint construction of the
participants (as suggested by Heritage and Sefi).

Many of our findings are in line with Heritage and Sefi's work. The
majority of advice sequences are initiated by the professional without the
client giving a problem-indicative response. Of the 61 advice sequences from
five centres analysed, a majority take form 4 where the professional gives
advice without any attempt to get the client to specify a problem. This is
shown in Table 6.1.

Table 6.1   *Forms of advice-giving in HIV counselling
data*

Patient-initiated 2
Counsellor-initiated 59
   of which: 16 full sequence (form 1)
              8 shortened sequence (forms 2 and 3)
              35 C-initiated without problem-indicative
                 response from P

Based on 61 advice sequences

In line with Heritage and Sefi, counsellor-initiated advice appears to get
little uptake (largely unmarked acknowledgments – henceforth UAs);
conversely, full sequences get marked acknowledgments (MAs). Predictably, the only example where a P implies that a C's advice is newsworthy (by

saying 'is that right', 'really') occurs when this P has himself made an observation on the topic covered by the advice and has twice been corrected by the C.

As in Heritage and Sefi's study, there is, however, little *overt* resistance to advice. The most common pattern is counsellor-initiated advice (not based on eliciting a perceived problem from the patient) interspersed with a series of 'mms' from the recipient (see Extract 6.3, pp. 113–4).

The data on uptake is shown in Table 6.2:

Table 6.2   *Form of advice and degree of uptake*

Advice-format	Number	Type of acknowledgment*	
		unmarked	marked
P-initiated	2	0	2
C-initiated:			
Step by step: full-sequence	11	1	10
shortened	5	3	2
Truncated:			
no P problem elicited	32	29	3

Based on 50 advice sequences.
*'unmarked' means *only* unmarked acknowledgments were given in the advice sequence; 'marked' means that at least *one* marked acknowledgment was given.

Table 6.2 shows a very clear correlation between the way in which an advice sequence is set up and the response it elicits from the patient. In the total of 32 cases where the counsellor delivers advice without attempting to generate a perceived problem from the patient, there are only three cases where the patient shows any sign of uptake. Conversely, in the other 18 cases, where the advice emerges either at the request of the patient or in a step-by-step sequence, there are only four cases where the patient does *not* show uptake.[5]

A further point needs to be made about Table 6.2. We have deliberately excluded one centre where we have examined 11 advice sequences. Here, although there are several examples of step-by-step advice packages, we find no marked acknowledgments and considerable overt resistance to advice. There is no space to look in detail at one of these deviant cases. It turns out that such advice packages do not get their predicted uptake because, although the advice follows a sequence of requests for specification, its content often does not take up, or even contradicts, the perceptions of the patient's problems that have been elicited. I have excluded these cases from Table 6.2 in order to show the more common pattern where advice sequences which follow step-by-step methods are constructed in terms of what the patient has just said. However, these cases will be discussed in detail in Chapter 7.

How, then, do our data differ from those of Heritage and Sefi? First, we have comparative material available from several centres. We find that counsellors at any one centre tend to construct their advice packages in a similar manner. This offers a useful opportunity to test hypotheses and to highlight the consequences of different ways of giving advice.

Second, we have fewer cases of patient-initiated advice and fewer displays of patient competence. We can speculate that the different context is important here. A hospital interview about HIV may discourage displays of competence or knowledge by patients. To talk about looking after one's own baby in one's own home is one thing; to discuss a sexually transmitted disease is quite another. As my earlier research showed, patients only go into detail on potentially delicate topics, like sexuality, when specifically requested to do so by a professional (see Table 4.1, p. 76).

Third, unlike Heritage and Sefi, in addition to our main sample (61 cases), we have seven further cases (from only two of five centres) where, although no advice is given by a counsellor, patients summarize what they have learned from the line of questioning. In Extract 6.7 we examined how one client can produce a version of what she has learned without any explicit advice sequence. As I argue later, this has clear practical implications. However, before we reach these implications, we must deal with one more extract that indicates a deviant case.

A deviant case

Even within the 50 cases used here, there are some unexpected examples. For instance, why should three examples of counsellor-initiated advice get marked acknowledgments, against the normal pattern? As Mitchell (1983) has forcefully argued, in case-study work we have an obligation to follow up all deviant cases in order to strengthen the explanatory power of our analysis.

Extract 6.8 below is a counsellor-initiated advice sequence. Although P offers no newsworthiness tokens ('oh'), unexpectedly, there is plenty of P uptake, involving completion of C's turns (lines 3–4, 14 and 27) and references to the applicability of the advice to himself (line 20). Moreover, unlike Heritage and Sefi's findings, after lines 3–4, 14 and 27, the professional acknowledges her client's display of competence.

```
        Extract 6.8 (UK1)
   1  C:      But we can't tell you know whether uh one individual
   2          is going to or whether they're [no:t.
   3  P:                                      [(It's just on
   4          proportions). =
   5  C:      That's ri:[ght.
   6  P:                [(        )
   7  C:      .hhhh A:nd obviously if someone looks after
```

```
 8              themselves they stand a better chance you know
 9              keeping fit and healthy.
10   P:         Ye:s.
11   C:         .hhhh The advice we give is common sense really if
12              you think about it.=To keep fit and healthy, (.)
13              eat a [well) a balanced di:et,
14   P:               [For your natural resistance.=
15   C:         =That's [right.
16   P:                 [Ye:s.
17   C:         .hh Plenty of exerci:[se:
18   P:                             [Right.
19   C:         [Uh::m or enough exercise.
20   P:         [(I already get that) hheh .hhh [hhh .hhhh Too=
21   C:                                         [Yeah.
22   P:         =much of it. hhuh=
23   C:         =Enough slee:p.
24   P:         Y[es.
25   C:          [You know. All the things we should normally
26              do[: to keep healthy,
27   P:            [Right. Rather than let yourself get run down.=
28   C:         =That's ri:ght.
```

Extract 6.8 is remarkable for the large number of marked acknowledgments given by the client (lines 3–4, 14, 20, 22, and 27). Many of these acknowledgments occur as overlaps and/or as candidate-completions of C's utterances, indicating a powerful claim to a mutual orientation.[6] Moreover, C embellishes this mutuality, in line 15, by agreeing with P's formulation.

How can we account for the far greater uptake of advice in Extract 6.8 compared to Extract 6.3? After all, both involve truncated counsellor-initiated advice sequences based in an Information Delivery format. Why should P display his perspective without any use by C of a PDS sequence?

The answer seems to lie in the hit-or-miss character of non-recipient-designed advice sequences like these. In most cases, as Table 6.2 shows, counsellor-initiated advice sequences, not based upon any prior elicitation of the client's perspective, will elicit a minimal response. In a minority of such advice-givings, however, a counsellor will fortuitously hit upon a topic upon which P has some prior interest and knowledge. This, I suggest, is why, in Extract 6.8, P offers his marked acknowledgments.[7]

However, in the Information Delivery format, unlike the Interview format, clients are only interactionally required to give response-tokens (unmarked acknowledgments) (see Chapter 3). This means that, in Information Delivery, it is *optional* whether patients offer marked acknowledgments.

When they do so (as in Extract 6.8, via statements and displays of knowledge), they do not implicate themselves in any future lines of action because they are only responding to what can be heard as information and not necessarily advice.

The optional character of the kind of patient uptake in Information Delivery may account for the variance between Extracts 6.3 and 6.8. However, it does not explain why counsellors would want to package their advice in a way which makes patient uptake less likely. In Chapter 8 I shall argue that, by constructing advice sequences that can be heard as information delivery, counsellors manage to stabilize advice-giving.

Practical implications

Throughout this book I have argued that we can develop the practical pay-off of counselling research by avoiding the language of 'communication problems' (which implies that professionals are bad at their job) and instead examine the *functions* of communication sequences in a particular institutional context.

An understanding of the institutional contexts of HIV test counselling allows us to move on from our necessary initial focus on how the participants organize their talk. As Maynard (1989: 139) argues: 'the structure of the interaction, while being a local production, simultaneously enacts matters whose origins are externally initiated'. Elsewhere Maynard (1985) has demonstrated how such a study of such 'externally initiated' matters can raise questions about the *functions* of communication patterns. Closely following Maynard, gathering ethnographic data on the clinics where these counsellors work allowed me to address the functions of counsellors' behaviour and, thereby, made possible constructive input into policy debates.

Counselling prior to the HIV-antibody test occurs within at least two major constraints. First, it is dependent upon patient-flow. This produces sudden periods of demand (usually immediately after the latest media advertising campaigns), interspersed with relatively quiet periods. The uneven flow of patients makes it difficult to design an effective use of clinic resources.

The second problem is that pre-test counselling is expected to cover a huge number of topics – from the difference between HIV and AIDS, to the meaning of positive and negative test results, to issues of insurance cover, confidentiality and 'safer sex'. The consequence is that, in most English testing sites, such counselling consists of largely stereotyped 'information packages' and is completed within 15 minutes. The lack of patient uptake of advice based within an Information Delivery format suggests that this may not very be a very effective method of getting clients to review their sexual practices. It is certainly a dull and repetitive task for the counsellors.

On the other hand, as Chapters 7 and 8 will show, personalized advice-giving can be unstable and, if the client's perspective is to be properly elicited, it takes a long time. Truncated, non-personalized advice sequences are usually far shorter – an important consideration for hard-pressed counsellors.

I suggest, therefore, that the character of HIV counselling as a focused conversation on mostly delicate topics explains why truncated advice sequences (like those seen in Extracts 6.3, 6.5 and 6.8) predominate in the transcripts. Clearly, such sequences are functional for *both* local and institutional contexts.

I return to the point about the need to locate 'communication problems' in a broader structural context. My research has much to say about how counsellors can organize their talk in order to maximize patient uptake. However, without organizational change, the impact of such communication techniques alone might be minimal or even harmful. For instance, encouraging patient uptake will usually require longer counselling sessions. Experienced counsellors will tell you that if they take so long with one client the waiting period for others increases, some clients will simply walk out – and hence may continue their risky behaviour without learning their HIV status.

Two possible solutions suggest themselves from the data analysed by this study. First, as in Extract 6.7, avoiding necessarily 'delicate' and unstable advice sequences but encouraging patients to draw their own conclusions from a particular line of questioning. Second, since both this method and step-by-step advice-giving take considerable time, finding ways of making more time available for more effective counselling.

One possibility that British centres might consider following is the US model of group pre-test counselling combined with the completion by patients of individual, confidential questionnaires about their reasons for wanting an HIV test. This is then followed by lengthy one-to-one counselling at the *post-test* stage. A second possibility is to retain pre-test individual counselling but to make more use of the time while patients are waiting. Interactive videos, although costly in the short run, might well turn out be cost-efficient in terms of covering a lot of the ground currently taken up by information delivery by the counsellor. Not only would this allow each counselling session to be structured more to the needs of individual patients; it would also make pre-test counselling far less repetitive and far less boring for the counsellor.

As our workshops with counsellors show, professionals respond to research that seeks to document the fine detail of their practice, while acknowledging the structural constraints to which they must respond. Put another way, this means that we should aim to identify the interactional skills of the participants rather than their failings. Although the researcher cannot tell practitioners how they should behave, understanding the intended and unintended consequences of actions can provide the basis for a fruitful dialogue.

Conclusion

Despite Nelkin's call for studies 'to evaluate diverse means of communicating information about sex' (Nelkin, 1987: 982), one is struck by the lack of research on the actual process of HIV counselling (but see Peräkylä, 1995). As Bor (1989: 184) has noted, research so far has concentrated on 'approaches to behavioural change, health education and psychosocial support rather than communication in clinical settings'.

Faced with this lack of knowledge, our study supports Green's (1989: 9) assertion that most counsellors have adopted a largely pragmatic approach. Counselling practice certainly varies from one centre to another. At some British and US centres and where counsellors are trained in methods deriving from family therapy, we find, as in Extracts 6.4 and 6.6, that advice is recipient-designed following extensive questioning of clients (see also Peräkylä, 1995). Conversely, at many British testing centres, given the huge agenda of pre-test counselling, counsellors seem to focus on health promotion in terms of a set of truncated sequences of counsellor-initiated advice. Yet, even the most directive counsellors do, occasionally, try interview-based advice sequences, not only, as in Extract 6.5, where C turns to a question when her advice fails to get any response at all.

The research has shown the practical skills of counsellors. For instance, by using truncated sequences they at least manage to produce relatively short counselling sessions with minimal overt conflict. Given the time pressures many of them face, this is no mean achievement.

In line with Bor, Miller and Goldman's (1992) text on HIV/AIDS counselling, our research has also revealed the nature and effectiveness of step-by-step methods of counselling based on question–answer sequences rather than on the delivery of information. Through such methods, clients do indeed learn *relevant* information. More important, following Stoller and Rutherford (1989: S294), they learn the skills to determine what is appropriate for themselves and their partners. Nonetheless, as the next two chapters show, in contexts like these, where clients do not necessarily present with a 'problem', personalized advice-giving remains a potentially difficult activity.

With greater knowledge of what is effective in HIV counselling, and better organization of time and other resources, there is thus some prospect of future modifications to counselling practice in this area.

Notes

1. For instance, Feltham and Dryden's *Dictionary of Counselling* defines counselling as: 'a principled relationship characterized by the application of one or more psychological theories and a recognized set of communication skills, modified by experience, intuition and other interpersonal factors, to *clients' intimate concerns, problems or aspirations*' (quoted by Feltham, 1995: 8, my emphasis).

2. In rational emotive therapy, Feltham suggests that a counsellor's comment like 'If you want to achieve your goals, then you had better do x' actually amounts to advice (ibid.: 18).

3. However, it may be felt that, in comparing Extracts 6.3 and 6.4 we are not comparing like with like. More specifically, it could be argued that P's uptake of advice in 6.4 and lack of uptake in 6.3 may simply reflect that the patient in 6.4 was a gay man at high risk from a seropositive partner.

This might have had two consequences. First, the greater uptake might not reflect how the advice package was set up but the possibility that this patient was paying more attention because he already had a perception of his own high risk of infection. Second, perhaps it is easier for counsellors to set up step-by-step advice sequences with gay men who come from a community already predisposed to take such advice seriously.

Nonetheless, our analysis suggests that the link between how advice is set up and client uptake holds whatever the gender or sexual orientation of the client. For instance, in an example where the client is a heterosexual young woman (Extract 6.6 pp. 121–4), we show how the step-by-step sequence is equally effective.

4. However, we ought to underline the point that there is also a less explicit character to the advice delivery in Extract 6.5, based on C's ambiguous appeal to 'this is why we say'. As already noted, this creates the possibility of P hearing C's utterance as information-about-the-advice-we-give-here rather than as personalized advice.

5. If we return to the interview-format based advice-giving found in Extract 6.4, we can note how it tends to produce marked acknowledgments of advice. The extract below comes immediately after the conclusion of Extract 6.4:

Extract 6.4 continued

```
82   C:              [So that's one problem. .hhhh The other
83                is that (.) if either of you was carrying another (.)
84                sexually transmitted disease or perhaps something else
85                could be transmitted .hh hepatitis (.)
86                [gonorrhoea syphilis or something like that.=
87   P:           [Mm hm
88   C:           =.hhh It would trigger the immune system
89   P:           Mm hm:
90   C:           a:nd (.) if that happe:ns what happens is that the
91                virus replicates more rapidly.
92   P:           Mm hm:
93   C:           So: y-you get more virus. .hhhh So one way or the
94                other yeah you can have sex but (.) safer sex is
95                probably: uh[:m
96   P:              [Yeah:. .h er[: What abou:t=
97   C:                        [(              )
98   P:           =er::: (0.6) oral sex without a condom. (0.2) er:
99                However::=
```

As C completes his advice, in lines 93–95, P produces an overlapping question (lines 96–99). Together with a later question (not transcribed here) which refers to C's advice, this indicates considerable P uptake.

6. Doug Maynard (personal communication) has noted how Sacks (1992) treats such overlapping remarks as powerful claims that 'my mind is with you'.

7. An alternative possible explanation is that this patient is simply a personality type that will intervene in this kind of way however C sets up her advice. CA, of course, cannot explain such variance – indeed it specifically avoids such issues.

7

Resisting Advice

In the previous chapter, we examined the link between advice-giving and advice reception. Outright advice rejections were noticeably absent from our data. At worst, clients were silent or produced minimal responses to counsellors' advice.

In this chapter, I focus on a small corpus of data in which advice resistance seems to be more open. Obviously, the character and circumstances of such resistance, as well as how episodes of resistance are resolved, will be of interest to practising counsellors.

I discuss the contribution that conversation analysis can make to our understanding of the mechanics of counselling. In addition, I show how micro-sociological ideas about the preservation of self-esteem or 'face' may also be relevant to these matters.

Mobilizing such perspectives, I show how the demands of maintaining self-esteem and social solidarity support a preference for the acceptance of advice. Curiously, such a preference organization is respected even when the advice is rejected or received equivocally.

Throughout, we observe the co-operative minimization of resistance to and rejection of advice. Clients opt for unmarked acknowledgments and silences much more frequently than they choose outright advice rejection. Where they reject advice, they lead up to it through delays and mitigations, and counsellors speedily back down. This kind of indirect resistance creates an environment in which all parties can seek to reaffirm social solidarity without directly acknowledging the existence of a disagreement. Equally, counsellors deploy a series of strategies for minimizing resistance: packaging their advice in questions or in an ambiguous format (potentially information delivery rather than advice-giving).

The chapter concludes by examining a deviant case, where an advice rejection is given without delay or mitigation, to examine the kinds of local conditions which threaten the displays of social solidarity observed elsewhere. Throughout, I show how these findings complement Heritage and Sefi's (1992) work on health visitor/client interactions, first discussed in Chapter 6.

Preference organization

In an early paper, Erving Goffman (1955) suggested that a persistent consideration of interactants is to protect one another's public self-esteem, or 'face'. In doing whatever people are doing, they take into consideration and project the moral standing of themselves and their co-interactants. In the ordinary course of events, this consideration entails the *protection* of the positive moral standing of the self and of others.

As many critics have pointed out, Goffman's observations are as ingenious as impressionistic (see e.g. Drew and Wootton, 1988). In particular, Goffman tends to globalize concepts like 'face', whereas concepts in CA have situated and local referents. Consequently, it can be suggested that the concept of 'face' is somewhat psychologistic, while CA concepts, like 'preference organization' (discussed below), refer to the social organization of conduct.

Nonetheless, decades after the publication of Goffman's initial observations, conversation analysts have been able to pick up themes related to his initial observations. In conversation analysts' rigorous empirical approach, some important implications of Goffman's impressionistic concept of 'face' have been encapsulated in the concept of 'preference organization' (see also Heritage, 1984).

In conversation analysis, 'preference organization' basically entails the distinction of two formats of action. Certain actions – typically actions that occur in response to other actions, such as invitations, offers or assessments – can be marked as dispreferred, that is, problematic in one way or another. Thus, rejections of invitations or offers, or disagreements with assessments, can be performed in a way that encodes their problematic status. Conversely, acceptance of invitation or offer, or an agreement with an assessment, can be performed in a way that does not exhibit such problematic status.

Conversation analytical research has identified a number of practices through which the dispreferred status of an action can be shown. According to Heritage (1984: 265–80), these practices include:

1 The action being delayed within a turn or across a sequence of turns
2 The action is commonly prefaced or qualified within the turn in which it occurs
3 The action is commonly accomplished in mitigated or indirect form, and
4 the dispreferred action is commonly accounted for.

In relation to the problems with psychological concepts of 'face', the concept of 'preference', therefore, does not refer to inner experiences of the actors about 'problems' or the lack of them involved in performing certain actions (Levinson, 1983). Furthermore, the distinction between preferred and dispreferred actions does not require an *a priori* categorization of actions as problematic or non-problematic. Rather, the distinction between a 'preferred' and 'dispreferred' action format is a resource for the interactants, through the use of which they can portray their actions as problematic, or not.

We can see this point clearly by referring to one of Heritage's examples of a rejected offer:

```
        Extract 7.1 (Heritage, 1984) (S's wife has just slipped a disc)
1   H:      And we were wondering if there's anything we can do
2           to help
3   S:      [Well 'at's
4   H:      [I mean can we do any shopping for her or something
5           like tha:t?
6           (0.7)
7   S:      Well that's most ki:nd Heatherton .hhh At the moment
8           no:. because we've still got two bo:ys at home
```

Heritage shows how S's refusal (lines 7–8) of H's offer displays three relevant features of preference organization. First, when S does not take an early opportunity to accept H's offer (after 'anything we can do to help', lines 1–2), H proceeds to revise it. Second, S delays his refusal via the pause in the slot for his turn at line 6. Third, he justifies it by invoking a contingency about which H could not be expected to know. Both parties thereby produce a 'no fault' account.

Extract 7.1 also exemplifies a recurrent feature of interactants' way of using the resources of preference organization. In this example, the action that is marked as dispreferred, or problematic, is *S's refusal of H's offer*. To put it in Goffman's terms, S's refusal *threatens H's face* as a potential helper and as a person who, through his offer, also claims certain closeness to S (see also Brown and Levinson, 1987). What is at issue in S's refusal is no less than the local social solidarity between H and S. In enabling the participants to display the problematic status of the refusal, the preference organization helps them to maintain H's face and to preserve the social solidarity, while performing the action that potentially threatens these.

Rejection of advice

As we noted in Chapter 6, Heritage and Sefi (1992) have analysed initial interviews between British health visitors and first-time mothers. They show how mothers are frequently given advice without having requested it. Offers of advice, just like offers of invitations, normally imply acceptance as the preferred response. Although mothers may indicate non-receptiveness to such advice, by merely replying 'mm hm' and the like or by showing that they already knew about the topic, they almost never explicitly reject it.

In their study, Heritage and Sefi mention only one instance where a mother overtly rejects the advice of a health visitor. It occurs where the health visitor is giving advice about when to pick the baby up:

Extract 7.2 (Heritage and Sefi, 1992)
HV = Health Visitor; M = Mother

```
1   HV:    No: I think it's a very important right from the
2          beginning to be fi:rm with 'em.=I(f) you firmly put
3          'em down you: TELL 'em (0.8) bedtime an' I'm not
4          pickin' you: up so you can: (0.5) you kno:w=
5   M:     =Tha:[t's i:t.
6   HV:         [do what you li:ke (.) and I'm goin' off to
7          (1.0) uh:m
8          (0.7)
9   M:     Oh I wouldn't let 'er cry too: long you kno:w.=
10  HV:    =No:.
11  M:     I mean (0.2) half an hou:r (0.5) y'know I- like to
12         you sa:y you look- you check them.
```

In Extract 7.2, after an initial affiliation ('Tha:[t's i:t.', line 5), the health visitor's advice is explicitly rejected by the mother (line 9).

Rejecting advice is an action that potentially threatens the face of the speakers, and thereby undermines local social solidarity. In this light, note that Mother's rejection is mitigated ('cry too: long', line 9), accounted for (by the laudable desire to 'check them', line 12) and delayed (by the affiliation and the 0.7 second delay before the rejection). We might also note that, at line 10, the health visitor affiliates to Mother's comment even though Mother is rejecting her advice. In sum, it appears that the speakers organize and revise their utterances so as to manage the rejection of advice in a way that preserves the preference for agreement.

Although Heritage and Sefi stress how their health visitors persist in giving advice, despite lack of uptake by their clients, their own data show how this persistence co-exists with maintaining such a preference organization. Even in this single case, where advice is explicitly rejected, both professional and client maintain a primary orientation to a world in which acceptance and agreement are preferred.

Now consider another example of rejected advice. In this case, the data are drawn from a pre-HIV test counselling interview between a patient (P) and a counsellor for HIV/AIDS (C) in a hospital clinic for sexually transmitted diseases.

Extract 7.3 (UK2)

```
1   C:     but you know it's important that you think about the
2          fact that it might be positive hh though >in the
3          majority of people< it comes back as totally
4          negative
5          (0.5)
6   C:     but we have [to discuss that bit
```

```
 7  P:                       [mm
 8  P:        (yes [I see)
 9  C:               [because in fact there there's nothing worse
10              than than sort of hh umm someone saying >oh no no no
11              you haven't been at risk< and then (0.3) them having
12              a problem later on to face [occurring
13  P:                                    [yeah
14  P:        um I mean I I should have thought let's cross the
15              bridge when we come to it heh is a better attitude
16              you know=
17  C:        =hh well:: everybody's different in their [attitudes
```

Once again, at line 14, we find a client resisting a professional's advice (lines 1–4). How is this managed? Note how P's explicit resistance to C's advice about thinking about a positive test result is delayed for several turns and is only produced after a further ten lines of transcript. Such delay can be monitored by C as implying implicit resistance.

First, P does not take up an available turn-transition point (the first gap of 0.5 seconds). C can now monitor the gap as implying a failure to affiliate to her advice. Indeed, there is evidence that she does hear it this way, because she temporarily abandons the advice for an agenda statement (line 6). P's subsequent utterances ('mm', 'yes [I see') can now be heard as response-tokens or continuers which acknowledge merely that he understands the agenda. Although such response-tokens give the floor back to C, P has not so far affiliated to the advice.

However, when C uses her next turn (lines 9–12) to deliver information which might serve to underline her earlier advice, P now resists. Note, however, that not only does P delay his rejection across several turns but, within this turn, he hesitates, prefaces it and mitigates it by laughter – all canonical markers of dispreferred responses. Moreover, although C marks the difference of views ('hh well', line 17), like the health visitor in Extract 7.2 she does not contest her client's rejection of her advice. Instead, she backtracks in a way which, while not rejecting P's utterance, preserves some saliency in her original advice (as relevant to other people).

Following Drew and Holt (1988), we should note that P's resistance in lines 14–16 is tied to a proverb ('let's cross that bridge when we come to it'). Drew and Holt suggest the possibility that such proverbs and idioms 'have some special resistance to being challenged with concrete, empirical facts'(1988: 411) and may arise in environments where the parties are not aligning themselves to one another in preferred ways (in Drew and Holt's data, as mutually affiliated to a complaint).

In Extract 7.3, P's initial implicit lack of alignment to C's advice (failing to take up the slot for an advice acknowledgment in the 0.5 second silence after C's first turn) becomes an explicit advice rejection. In this local context, P's use of a proverb may have at least three functions. First, it provides grounds for his non-alignment couched in an appeal to 'what everyone knows' about human affairs. Second, therefore, it creates difficulties if C wants to challenge P's line – because C must attend to 'what everyone knows' rather than just P's own views. Third, as Drew and Holt demonstrate, such idioms have a topically terminal character, allowing, as here, for the parties to come to a very general agreement about 'what everyone knows' prior to shifting away from the topic associated with the misalignment. Note here how C responds with an idiom of her own ('everybody's different in their [attitudes'). This is preparatory to a topic switch (data not shown).

In both Extracts 7.2 and 7.3, then, professionals and clients demonstrably accommodate advice rejections to the demands of social solidarity, through the means of preference organization. In the rest of this chapter we will examine a small data-base of advice sequences in order to show in detail how the preference for the acceptance of advice is preserved and oriented to, when the advice is rejected, indirectly or equivocally.

Data-Base

Our data are all drawn from a British sexually transmitted diseases clinic in a department of genito-urinary medicine in a metropolitan teaching hospital (UK2). The counsellor (C) has previously worked as a contact-tracer in the department. With the emergence of HIV and AIDS, she has taken on the role of pre- and post-test HIV counselling as well being a health adviser to seropositive patients seen in the department. To complement her earlier experience, she has attended HIV training courses run at a national centre, as well as having some training in the family therapy methods used in HIV counselling in another nearby centre.

In the previous chapter we examined 50 advice sequences drawn from three different centres in Britain and the USA which offered HIV testing and counselling. The present sample, discussed here, is drawn from only three pre-test counselling interviews (lasting 26, 17 and 6 minutes each) by the health adviser mentioned above. This has generated 18 advice sequences.

This small data-base was chosen because it was relatively rich in outright rejections of advice. For instance, while Heritage and Sefi cite only one such rejection out of 70 advice sequences (or 1.4 per cent of the total) and our earlier sample contained no such rejections in 50 cases, the present corpus includes four outright rejections out of 18 advice sequences (or 22 per cent of the total).[1]

Forms of resistance

In this chapter we will be concerned with how counsellor and client maintain social solidarity by constructing their talk so as to minimize disagreement and to manage whatever disagreements or conflicts surface during the interview. I therefore focus on the different forms of resisting advice, which involve the management of sequences which are recognizably produced as 'dispreferred'.

Apart from the outright rejection of advice, as we saw in Chapter 6, Heritage and Sefi (1992) identify two forms of indirect resistance to advice: the first is *an unmarked acknowledgment* which can be done through response tokens such as 'mm', 'yeah', 'right'. These are minimal response tokens which have a primarily continuative function; they do *not* either acknowledge the advice-giving as newsworthy to the recipient or constitute an undertaking to follow the advice. They can be heard as a form of resistance in themselves because, implicitly, such responses are refusing to treat the talk as advice.

The other form of indirect resistance takes the form of *assertions of knowledge or competence* by the advice recipient. These indicate that the advice is redundant – hence they also may be taken as resistance.

The forms of indirect resistance are to be distinguished from what Heritage and Sefi (ibid.) call *marked acknowledgments*. Marked acknowledgment can be done for example through 'oh right' or repeats of key components of the advice. These acknowledge the informativeness and appropriateness of the advice and constitute the form of advice reception that does *not* involve resistance.

We now turn to examples where patients in HIV counselling sessions resist advice. We first consider cases of indirect resistance, moving on to examine outright rejections of advice. How do the parties manage each of these forms of resistance and what does that management tell us about preference organization?

Resistance by unmarked acknowledgments

As already noted, Heritage and Sefi (1992) identify unmarked acknowledgments of advice by the use of such receipt objects as 'mm hm', 'yes' and 'that's right'. We will see how such tokens and silences work to mark out a dispreferred action in a mitigated and indirect form. Furthermore, we will show how the downgrading of advice that usually follows demonstrates how such responses are monitored as indirect resistance by the counsellors. This kind of indirect resistance thus creates an environment in which all parties can seek to reaffirm social solidarity without directly acknowledging the existence of a disagreement.

The following extract, from Heritage and Sefi's (1992) data, gives several examples of both unmarked acknowledgments and no acknowledgment at all to a piece of advice about immunization:

Extract 7.4 (Heritage and Sefi, 1992)
1   HV: but it is recommended that if possible (0.2) all of
2   them are better than: (0.7) i- it's better to have
3   them all than (0.5) uhm: (0.7) no:t,=

```
 4  F:        =(      [         )    ( (to baby))
 5  HV:                [whooping cough can be a killer in the baby
 6            under one.
 7  -->       (1.0)
 8  HV:       Uh:m (1.2) but it m- (0.2) maybe you'd like to have
 9            a think about it and=
10  M: -->    Mm hm
11  HV:       uh:m talk it over with the doctor
12  -->       (1.0)
13  HV:       when you see him at clinic
14  M: -->    Mm hm.
```

At four different times in this extract (shown with arrows), the clients (father = F and mother = M) either say nothing at a possible turn-transition point or offer only the response-token 'mm hm'. Using a longer extract (not shown here), Heritage and Sefi (ibid.: 399) argue that: 'the(se) forms of acknowledgment are consistent with the tacit expression of parents' resistance to making a quick decision about their child's vaccination'.

Such silences or unmarked acknowledgments (UAs) attend to preference organization because they give an opportunity for the advice-giver to monitor the recipient's unreceptiveness and so to modify the advice or even to change topic.[2]

These kinds of display of unreceptiveness to advice are also visible in our data. Extract 7.5 below involves a piece of advice to a man who has already told the counsellor that, apart from one time when he stopped using a condom after some months in a relationship, he always uses them:

```
    Extract 7.5 (UK2)
 1  C:        =it's gotta be a little bit longer
 2        1->(1.0)
 3  C:        tt you know
 4  P:2->     [yes
 5  C:        [you've got to actually (1.5) be using a condom hh
 6            for a lot lot longer than (.) [than people think
 7  P:2->                                   [yeah
 8  C:        (.) that you should (.) I mean de >there's no way
 9            there's no flashing lights< over somebody's head
10            that's gonna sort of give you any indication
11        1->(0.4)
12  P:2->     yeah
13  C:        of anything wrong hhh um (.) this is for future
14            reference rather than (0.7) you know anyone sort of
15            (.) telling you what (.) what's been in the past (.)
16            just just bear in mind that it will be useful to use
17            condoms (.) all the time
18  P:2->     mm
```

Like Extract 7.4, Extract 7.5 shows a combination of no acknowledgment (arrow 1) and minimal UAs (arrow 2). However, here we can see how C monitors P's indirect resistance and reformulates her advice as 'for future reference' (lines 13–14), thereby removing any implied criticism of P's past behaviour. Predictably, however, when she returns to her advice, even possibly upgrading it at line 17 ('all the time'), she still only gets another unmarked acknowledgment (line 18).

In Extract 7.6, C returns to her earlier advice, still receiving no marked acknowledgment:

> Extract 7.6 (UK2) (Extract 7.5 continued)
> 1   C: you're <u>not</u> (.) okay (0.7) umm (.) so really you you
> 2   know you're (.) out looking for another heh heh
> 3   <u>relationship</u> really aren't you=
> 4   P: =sort of
> 5   C: so
> 6   P: yeah:
> 7   C: basically you've just got to (0.5) use (.) be a bit
> 8   selfish and and use self protection
> 9   P: mm
> 10 C: you know
> 11 P: mm
> 12 C: okay:?
> 13 P: yeah

Extract 7.6 begins with C formulating the gist of an earlier statement by P (data not shown). This gist is indirectly resisted by P's 'sort of' (line 4). Note, however, the beauty of this utterance. It implies but mitigates the dispreferred action (rejecting C's account).

Nonetheless, C now moves into an advice package (lines 7–8) which she links to P's answer (by her 'so' on line 5). This generates two unmarked acknowledgments (the 'mms' in lines 9 and 11). Exhibiting an understanding of these 'mms' as resistive by her 'okay?' (line 12), C now requires and gets an upgrade from P ('yeah', line 13).

However, although P has maintained a minimal level of social solidarity, his display of resistance makes it difficult for C to pursue this line of advice fruitfully. Not surprisingly, in data not shown here, C now initiates a move to close the topic, which P accepts.

In Extract 7.7 below, unmarked acknowledgments are followed by C downgrading her advice and closing the topic:

> Extract 7.7 (UK2)
> 1   P: and I don't know I don't know probably this movement
> 2   I don't know really if I (0.5) what if I'm not doing
> 3   it <u>right</u> but I don't think I put it on the wrong way
> 4   round=
> 5   C: =hh maybe if you (.) think about it in a different

```
 6              way and incorporate your (0.7) putting on the condom
 7              in your lovemaking
 8    P:        mm
 9    C:        and I think perhaps (.) a̲ you can change your
10              attitude to (.) what you're (.) using
11    P:        yes
12    C:        and (.) b̲ (.) it'll (1.2) actually give you more
13              pleasure
14              (.)
15    C:        I mean it it's a question of really er putting it on
16              properly I mean if you're putting it on in in a
17              lovemaking situation then you will know very well
18              that it's on (.) properly
19              (0.7)
20    C:        umm and I think [[softly]] it's well worth trying
21              really
22              (1.0)
23    C:        hh how much do you know about the virus apart from
24              the (0.5) [what you've
```

Extract 7.7 begins with P delivering a statement which is advice-implicative in that it gives information about his problems in using condoms. C monitors P's talk this way, offering a personalized advice sequence (beginning in line 5). However, it appears that C's advice is not terribly well fitted to P's query. For, while it seems that P is seeking information about the mechanics of getting a condom on, C appears to suggest that in a 'lovemaking situation' the mechanics take care of themselves.

In this environment, predictably C's advice elicits only two minimal response tokens from P (lines 8 and 11). Nonetheless, C continues her advice sequence using a list form ('a' and 'b'). However, when P fails to use the possible turn-transition point on line 14 to acknowledge C's advice, C reformulates it using much of the original content. Once again, however, P does not enter at the next possible turn-transition (line 19). At this point, C downgrades her advice, using a lowered voice: it is now only something 'well worth trying really'. Finally, when P doesn't use the 1.0 slot (line 22) to offer any response token, C switches topic.[3]

Such pauses here serve to maintain the preference for agreement. They avoid the dispreferred option of open disagreement and they allow the advice-giver to reformulate or abandon what she is saying. As Heritage (1984: 274) argues:

> if first speakers can analyse a pause as prefatory to rejection, they can use the time to step in to modify and revise the first utterance to a more 'attractive' or 'acceptable' form.[4]

Pauses work in a similar way in Extract 7.8 below where C has been suggesting that P visit a marriage guidance organization (data not shown):

Extract 7.8 (UK2)

```
 1  C:    em- em: or or: a citizen's advice bureau (0.4) would
 2        tell you where the nearest (0.7) one (.) was and
 3        then you'd be able to set up the appointment if they
 4        suggested that
 5        (0.8)
 6  P:    mm
 7        (0.8)
 8  C:    I think it's well worth trying if if that's what you
 9        wish
10        (1.0)
11  C:    but you know only you can make these decisions
12  P:    well [you (    )
13  C:         [we can't [insist you do anything
14  P:                   [(          )
15  P:    (      )
16  C:    you know if it's a problem to you
17        (0.8)
```

Once again, P receives an advice sequence with silence. Only after the 0.8 second pause (line 5) does he produce a minimal response token. C now delays her next turn (line 7) but P declines to expand his response. At this point, C downgrades her advice, making it a matter of P's 'wish' (line 9). When P passes his next turn (line 10), C removes the advice component altogether (line 11), simply referring to the primacy of P's own decisions. Only after this, at line 12, does P start to produce an utterance which, through its delay and mitigated form ('well') carries many of the hallmarks of dispreferred actions.

P's pauses here allow C to monitor an implicit local but cumulative trouble and to manage it by backing off from any strong urging of the advice upon P. In line with the preference for the acceptance of advice, both P and C attend to the interactional management of a disagreement which is never openly stated.

In Extract 7.9 we see a further example of such management:

Extract 7.9 (UK2)

```
 1  P:    yeah I've been talking to lots of friends (.) you
 2        know friends can be pretty good=
 3  C:    =friends get emotionally involved
 4  P:    umm
 5  C:    and sometimes it's best to be somebody (0.3) who's
 6        outside the situation in the relationship (0.5) and
 7        who can stand back and say well (.) you know do you
 8        think you might handle this (.) a different way if
 9        you do so and so
10        (0.5)
11  C:    do you see?
```

```
12   P:      umm (   )
13           (1.0)
14   C:      it's well worth trying (.) any-anyway I'll leave it
15           to you to decide
16   P:      all rig[ht
17   C:           [what you want to do
18   P:      yes [yes
19   C:          [but umm (0.7) you- when are you coming back
20           again X?
```

At line 3, C continues P's topic of 'friends' but in a way that seems to 'correct' P's observation.[5] However, P offers only a minimal acknowledgment of this 'correction' ('umm' in line 4). This creates a potentially unfavourable environment for advice, revealed in the lack of any uptake by P at line 10.

P's failure to use the slot at line 10 is monitored by C. But her prompt 'do you see?' (line 11) only gets minimal uptake which P does not expand in the 1.0 pause that follows.

As in Extract 7.8, C downgrades her advice and exits from the topic. However, here C gets stronger alignment to this downgrade via P's 'all right' (line 16) and 'yes yes' (line 18).

Resistance which implies the redundancy of the advice

We have seen that unmarked acknowledgments and failures to take an available turn at talk mark and manage dispreferred actions in a mitigated or indirect form. I now turn to the other form of indirect resistance.

In Heritage and Sefi's (1992: 403) data, mothers often 'respond to advice giving with some assertion of knowledge or competence'. Heritage and Sefi suggest that this happens because mothers want to display their 'capacity to cope with matters concerning their babies' health' (ibid.).

In the extract below, the health visitor is giving advice about the treatment of eye infections:

```
     Extract 7.10 (Heritage and Sefi, 1992)
 1   HV:     Ye:s if they- if they: (0.2) if you think they're
 2           pussie
 3           (0.8)
 4   M:      Yea:h
 5   HV:     then you must used boiled wa:ter wi[th a
 6   M:                                        [Yeah I know
 7   HV:     ((details advice))
 8   M:      Yeh I do that now. (0.2) I use a separate thi:ng
 9           (0.2) with a bit of wa:rm warm water.=
10   HV:     =Mm.
```

At lines 6 and 8, Mother twice displays prior knowledge and competence about the advice that HV is delivering. By attending to the redundancy of the advice, she resists it. When resisting the advice, however, the mother also orients to preference organization. Not only does she give an account of her resistance but the account is couched in terms of her contingent knowledge of her own circumstances. Since the health visitor could not be expected to know of these circumstances, Mother preserves the 'no fault' nature of giving-advice-which-turns-out-to be-redundant.[6]

In the different environment of an HIV test in a sexually transmitted diseases clinic, patients may be less concerned to display their knowledge and competence in sexual matters. This may account for the lack of such instances in the sample of 50 advice sequences discussed in the previous chapter.

However, in the present sample, there are two instances of patients asserting prior knowledge or competence; space will allow us to examine one of them. In Extract 7.11, C has been advising the use of condoms to an American visitor:

```
      Extract 7.11 (UK2)
 1   C:       umm Dr X said that you have had several partners (.)
 2            in (.) America umm but that you've used been using
 3            (.) a form of protection=
 4   P:       =all the [time
 5   C:                [mm
 6   P:       except that time (0.5) that (.) was the only time
 7            that happened
 8            (1.0)
 9   C:       you see (1.0) that cuts down the chances of of being
10            at risk (.) obviously I mean (.) people have got to
11            be (0.7) practical and (.) and use these sort of
12            forms=
13   P:       =well coming from ((city)) you know I've=
14   C:       =mm=
15   P:       =had a sort of education
16            (0.8)
17   C:       yes
```

At line 9, C is starting to build a piece of advice on P's previous admission (lines 6–7) that at one time he did not use 'protection'.[7] Notice, however, that the advice sequence is generalized – referring to 'people' rather than 'you'. This makes the sequence hearable as informational with a very general 'target' – thereby avoiding singling out P as the advice recipient. Consequently, C constructs what she is saying as compatible with merely a response-token from P.

Despite this, P attends to what is being said as advice and marks it as redundant (lines 13 and 15). But note that P attends to the dispreferred nature of his assertion of competence, prefacing it within the turn in which it occurs ('well') and accounting for it by his personal circumstances. To summarize, in Extract 7.11, the reception of redundant advice is marked and managed in a way which respects the preference for acceptance.

Outright rejections

Extracts 7.2 and 7.3 examined in detail two examples of such resistance. Unlike both Heritage and Sefi (1992) and the data discussed in Chapter 6, the present data offer multiple examples of explicit rejections of advice. Moreover, in each case the rejection is attended to as resistance by C.

In Extract 7.12, C is suggesting that P and his wife should visit a marriage guidance counsellor:

```
      Extract 7.12 (UK2)
  1   C:      do you think that somewhere like (0.3) Relate which
  2           is the old Marriage Guidance people=
  3   P:      =em[:
  4   C:         [(    [ )
  5   P:         [we've gone beyond that now I mean as she's been
  6           to a medium [de
  7   C:                  [mm
  8           (1.0)
  9   P:      I've (got rid) of Tarot I mean she's (0.7) now she's
 10           got her own place >we used to live together< (0.5)
 11           but she's recently got her own place
 12           (1.0)
 13   P:      and er: she's (0.4) independent now you know
 14           (1.0)
 15   P:      she's finding her feet
 16           (1.2)
 17   P:      yer know
 18   C:      (                      ) to your relationship?
```

In Extract 7.12, note, initially, C packages her (uncompleted) advice as a question (lines 1–2). This kind of question format works, like the perspective display series (Maynard, 1991) discussed in Chapter 2, by allowing the answerer to provide his own perspective prior to the explicit delivery of some advice or information.

Before C has completed her question, P's 'em' (line 3) marks a claim to an early turn at talk, while allowing C to retain the floor to finish the question. Now, at line 5, P resists the advice implicit in C's question. In line with preference organization, however, the advice rejection is mitigated – P's reference to 'now' implies that C's advice might have been relevant before.

Having monitored P's answer as resisting her implied advice, C now allows P to display more of his own perspective by passing her turn on four successive occasions (shown by the pauses after P's subsequent turns). Now P's extended answer can be heard as a problem-statement, to which C responds in a turn which seems to involve a request for specification (line 18) before an actual package of advice is delivered (data not shown).

In all three examples of advice rejections shown thus far (Extract 7.2 from Heritage and Sefi's data; Extracts 7.3 and 7.12 from ours), professional and client collaborate in containing and smoothing over their disagreement. Shortly, we will examine a deviant case where it *appears* that the rejection of C's advice is immediate and open. However, it will be helpful to preface discussion of this case with a more general examination of the local circumstances in which advice rejections may occur.

Multiple advice rejections

The presence of four rejections out of 18 cases in our corpus is best explained by considering shortly an example of advice *acceptance* from the same corpus. Take Extract 7.13:

```
        Extract 7.13 (UK2)
  1  C:      em I'm picking up that (0.8) it's your emotional
  2          problem that that's [a problem rather than
  3  P:                          [mm
  4  C:      rather than: your sexuality=
  5  P:      =oh yes: (0.5) very much (0.5) I mean you know heh
  6          I'm er eating my heart out as it were
  7  C:      well then why don't you do something positive by
  8          going in
  9          (0.7)
 10  P:      yes::
 11  C:      having a chat with [somebody
 12  P:                         [I should really=
```

Here C establishes a favourable environment for advice-giving by first generating an early and strong agreement (line 5) with her formulation of P's 'problem' (lines 1–4). In and through the agreement displayed by P, the participants have established an alignment in their perceptions of the problem at hand. When the counsellor thereafter delivers her advice which is related to the matters that the participants have just agreed upon, she gets a marked acknowledgment, delivered early (line 12) which employs the *preferred* action format.

Conversely, resistance to advice is found where C produces advice in environments characterized by displays of non-alignment or disagreement. Take Extract 7.14:

```
        Extract 7.14 (UK2) (Extract 7.6 continued)
  1  C:      are talking to someone about which you know [(   )
  2  P:                                                  [well in
  3          Y I've been involved only with one girl
```

```
 4   C:      mm
 5   P: .    for (0.5) for a long time (.) so a few years=
 6   C:      =is she your regular girlfriend?
 7   P:      yes=
 8   C:      =you're still involved with her are you?
 9   P:      no not any more heh
10   C:      you're not (.) okay (0.7) umm (.) so really you you
11           know you're (.) out looking for another heh heh
12           relationship really aren't you=
13   P:      =sort of
14   C:      so
15   P:      yeah:
16   C:      basically you've just got to (0.5) use (.) be a bit
17           selfish and and use self protection
18   P:      mm
```

In Extract 7.14, C uses the information provided by P to her two questions (at lines 6 and 8) to formulate P's intentions (10–12). However, this formulation has not been directly warranted by P's two answers and so works more as a 'guess' rather than a 'summary'.

P now indicates the limitations of C's guess by his response of 'sort of' (line 13). Note, however, that P's response is hearable as a disaffiliation from C's assertion, given how it serves to downgrade it.

Now when C offers her advice (lines 16–17), linked to an unsupported formulation of P's perspective, P gives only an unmarked acknowledgment (line 18) implying indirect resistance. Thus, in Extract 7.14, a formulation of P's intentions which partially misfires leads to resistance to subsequent advice.

Although Extract 7.14 gives us a clue about the reason for the presence of multiple advice rejections in these data, it contains only an implicit resistance to advice. We can learn more about advice rejections in Extract 7.15 below. C has been reviewing P's many previous visits to the clinic, building up a case for viewing him as one of the 'worried well'. She then delivers her advice, clearly directed against this behaviour (lines 23–7) but gets an outright rejection (line 28). In terms of preference organization, Extract 7.15 below is, then, our deviant case.

```
     Extract 7.15 (UK2)
 1   C:      you can actually [create your own NSU by by stress
 2   P:                       [mm
 3   C:      and worry
 4   P:      mm I see I'm not the type of person to heh heh ( )
 5                                                    [stress
 6   C:      [yes but it might be [something you're submerging up
 7   P:                           [get stressed
 8   C:      here you see
 9   P:      mm [hmm
```

```
10  C:              [and (.) mixed up with that is is (.) the worry
11                  about (.) what you hear on TV and radio and (.) and
12                  what you read in the news[papers
13  P:                                       [mmm
14  C:              and magazines hh and so (0.5) mi there's a great
15                  complete (.) mixmatch of of (.) what's actually
16                  happening to human beings at the moment in (.) in GU
17                  medicine because they're still worried [about
18  P:                                                     [mm
19  C:              HIV as >a sexually transmitted disease< so so it
20                  might be one of these you know=
21  P:              =mm
22  C:              that that's creating the problem (0.5) so hh um
23                  (1.0) I think what you have to do is (.) when you've
24                  had your clean bill of health this time
25                  (0.4)
26  P:              yes
27  C:              is (.) [[softly]] get on with living
28  P:              I do live my life anyway so
```

Let us inspect the environment in which P's rejection of C's advice at the end of this extract occurs. Extract 15 begins with the counsellor delivering information to the patient. In principle, it might seem that acknowledging information need not commit P to a course of action. However, here C's observations on the link between a sexually transmitted disease (non-specific urethritis or NSU) and 'stress' are hearable by P, who has had treatments for NSU, as bearing on the cause of his own condition.

P might want to resist not only the implication (that he is a hypochondriac) but also the possible piece of advice (don't get stressed and you won't get ill) that follows from the implication. So P's response (lines 4–5) works towards resisting both the version of himself already proposed and the advice that might follow it.

Nonetheless, C contests P's interpretation in a long series of turns beginning at line 6. Rather than affiliate to C's account, P throughout only offers minimal response-tokens. By resisting P's answers about his problem, C has created an environment of disalignment in the participants' perceptions of the issue at hand. Clearly, this constitutes an unfavourable environment for delivering advice about the solution of P's problem.

When, finally, C delivers the advice to which she has been leading (lines 23–7), she gets an outright rejection in which P points out that the advice is not suitable for him (line 28).[8]

P does not, in this extract, delay, preface, mitigate or account for his rejection of C's advice. Thus, one might suggest, P seems not to attend at all to the rules of preference organization. However, we must bear in mind that, like any human rule-system, preference organization does not determine behaviour but provides a way of making behaviour accountable.[9]

Therefore, rather than ignoring preference organization, P can be heard to express an extraordinarily strong rejection of C's advice through expressing it in the *preferred* action format. It is the very lack of delays, prefaces, mitigation or accounts that constitutes this format; and thereby, it establishes the extraordinary strength of P's rejection.[10]

It appears that the unfavourable environment of advice-giving in Extract 15 makes relevant such extraordinary rejection. As we have already remarked, C's advice is embedded after a sequence in which P has formulated his own experience (line 4). However, this formulation has been resisted by C. Thereby, an environment has been created in which the participants disagree about what P's perspective is. As C's advice is embedded in her version of P – a version already refuted by P himself – a local environment now exists where C's advice can be rejected in the strongest available way. We can conclude that it is not that preference organization is irrelevant here but rather that P displays, through his disattendance to some of the ordinary practices in using this organization, that something out of the ordinary has been going on.[11]

Conclusion

Advice sequences about babycare and sexual behaviour have one thing in common. Both deal with matters that are directly hearable as related to the moral standing of the advice recipients.[12] Despite this, the most striking aspect of Heritage and Sefi's data and our own is that both parties respect the preference for agreement. Outright resistance is far less common than implied resistance. Where advice rejections occur, they are normally accomplished in dispreferred action format. Even the single deviant case (in which the advice rejection occurs in the preferred action format) is analysable in terms of the speakers' orientation to preference organization in choosing that format to display the extraordinary strength of the rejection.

Throughout, we have observed the co-operative minimization of resistance to and rejection of advice. Clients opt for unmarked acknowledgments and silences much more frequently than they choose outright advice rejections. Where they reject advice, they normally lead up to it through delays and mitigations, and counsellors speedily back down. Equally, counsellors deploy a series of strategies for minimizing resistance, sometimes packaging their advice in perspective display sequences or using an ambiguous format (potentially information delivery rather than advice-giving).

Heritage discusses preference organization in the context of 'the timing of social solidarity' (1984: 265). This is precisely what we have observed in examining how advice is given and received. Taking a direction from French sociology, we might say that counsellors and patients attend to the

Durkheimian principle of social solidarity, not as automatons but 'by playing with the tempo of the exchange' (Bourdieu, 1979: 15).

From a practical point of view, however, the presence of advice resistance is probably more important than how it is smoothed over. As already implied, such resistance seems to emerge here where a counsellor embarks on a piece of advice that has not been grounded first in her client's own perspective. Sometimes, as in Extract 7.15, this happens because C tries to legislate about P's underlying emotions. Elsewhere, as in Extract 7.14, C uses questions to obtain P's perspective but then jumps to an early formulation of it which P resists.

On other occasions such resistance is minimized, either by packaging a piece of advice as a question about P's perspective (Extract 7.12) or by C offering a candidate formulation of P's perspective to him (as in Extract 7.13).

On both these occasions, we see the way in which perspective display devices (Maynard, 1991) may align clients to an upcoming piece of advice or, presumably, allow that advice never to be explicitly offered. However, as noted in the previous chapter, obtaining the client's perspective can be a slow procedure. Once again, we come to the conclusion that devices which may function well for counsellors' purposes depend upon the kind of leisurely interview which circumstances do not always allow.

Notes

1. A fascinating example of resistance is found in two of our Trinidad extracts where patients overtly resist question–answer sequences about 'safer sex' by asserting that the counsellor should not be asking about their behaviour and knowledge but, as the expert, telling them directly (see Youssef and Silverman, 1992).

2. It is noteworthy that, in Extract 7.4, the HV formats her advice in an ambiguous way. Like many HIV counsellors, what she says to her clients is hearable not only as advice but as *information* about the kind of advice that is 'officially' given. Consequently, if F had produced just an unmarked acknowledgment after HV had completed her observations about 'whooping cough', this would have served to maintain a proper alignment to information delivery. Hence, *contra* Heritage and Sefi, where the communication format is ambiguous, unmarked acknowledgments may not necessarily be heard as resistance to advice but as continuers which stably maintain information delivery. Through maintaining such ambiguity, these professionals skilfully manage to skip over some of the interactional traps of giving advice. In fact, because F fails to say anything here, there is an interactional problem whether the format is heard as information delivery or advice-giving. Hence, in this instance, Heritage and Sefi have grounds for arguing that HV hears resistance at this point. We take up this issue of ambiguous advice packages in the next chapter.

3. C's use of an information check here is a nice, commonly used, device to warrant the shift of format away from the interactionally perilous advice-giving to a more stable format. The information check means that the upcoming information delivery can be presented as implicitly requested by P.

4. Given the lack of fit between C's advice and P's question, noted above, P's minimal uptake might demonstrate a lack of understanding, involving a puzzlement over 'how is this an answer to my question?' rather than an advice rejection *per se*. In this case, social solidarity is still being maintained but in relation to not confronting the irrelevance of advice rather than avoiding

disagreement with advice. I am grateful to an anonymous reviewer for this suggestion.

5. At line 3, C appears to disagree with P without any dispreference markers such as delay or mitigation. However, it is possible that C's utterance may be read as an elaboration of P's observation about 'friends' i.e. to the extent that friends are 'pretty good', this may be because they 'get emotionally involved'. To this extent, C *is* attending to the preference for agreement.

6. This discussion draws heavily on Heritage, 1984: 271–2. See Extract 7.1 above for a further example of a speaker using knowledge of his own circumstances to manage a dispreferred action.

7. Notice how P beautifully attends to the preferred answer built into C's question. He first produces this answer, marking his subsequent revision as dispreferred by delay and a lowered voice.

8. P's resistive utterance ('I do live my life anyway so') appears to be an instance of asserting previous knowledge or competence and thereby fits the second form of resistance discussed earlier.

9. Rules are never exhaustive; they cannot cover every instance. Given particular circumstances, they seem more or less appropriate. As Wittgenstein points out: 'we must be on our guard against thinking that there is some *totality* of conditions corresponding to the nature of each case (e.g. for a person's walking) so that, as it were, he *could not but walk* if they were all fulfilled' (1968: 74, para. 183).

10. Nonetheless, P formulates his rejection by appealing, as elsewhere, idiomatically to a self-evident statement of affairs ('I do live my life anyway').

11. I am grateful for John Heritage's help with this point and also for drawing my attention to Christian Heath's (1992) analogous finding that open resistance to medical diagnoses is only found where the diagnosis suggests that there is nothing wrong with you.

12. Compare these settings to, say, a doctor giving advice about the treatment of a physical injury or an accountant giving advice about taxation. Although issues regarding clients' moral standing may, of course, arise in such settings, they may not be so directly implied as in the counselling and health-visiting environments.

8

Concealing Advice: the Advice-as-Information Sequence

The previous two chapters have examined the link between different forms of advice-giving and advice reception. In particular, in Chapter 7, we looked at how, in certain conversational environments, resistance to advice may assume quite spectacular proportions. This concluding chapter on advice seeks to pull these threads together and to advance the argument by spelling out a device used by counsellors to stabilize advice-giving.

This chapter is organized in four related sections:

- It summarizes what we have learned so far about the interactional difficulties that can arise in personalized advice-giving.
- It analyses favourable environments for the uptake of advice.
- It shows the instability of maintaining an unambiguous advice-giving format.
- It identifies an interactional solution for advice-givers and advice recipients to the problem of the non-uptake of advice.

The bulk of the data discussed in this chapter is drawn from 21 pre-HIV test counselling interviews in a US city (US2). Some data from a UK testing centre (UK1) are introduced for comparative purposes.

Slightly different procedures are used at each centre. In the US clinic, Ps fill in a questionnaire prior to the interview and Cs refer to Ps answers during counselling. In the UK clinic, Ps are usually seen 'blind' – although some come with referral note from a doctor at the clinic.

Categorization and advice-giving

In professional–client encounters, even apparently straightforward information delivery can imply a categorization which the speaker might not want to imply. For instance, in the extract below from a British HIV test counselling interview, the counsellor (C) is outlining her agenda to the client (P):

Extract 8.1 (UK1)
1   C: we also need to go over with you what <u>happens</u> (.)
2   when someone gets a positive test result,

```
3    P:        Yes.
4    C:        but plea:se remember we have to do this with .h
5              everyone who's tested .hh[h and we're not saying=
6    P:                                [Ri:ght.
7    C:        =that we think you know you're in (.) any greater
8              ris[k (of uhm of a) positive result. .hhhhhh=
9    P:           [No (            )
```

Notice how C attends to the implications of her 'need to go over with you what happens (.) when someone gets a positive test result'. P is told that this is an activity that arises from the category 'someone having an HIV test' and not from the category 'likely to be infected with HIV'. Through this postscript, C neatly marks and manages the implications of her agenda-statement which imply that P is 'someone (who might) get(s) a positive test result'. Notice also how P collaborates with this (re)categorization by his overlapping acknowledgments in lines 6 and 9.[1]

Asking a particular question of someone can also be rich in implications. For instance, by asking the question, you imply that the question uses categories which are relevant to the person at whom such a question is directed. Such an issue arises when Cs ask Ps about their possible drug use. Note the preface (line 1) and the postscript (line 4) to the question here:

```
     Extract 8.2 (UK1)
1    C:        er: I have to ask you this have you ever injected
2              drugs.
3    P:        No.
4    C:        Because they're the sort of highest ris:k (.)
```

As with questioning, advice-giving can imply particular categories through which the advice recipient is being defined. For instance, if a counsellor advises me 'to be sure to have safer sex in future', the implication may be that I have not been having safer sex in the past.

A second problem, which is peculiar to advice-giving, is that it seems to require strong uptake from its recipient if the advice-giving is going to persist over many turns. For instance, as I noted in Chapter 6, Heritage and Sefi (1992) argue that the absence of clear uptake markers (like 'oh really' or 'I think you're right' or 'how do you mean?') is strongly implicative of a client's resistance to the advice offered.

Throughout our corpus of examples, counsellors exit quickly from personalized advice-giving when patients offer only minimal response tokens or when they display overt resistance. By contrast, according to Jefferson and Lee (1981), advice is most likely to be well received where it is 'initiated by the troubles-teller' and emerges:

> as the logical outcome of a diagnosis offered by the troubles-recipient and concurred in by the troubles-teller; i.e. the advice is sequentially appropriate and the talk is interactionally 'synchronous'. (1981: 408)

This suggests the possibility that, where these features are absent, i.e. advice is delivered 'prematurely' and/or without a 'trouble' being presented by the client, we are likely to find that it is rejected.

Heritage and Sefi's (1992) account of health visitor/mother interactions entirely fits this explanation of advice rejections. Unless the client seeks advice, she will usually resist advice which is not recipient-designed to an elicited 'problem' or sequentially appropriate.

Extract 8.3 below shows how advice reception is organized in these circumstances, i.e. the health visitor (HV) has not based her advice (lines 1–3 and 5–6) on any 'diagnosis' or problem provided by the mother (M) or father (F):

```
      Extract 8.3 [Heritage and Sefi, 1992]
 1  HV:    but it is recommended that if possible (0.2) all of
 2          them are better than: (0.7) i- it's better to have
 3          them all than (0.5) uhm: (0.7) no:t,=
 4  F:     =(        [      )     ( (to baby))
 5  HV:               [whooping cough can be a killer in the baby
 6          under one.
 7          (1.0)
 8  HV:    Uh:m (1.2) but it m- (0.2) maybe you'd like to have
 9          a think about it and=
10  M:     Mm hm
11  HV:    uh:m talk it over with the doctor
12          (1.0)
13  HV:    when you see him at clinic
14  M:     Mm hm.
```

Heritage and Sefi focus on the 1.0 second post-advice pause at line 7. They argue that HV's subsequent downgrading of her advice (line 8 onwards) shows that she monitors the parents' failure to use the 1.0 second slot as indicating resistance to it.

Following Jefferson and Lee (1981), Heritage and Sefi (1992) show how a more favourable environment can be created for advice-giving by the establishment of an agreed 'problem' being experienced by the potential advice recipient. As we saw in Chapter 6, advice is much more likely to be well received when it is addressed to a client 'problem' elicited by a series of questions and a request for specification.

Favourable environments for advice-giving

In Chapter 6, I noted Heritage and Sefi's (1992) identification of what they called a marked acknowledgment of advice (e.g. 'oh right' or repeats of key components of the advice). Heritage and Sefi argue that such utterances acknowledge the informativeness and appropriateness of the advice. Like Heritage and Sefi, in Chapter 6 we found a strong association between the presence of marked acknowledgments and two environments in which the advice-giving took place:

a question from the client;
questions from the counsellor which elicit a problem which the client is then asked to specify.

Let us review each environment in turn, in relation to the new data being discussed here.

A question from the client

Extract 8.4 below illustrates why Heritage and Sefi argue that a client's request for information or advice creates a highly favourable environment for advice-giving:

```
        Extract 8.4 [Heritage and Sefi, 1992]
 1   M:      I haven't ba::thed her yet. Is once a week enough.
 2           (0.7)
 3   HV:     We::ll (0.2) babies do: sweat a lo:t. (0.3) So I
 4           would recommend giving her a ba:th every da:y.
 5   M:      Every da::y.
 6   HV:     So that she gets used to it and sh- that's her
 7           little pl:aytime for he[r.
 8   M:                             [Oh ri::ght.
```

Notice here how HV's advice (lines 3–4) directly responds to the question asked by the mother (M). Now M offers a marked acknowledgment (MA), repeating a key component of the advice ('Every da::y'.). When HV explains her advice (lines 6–7), M provides an overlapping MA ('Oh ri::ght.').

The US counselling data reveal how advice related to a client's question often produces an MA from the client. In Extract 8.5 the client begins by asking a question about oral sex:[2]

```
        Extract 8.5 (US2)
 1   P:      what ahm what if you do not use a condom to the
 2           point of when they're ready to ejaculate?
 3   C:      okay, pre ejaculation fluids also contain the virus
 4   P:      okay
 5   C:      obviously there would be more fluid and more
 6           possibility of infection with the ejaculation
 7   P:      right
             ((More detailed transcription))
 8           (0.4)
 9   C:      a:nd (0.4) so you know there: (0.4) still would be
10           some risk involved (0.6) obviously it would be
11           reduced considerably.
12   P:      mmhmm
```

```
13  C:      and that probably is (.) in mo:st cases what the
14          recommendation ah- would be is to .hhh not accept
15          (1.0) the ejaculation in your mouth.=
16  P:      =right right
17  C:      okay
```

In Extract 8.5, as C completes an advice-sequence (lines 13–15) directly tied to P's initial question, P is in early with an MA ('=right right').

A little later in the same session, P volunteers a further example of safer sex (covering parts of the body in 'saran wrap') but is corrected by C (lines 3–4):

```
    Extract 8.6 (US2)
    C:      okay, I will give a little demonstration ahm
            ((More detailed transcription))
2   P:      =liddle (0.4) plas- ah, saran wrap wo- does wonders.
3           (1.0)
4   C:      sara:n wrap doe- is not safe.
5           (1.4)
6   P:      no?
7           (0.2)
8   C:      no.
9           (0.8)
10  C:      okay, THE FIRST PREFerence: (.) is a little piece of
11          latex called a dental dam
```

Predictably, given the positioning of C's information/recommendation (line 4) as an immediate correction of P's volunteered version of what is 'safe' (on a topic initiated by P himself), P offers a marked acknowledgment, producing a newsworthiness token ('no?', line 6).

These two extracts, from the same session, support Heritage and Sefi's arguments about the linkage between marked acknowledgments and advice deriving from clients' questions. However, it is important to note that, in both cases, C shapes his advice in a different form to that of Heritage and Sefi's health visitor. Thus, in the HIV test extracts, C says: 'in mo:st cases what the recommendation ah- would be' and 'THE FIRST PREFerence: (.) is'. On the other hand, the health visitor says: 'I would recommend'. We can note C's use of a passive voice, compared to HV's formatting of her advice in her own, emphasized ('I') voice. So despite the similar and, apparently, favourable environment of P's request for information, C is still cautious.

These data cannot demonstrate whether the different institutional functions and environments of HIV counselling and health visiting are associated with different levels of caution. This means that any attempts to explain these differences would be speculative. Indeed, although it would be tempting to explain C's caution in the light of the US legal environment, our data suggest that British counsellors also quite often proceed with caution in giving advice even when, as here, specifically asked for it by their clients.

The caution demonstrated here will be taken up in the final section of this chapter. We need only note at this stage that the use of the passive voice by this C neatly establishes an ambiguity about whether this is his personal advice to this particular client.[3] Given this ambiguity, an unmarked acknowledgment from P need not damage the format.

Let us return to the issue of the link between the reception of advice and the form of its delivery. A further difference from Heritage and Sefi's data is that advice based on an earlier question from a client does not always produce a marked acknowledgment. In the US pre-test counselling data below, C delivers advice related to P's question but only gets an unmarked acknowledgment ('=yeah'):

```
     Extract 8.7 (US2)
 1   C:      .h do you have any questions.
 2           (4.1)
 3   P:      well uh: (1.2) so:- eh even if I did uh::i (0.7) end
 4           up testing po:sitive or something like that the:nd.
 5           (1.2) u:::::m::: say my wife: is still willing to
 6           live with me and everything like that nice, eh I
 7           think she would.
 8                   (0.2)
 9   C:      mm [hmm]
10   P:         [but] ah:: eh how much of ah at risk would she be
11           (0.5) you know if- if: ah:: (0.8) I mean how sa:fe
12           do you have to be with a:: [person]
13   C:                                  [any ti]me that you're
14           invo:lved with her: (1.3) i:n (0.8) vaginal or anal
15           intercourse: (1.3) I would r:ecommend that you
16           always use a rubber.=
17   P:      =y:eah.
18                   (0.7)
19   C:      'k[ay
20   P:        [okay:: (    )
```

In Extract 8.7, C personalizes his advice ('I would r:ecommend', line 15). However, despite the favourable environment created by P's (invited) question, P only offers, at line 17, 'y:eah'. As already noted, Heritage and Sefi argue that such an acknowledgment does not mark the advice as newsworthy or constitute an undertaking to follow it.

On the other hand, P's 'y:eah' is stronger uptake than the 'mms' we noted in many extracts in earlier chapters and its early delivery makes it hearable as possibly taking up C's advice. This makes the extent of P's uptake somewhat ambiguous. There is evidence that C analyses P's 'yeah' in the same way, pursuing a stronger acknowledgment which he gets in P's overlapping 'okay::' at line 20.[4]

Analysis of these counselling extracts suggests two modifications of Heritage and Sefi's argument. First, while advice based on a client's question may be more likely to generate a marked acknowledgment, we may expect to find variations in the strength of that uptake. Second, two different advice formats have been identified – the 'institutional' or 'passive' voice and the personal voice. It is important to examine the functions of each voice.

A counsellor's question elicits a problem

Heritage and Sefi discuss an 'extended sequence' of advice-giving. In this sequence, the professional only delivers advice after a 'problem' has been identified in an answer to the professional's question. More questions are then asked to further specify the problem and advice is then delivered in a highly recipient-designed form. As already noted, this structure is similar to the perspective display sequence identified by Maynard (1991, 1992) in doctors' delivery of diagnosis statements. The outcome is usually uptake of the advice (or diagnosis), indicated by the presence of marked acknowledgments from the client.

We have already identified such a sequence in HIV test counselling in Chapter 6. Our present data confirm that the extended sequence is indeed an effective means of obtaining uptake of advice. We can demonstrate this, using extracts from two US counselling interviews.

In Extract 8.8 below, C is topicalizing 'safer sex'. C has already learned that P does not currently use condoms with his partner (not transcribed). However, it is noticeable that C abstains from delivering explicit advice on the topic. Instead, he asks a question about condoms which sets up a perspective display sequence:

```
Extract 8.8 (US2)
 1  C:      now, as far as you're- as far as safer sex is
 2          concerned, hh because you have been in a twelve or
 3          whatever month relationship with this person, how
 4          would you feel about putting the condoms back on?
 5  P:      I'd prefer not to actually, um
 6  C:      and how does she feel?
 7  P:      well the same way
 8                  (0.3)
 9  C:      awr:ighdy.
10                  (1.0)
11  C:      here's what I would recommend then (0.1) obviously:
12          (0.6) you folks have been (1.4) not (0.7) using
13          protection (0.5) for a year now.
14                  (2.0)
15  C:      ((tch)) wha' do you use for birth control?
```

This is a fascinating extract in the way in which C attempts to move towards a recipient-designed advice sequence. Notice how C bases his question about condoms (lines 3–4) on information that he has already gleaned from his client.

However, C's question is highly implicative of a piece of advice (i.e. 'I think you should put the condoms back on'). P shows he monitors the question the same way using 'actually' to mark his answer as the dispreferred one.

Nonetheless, C still abstains from explicit advice-giving. At line 6, he extends the PDS by asking a question about P's partner. When this produces the same answer (marked as dispreferred by 'well'), C simply acknowledges that he has heard what P is saying ('awr:ighdy.').

Although C now starts to deliver personalized advice (line 11), this is then aborted by a further question from C ('wha' do you use for birth control?'). If C wants to advise the use of condoms, his questions have created a highly unfavourable environment. To achieve uptake of that advice, he will need to align P much more with his perspective.

This is how the interview continues:

```
        Extract 8.9 (US2) (Extract 8.8 continued)
15  C:      ((tch)) wha' do you use for birth control?
16              (1.6)
17  P:      pi:lls.
18          ((C asks more questions and then delivers information
19          about the likelihood of passing HIV in a monogamous
            relationship))
20  C:      .hhh the moral of this story is that we really don't
21          know: (1.2) whe:n or why: (1.1) an HIV infection is
22          spread (0.3) between a man and a woman. (1.3) .h
23          sometimes it happens and sometimes it doesn't. (1.1)
24          .hh so that if: (1.1) you: (0.5) are in fact HIV
25          po:sidive and we- we don't know that yet do we?
26              (1.0)
27  C:      .hh that although you have had maybe hundreds of
28          sexual relationships: (0.5) with your girlfriend.
29          (1.2) .h she may still be HIV negadive.
30              (2.2)
31  C:      okay:? (0.6) .h and that if you were to put on the
32          condoms for the next two weeks: (1.0) .h you would
33          (0.2) sto:p (0.6) any po:ssiblidy (0.8) of infecting
34          her. (0.2) see what I'm saying?
35              (0.2)
36  P:      I understand, [yeah.]
37  C:                   [.hhh ] so ho:w would you
38          feel about using co:ndoms for the next couple of
39          weeks:?
40  P:      =('at 'ould) definitely make sense:.=
41  C:      nkay,
```

At the end of this extract, notice how P finally provides a marked acknowledgment of C's implicit advice (=('at 'ould) definitely make sense), indicating that his answer is preferred by his early entry and upgrade ('definitely').[5] However C's final question about condom use ('ho:w would you feel about using co:ndoms for the next couple of weeks:?') has been delayed through many turns and is now limited to the period during which the test result is unknown (to 'the next couple of weeks').

Following Heritage and Sefi (1992), this extract shows how a sequence whereby the parties establish a shared alignment to a problem is likely to be associated with client uptake of the advice. It also underlines Maynard's (1991,1992) point that, where a PDS delivers a 'misaligned' P perspective, further questions may align the client to the professional's perspective.

Following Chapter 7, the analysis also shows how a question can be heard as advice, without the need for clearly marked advice to be delivered. Thus we have identified a further means through which professionals can manage the problematic character of constituting themselves as advice-givers.

However, sometimes advice-giving can be less problematic because a client's answer to a question has indicated an overall alignment to the professional's perspective. We see such an alignment being established in Extract 8.10 below in relation to the topic of 'oral sex':

Extract 8.10 (US2)

```
1   C:      what about oral sex?
2   P:      oral sex, except for that one time, it has been I
3           will- I will let my partner go down on me or I will
4           go down on my partner, but I will- except for that
5           one time, not let him come in my mouth. I will get
6           close and then I will jack him off
7   C:      good, okay, all righty, so I would tend to agree
8           with you that your risks are relatively low as far
9           as as the clients that we see.
```

Here the question, 'what about oral sex?', generates an answer which C favourably evaluates ('good, okay, all righty, so I would tend to agree with you').[6]

Having established that his P is already favourably disposed to 'safer sex' in an area often defined as 'less risky', C now delivers a long advice sequence on another 'low risk' activity:

Extract 8.11 (US2) (Extract 8.10 continued)

```
50   C:      .hhh S:O. (.) when you're playing
51           (0.3)
52   P:      mm hmm=
53   C:      =play away. .hhh take that fifteen or thirdy second
54           break again=
55   P:      =yeah.=
56   C:      =to clean up the ha:nds the co:ck the ba:lls the
57           butt the chest the- the whadever go:t messed up .hh
58           and go back and play some more:.=
```

```
59  P:      =okay
60  C:      .h but do:n't be cavalier about (0.6) mutual
61          masturbation being so incredibly safe it could never
62          happen. .hh 'cause in my experience that's not
63          true:.
64          (0.2)
65  P:      o:kay=
```

Up until the end of Extract 8.11, P offers only response tokens (mm hmm, yeah, okay) which serve as continuers rather than as marked acknowledgments of the advice. However, when C continues, P's responses are considerably upgraded:

Extract 8.12 (US2) (Extract 8.11 continued)

```
65  P:      o:kay=
66  C:      =okay? .hhh again if your hands are in really bad
67          shape, .hhh not tonight? dear.=
68  P:      =yeah, understood.=
69  C:      =okay?
            ((rough transcription))
70  P:      sorry I have a headache or whatever
71  C:      or yeah or whatever huh huh
72  P:      huh huh
```

In this final part of the extract, P provides two unmistakable marked acknowledgments to C's advice: 'yeah, understood.'(line 68) and 'sorry I have a headache or whatever'(line 70).

C's 'not tonight? dear.' is hearable as an idiomatic expression – the kind of thing a wife says when she doesn't want to engage in sexual relations. In the vocabulary of gay sex, such an expression may be used because each party may play with the gender roles established in the 'straight' community. Indeed, this is precisely what happens here as P matches C's idiomatic 'not tonight? dear.' with his own idiom 'sorry I have a headache'.

We can now start to see a local explanation for why MAs are placed here. Drew and Holt (1988) have pointed out that the use of such idiomatic expressions can be heard as pre-closing invitations. P's responses after C's 'not tonight? dear.' indicate that he monitors the talk in this way. First, he takes what may turn out to be the last opportunity to show his full alignment with C's advice through the utterance 'yeah, understood.' (line 68). Second, he aligns to C's advice and accepts his pre-closing invitation through 'sorry I have a headache or whatever' (line 70). Predictably, in the next few lines (data not shown), C exits from this topic.

This extract is an outstanding example of the collaborative production of advice reception. As in the earlier research, it shows how a question can establish the client's perspective and thus be a favourable environment for advice delivery aligned to it. The specific contribution of this analysis, using Drew and Holt's (1988) paper, is that it suggests local explanations of the positioning of different kinds of advice acknowledgments, while pointing to how Cs can close particular advice sequences.[7]

The delicacy of formulating advice

So far, we have been looking at how *favourable* advice-giving environments may be collaboratively established. We now move on to our second topic concerned with the local conditions associated with advice resistance. Two such conditions are discussed here:

entry into advice prior to obtaining the client's perspective;
personalizing advice to the client, drawing upon formulations to which the
   client may not be aligned.

Advice without knowing the client's perspective

This situation was discussed fully in Chapter 6. Our US data are fully in line with this earlier research: namely, such advice is associated with unmarked acknowledgments implying tacit resistance. One example from our data will suffice. Extract 8.13 begins with C asking a question:

```
       Extract 8.13 (US2)
 1   C:        you do use co:ndoms now?
 2                 (1.0)
 3   P:        on occa:sion, yes.=
 4   C:        =on occa:sion. (0.5) uhh
 5                 (0.5)
```

At this point, C could have sought further specification of P's answer ('on occa:sion, yes'), thus turning it into a gloss needing to be unpacked. In this way, it might have been possible to align P to a piece of advice. However, as the extract continues, we see below that, after repeating what P has said, C immediately offers an advice package which runs contrary to what P has said he is doing:

```
       Extract 8.14 (US2) (Extract 8.13 continued)
 6   C:        .hhh um (0.7) works >bedder< if you use 'em all the
 7             ti:me.
 8                 (2.7)
 9   P:        it's the heat of the mo:ment sometimes.=
10   C:        =tch .hh (0.5) n'kay, and then we'll ta:lk about
11             tha:t, too:.
```

The 2.7 second pause (line 8) after the advice is given is highly implicative of an upcoming dispreferred action. Indeed such an action (resistance to advice) is what we get when P eventually delivers his response (line 9). Now C extracts himself from further immediate discussion of the topic by an agenda-statement (lines 10–11).

This extract shows how advice-giving can come unstuck when a client's perspective turns out to be opposed to the advice *after the advice is delivered*. However, another problem with unaligned advice packages is that they may turn out to deliver advice which is already known to the client.

The possible *irrelevance* of advice to clients had already been identified by Heritage and Sefi in their English health visitor data. In our US counselling data, there is no evidence of clients suggesting the irrelevance of advice to them. However, what we do find are pre-emptive strikes by counsellors to show that they are aware that their advice may be irrelevant and hence to manage or prevent subsequent resistance.

All such cases arise where the client is a gay man.[8] For instance, in Extract 8.15 below, the client is a gay man whose partner has just tested positive. Very early on in the interview C observes:

Extract 8.15 (US2)
```
1   C:      I have a feeling you could probably give me the same
2           talk that I could give you about safer sex
3   P:      yeah, we're very careful
4   C:      okay, do you have any questions about safer sex,
5           what's considered safer, what is not?
```

C's observation (lines 1–2) works as a nice way of establishing P as a knowledgeable person. When this is confirmed, C allows P the opportunity to request advice if he wants it.

With another gay client, C also gives the floor to P to ask questions but then reverts to information about 'risky' sex (lines 2–4 below):

Extract 8.16 (US2)
```
1   C:      right right. okay do you have any other questions
2           about sexual activities? there's a couple more
3           activities that are pretty high risk, those would be
4           ah fisting or rimming
5   P:      mmmm
6   C:      okay, ah I got a nod of the head so I won't even
7           give you the gorey details on how to do that safely
8           so
9   P:      well ah the rimming I know how to do safely
```

However, when C takes a client's body movement as indicating prior knowledge ('I got a nod of the head', line 6), he makes it clear that he is not going to give advice on the topic. But P's response (line 9), marked as dispreferred ('well ah'), implies that he only has knowledge of one of the 'activities' to which C has referred. Now C has created a favourable environment to give advice about the other activity (data not shown).

Non-aligned personal advice

As already noted, the US clinic discussed here asks clients to complete a questionnaire prior to counselling. This may help counsellors to align their advice to the client's perspective. Another possibility this creates is that, if Cs do not check out their interpretation of Ps' answers with the P, they may severely misalign their advice.

This arises in the following extract. The misalignment, identified by the client is marked >:

```
        Extract 8.17 (US2)
  1   C:      .hhhhhh (1.0) u::m:(hhh) (2.9) >we would also<
  2           encourage that a person: (0.7) would seek some
  3           counse>ling?< (1.0) because being an'ibody positive
  4           i:s difficult news usually for people to: (1.3)
  5           assimilate what that all means. [.hhhh]
  6   P:                                      [ (  )]
  7               (0.3)
  8   C:      a::nd we would a:lso encourage a person to take a
  9           look at some of the behavior patterns that might
 10           have introduced them to the virus in the first
 11           place. .hhhhh (0.4) a::nd (1.6) being that u::m
 12           (0.4) you have uh:: (0.3) an addictive problem?
 13           (0.5) in your life? (0.9) we would suggest tha:t
 14               (0.5)
 15   P:>     we[ll that]'s debadable.
 16   C:        [perhaps]
 17               (0.9)
 18   C:      oh okay.
 19               (1.1)
 20   C:      well you were shooting up a month ago.
 21   P:      yeah but it's not like I'm strung out or anything. I
 22           don't do it very often, it's a couple times a month
 23           or something.
```

Extract 8.17 begins with C using what can be called an 'impersonal' format expressed in C's 'we would also encourage' (lines 1 and 8) . As we shall see, the advantage of such a format is that it shelves the issue of Ps' alignment to the advice. Because it is ambiguous whether C is delivering advice or information-about-the-advice-that-we-give, everything can proceed smoothly with only the minimal uptake required to support Information Delivery.

However, between lines 11 and 13, C introduces a formulation of the P related to P's drug use (presumably, as described on his completed questionnaire). This formulation ('being that u::m (0.4) you have uh:: (0.3) an addictive problem? (0.5) in your life?') is introduced very tentatively, with a raised intonation (inviting correction) and perturbations serving to mark a delicate object. And, indeed, it does receive a correction ('we[ll that]'s debadable.'), with P's 'well' and his 'debadable' serving to mitigate a dispreferred object. Even when C tries to warrant his formulation ('well you were shooting up a month ago.'), presumably referring to the questionnaire, P again resists it.

With C's (premature) formulation of P's self-perceptions now under-mined, we have a very unfavourable environment in which to deliver advice. And so, indeed, it turns out to be. As C persists in giving advice (albeit hedged around), he gets a single unmarked acknowledgment (line 27 below), followed by no further acknowledgment, despite slots at lines 33 and 35:

Extract 8.18 (US2) (Extract 8.17 continued)
```
24   C:      well a'yway we would suggest that you know that- if
25           that were to be a continuing
26                  (0.4)
27   P:      mm hmm
28                  (0.8)
29   C:      Issue (0.5) that perhaps that (0.5) needs to be
30           looked at. (1.2) *y'kn'* so that you don't continue
31           to put yourself .hhh in what would be considered
32           high risk situations:.
33                  (1.1)
34   C:      okay?
35                  (1.1)
```

Despite the misalignment of P to advice based on unchecked formulations, C later attempts a further formulation, now expressly warranting it in terms of P's questionnaire:

Extract 8.19 (US2) (continued)
```
1    C:      .hhhh (0.5) u::m:(hhhh) also looking: (0.5) at this:
2            uh (0.6) questionnaire: (1.3) you're (2.0) quite a
3            gymnast when it comes to(hh) se(hh)xual actividies.
4            .hhh
```

Without any alignment from P to this formulation (in the slot during C's breath on line 4), C now starts to launch into another piece of advice (once more hedged). Once again, a misalignment identified by the client is marked >:

Extract 8.20 (US2) (continued)
```
5    C:      so: (0.4) we might suggest (0.5) tha' cha- ya::
6            (2.2) just sord of-
7                  (2.1)
8    P:>     oh eh: I didn't mark >anything like that.<
9            I m[ean ] I don't- I only have my one partner=
10   C:         [well?]
11   C:      =y:eah?
12                  (0.2)
13   P:      that's all.
```

```
14  C:      (   )
15  P:      and since I encountered this ah possible exposure,
16          I've been using condoms.
17  C:      okay, does does your partner, your wife
18  P:      yeah
19  C:      um does she, is she somebody who is- is she
20          straight.
```

C hedged advice-giving ('we might suggest (0.5) tha' cha- ya:: (2.2) just sord of-', lines 5–6) lapses into a 2.1 second pause after which P actively resists C's formulation (lines 8–9). Now C abandons his advice and moves on to a further question.

In this section we have looked at how resistance to advice can arise where the advice is not aligned to the client's expressed position or perspective. In these circumstances, whether or not the counsellor attempts personal formulations of the client, resistance often follows (usually more actively expressed where a prior personal formulation has been offered – see Chapter 7). We now turn to how advice-givers can stabilize advice reception.

Stabilizing advice-giving: an interactional solution

Given the sort of difficulties in obtaining uptake that we have been examining, the data suggest a number of strategies that professionals can use to stabilize advice-giving. For instance, as we have already seen in Extract 8.8 above, implied advice can be packaged in the form of a question about a client's personal dispositions. The advantage of this strategy is twofold. First, because questions are part of an adjacency pair of question and answer (Sacks et al., 1974), some sort of recognizable answer can be expected. Second, resistance by the answerer to the advice implied in the question need not be threatening to further pursuit of the topic precisely because it is ambiguous whether advice has been given in the first place.

Here we are concerned with another interactional solution to the instability of advice-giving. As with framing advice as a question, it plays with the ambiguity of how a minimal client response might be heard. In this case, the issue is advice which is packaged to allow multiple responses to be managed. The point here, as noted earlier, is that personalized advice-giving requires far stronger uptake to stabilize itself than does information delivery. So, if a set of turns are hearable as perhaps information delivery, then they can follow one another without any difficulty, given only an occasional response-token from the other party. I refer to this as an Advice-as-Information Sequence, or AIS.[9]

The following data from a British clinic show how the AIS works. It involves 'advice' about pregnancy to a female client.

```
    Extract 8.21 (UK1)
1   C:      (0.8) Uh:m the other a:spect that I must cover with
```

2		you as far as the fact that you're fema:le .hhh is:
3		(.) with (.) any females who're having the test if
4		the test is positive .hhh we do tend to advi:se
5		against becoming pregnant.
6		(0.4)
7	P:	Mm [hm
8	C:	[Uh::m having said that (0.8) the statistics are
9		showing about a one in six risk to baby.=t- It
10		depends on whether: that person is an optimist or a
11		pessimist you know as to how they look on that.
12		.hhhh So if a woman really wants a chi:ld (.) then
13		we advise her becoming pregnant sooner (.) rather
14		than leaving it.
15		(.)
16	P:	Mm hm=

In Extract 8.21, C begins by aligning P to the next topic by invoking P's gender, allowing C to appeal to one of the category-bound activities associated with that gender (i.e. 'becoming pregnant', line 5). This activity is embedded in what is hearable as a piece of advice bearing on a fundamental matter ('we do tend to advi:se against becoming pregnant.')

However, note P's very limited uptake of the advice. After a 0.4 second pause, she simply produces the utterance 'mm hm'. This sort of response token works only as a continuer; it does not indicate any uptake of the advice. Yet C continues her flow of talk in an undisturbed way, overlapping with P's response token and going on to produce a modified piece of advice on the same topic. Once again, this elicits only a response token from P.

Here is, presumably, an important body of advice. Although it receives very limited (unmarked) acknowledgments, possibly indicating passive resistance (Heritage and Sefi, 1992), no interactional difficulties are observed.

How can this be? For instance, in Extract 8.14 above, we saw how a client's 2.7 second pause after advice is given was highly implicative of resistance to advice about condoms:

Extract 8.14 (US2) (Extract 8.13 continued)		
6	C:	.hhh um (0.7) works >bedder< if you use 'em all the
7		ti:me.
8		(2.7)
9	P:	it's the heat of the mo:ment sometimes.=
10	C:	=tch .hh (0.5) n'kay, and then we'll ta:lk about
11		tha:t, too:.

P's response is followed by C extracting himself from further immediate discussion of the topic by an agenda-statement. Given this, how can advice-giving proceed smoothly with only minimal response-tokens from P in Extract 8.21?

I suggest that the character of the communication in Extract 8.21 is hearably much more ambiguous than in Extract 8.14. First, there is not a complete fit between the categories used in the 'advice' and the advice recipient. Although P is identified as 'female' (and thus someone who may become pregnant), she has not had her HIV test yet and, indeed, may not even decide to have one. Thus, when C invokes the category 'the test is positive' (line 4), this links her advice to a category that P does not now (and may never) occupy. This means that it is hearable as the advice C 'would give' if certain things were to happen to the client (i.e. as conditional advice). Such a tentative formulation of a situation which might be appropriate to someone but not necessarily the client has been identified in HIV counselling as a 'proposal of the situation' or POTS device (Kinnell and Maynard, 1996).

Given the implied non-relevance of the 'advice' to P's *present* situation, what C says about pregnancy is hearable not as personalized advice at all but as   information-about-the-kind-of-advice-we-give-to-people-in-this-clinic. This way of hearing C's utterance is further strengthened by her preface to it: namely 'we do tend to advi:se', where the use of 'we' and 'tend' implies a general policy rather than recipient-designed, personal advice for this client. So what C says about pregnancy is doubly hearable as information about advice rather than unambiguous personal advice.

This has crucial implications for uptake. Given that what C is saying is hearable as information, P need only offer minimal response tokens to maintain the format. Moreover, apparent 'advice' about a highly sensitive topic can proceed in a way that manages the delicacy of what is being said.

So the AIS works by shielding both C and P from the implications of non-uptake of advice, given that such non-uptake is highly likely where the 'advice' has been delivered without any attempt by C to discover P's perspective on a presumably sensitive matter. In this environment, C's response tokens need *not* be heard as the implicit resistance that Heritage and Sefi (1992) suggest. On the contrary, they are hearable as sustaining information-about-the-kind-of-advice-we-give-to-people-in-this-clinic. Hence, through the AIS, everything can proceed smoothly and C can safely complete her counselling agenda.

The remainder of this chapter is devoted to showing how the AIS works in the US data. We begin with an extract where the American counsellor is addressing the same possibility – a positive HIV test. Here, however, with a male client, C is discussing the medical needs of someone who tests positive:

Extract 8.22 (US2)
            ((Near the start of the interview; C has just emphasized the
            importance of early detection))
1   (0.6)
2   C: a::nd (1.5) u::m some- okay, if a person (.) should
3   happen to test >an'ibody< po:sitive .hhh we would
4   strongly encourage them to seek out a a physician

```
 5              (.) particularly physicians who work in infectious
 6              disease .hhh u:m because they seem to: (1.0) uh:: be
 7              m:ore on top of what's happening in the world of:
 8              viral infections and things like that. (0.4)
 9   P:         mm hmm=
10   C:         =and medications .hhhh we would also encourage a
11              person certainly to take a look at some of their
12              behavior patterns .hhh u:m encouraging them to: .hhh
13              look at things that might have in fact (0.5) caused
14              them to (feel) infected in the first place whether
15              that be sexual practices that were not particularly
16              safe? (0.7) o:r (0.6) u:m (0.5) drug use: (0.4) *or
17              (0.7) um* (1.0) well those two basically (0.4) *I
18              m'n not much you can do about transfusions.*
19                   (1.5)
```

Let us look at C's first turn. As in the British extract, C's advice commences with an 'if' given in regard to a category (testing antibody positive) with only a possible relevance to the advice recipient, i.e. a POTS sequence. Moreover, once again, the 'advice' is not personalized but addressed to 'a person' (line 2) and 'them' (line 4), in the same manner as C's use of 'any females' in the previous extract. Similarly, just as the British counsellor says 'we tend to advise', her American colleague says 'we would strongly encourage' (lines 3–4).

Once more, we have a C packaging what she is saying as, at best, ambiguous advice-giving, hearable as information-about-the-advice-that-would-be-given. The evidence that both parties monitor C's talk in this way is found in the lack of local problems created by P's minimal uptake – no response at the candidate completion point of the 'advice' during the micro-pause after 'seek out a a physician' (line 4) and the presence of only a response token on line 9.

Now C takes a second turn without any noticeable turbulence in the design of her utterance. In this second turn, she introduces fresh topics (safer sex, drug use, transfusions) but they are all referred back to the category 'testing positive' and packaged via the same indefinite nouns or pronouns ('person', 'their' and 'them'). Despite the presence of two slots where P might have taken a turn (after 'drug use', line 16 and after 'transfusions', line 18), not even a response token is contributed.

These last two sequences have shown that the AIS is a powerful device which manages the potentially difficult interactional problems of advice-giving and advice reception about presumably delicate topics. It constitutes the professional as a mere reporter on the-advice-we-give-in-this-clinic rather than as a potentially intrusive personal advice-giver. It allows the client to be defined as an acceptably passive recipient of information about the kinds of things that other people get told (or that she may get told in future). Finally, and most significantly, it overcomes the potentially damaging local implications of minimal client uptake which would arise if Cs' could be heard to be giving clear-cut advice.[10]

So far, we have been only dealing with advice about a category which P does not currently occupy ('positive person') packaged as a proposal of the situation. Let us turn to examples of advice on categories which may be more relevant to P, albeit often constituted in a conditional way. We will focus on the topics of frequency of HIV testing and condom use. Is the AIS found here and, if so, how does it work?

We begin with two examples of 'advice' about the frequency of HIV testing. In Extract 8.23, this is packaged as 'the recommendation is':

```
        Extract 8.23 (US2)
   1  C:       THE RECMMENdation is: (0.2) uh: fo:r people: (0.8)
   2           who have been been at risk any time=
   3  P:       =mmhmm=
   4  C:       =regardless of: (0.4) uh::m (0.6) their (1.2) sexual
   5           ac[tividy] whether it being- going from you know=
   6  P:         [mmhmmm]
   7  C:       =z:ero to very active .hhh ah the recommendation is
   8           still that everyone be retested once a yea:r=
   9  P:       =yeah
  10           (0.4)
  11  C:       until there is actually a test for the virus itself=
  12  P:       =right
  13           (1.6)
  14  P:       (tch)okay=
  15  C:       =okayˆ (.) any other questions?=
```

From this extract onwards we are dealing with advice based on categories which are made directly relevant to clients. Here this relevance to the client is asserted by C's reference to 'people: (0.8) who have been at risk any time=' since Cs can usually assume that clients present themselves for an HIV test because they feel that they have been 'at risk'.[11]

Nonetheless, C does not address his 'advice' directly to P but to 'people' (line 1) and 'everyone' (line 8). Moreover, the author of this 'advice' is impersonal and hearable as some official body ('the recommendation is', line 1, repeated in line 7).

This way of setting up advice follows Peyrot (1987) who noted how psychotherapists made propositions concerning 'some people' without personalizing them to their client. Peyrot calls this an 'oblique reference'. As such, it may take the form of a reference to 'people' (as in Extract 8.23, line 1) or to a 'you' which may be heard as an indefinite 'one'.

Such advice-giving by 'oblique reference' plays with the ambiguity between advice and information-about-the-advice-that-we-give-here-in-the-clinic. Thus, as an AIS, response tokens (like 'mm') will satisfactorily maintain the format.

In Extract 8.23, at the first hearable completion point of C's 'advice', 'retested once a year' (line 8), P provides such a response token ('yeah', line 9). When C adds another piece of information ('test for the virus itself'), P offers 'right' and adds '(tch) okay' (line 14) when C does not take up the 1.6 second slot for a turn on line 13.

Given the ambiguity of the format, built into an AIS, P's response tokens are hearable as merely indicating recipiency of C's flow of information rather than as resistance to advice. It should be emphasized, however, that there is no *automatic* association between an AIS and minimal client uptake, like response tokens. Once a turn (or series of turns) is hearable as 'information', then a whole range of responses, from response tokens to newsworthiness tokens, satisfactorily maintain the format. Information receivers minimally need to indicate recipiency, but they can do many other things as well without challenging the format.

In Extract 8.24 below, also concerned with a recommendation about repeat testing, we find an extended response from the client:

```
      Extract 8.24 (US2)
1     C:       (.hh)so: ((cough cough)) if you have had any possible
2              exposure we do recommend that you:: be testedt
3              (.h)um:: every six months fo:r at least ah a year t-
4              to: (.) two years
5              (1.0)
6     P:       no: I don't think that I- (2.0) I have but I- (1.0)
7              (h) it's jus something I feel bedder about=
8     C:       =mmhmm=
```

Here C packages his 'advice' slightly differently to the previous extract. Although he still uses an 'impersonal' voice ('we do recommend', line 2), the recommendation is now addressed rather more directly to P (C says 'you' – line 2 – rather than 'people'), but made conditional by C's reference to 'if you have had any possible exposure'.

P monitors the talk in this way, questioning whether the category 'any possible exposure' (lines 1–2) applies to him: 'I don't think that I- (2.0) I have' (line 6). However, P now characterizes his motivation in a way that potentially aligns himself to C's 'advice': 'it's jus something I feel bedder about' (line 7).

Even if it turns out that P is resisting the 'recommendation' of follow-up testing, this need not challenge the communication format established here. For, in an 'information' sequence, an information recipient can *choose* whether to hear the information as personally relevant. Conversely, in an unambiguous advice sequence, unless the advice recipient shows that he hears the advice as personally relevant, the very advice-giving format is challenged. The beauty of the AIS is that it allows both parties to steer an untroubled course through the potentially choppy waters of advice-giving.

Advice-giving about the topic of condom use offers further examples of the AIS. In Extract 8.25, notice how C formats a 'recommendation' about condoms:

```
        Extract 8.25 (US2)
1               (10.6)
2   C:          we recommend tha'chu use co:ndoms
3               (1.0)
4   C:          ah:: if you are not su:re about your partner's:
5               (0.2) status.
6               (.)
```

Although C's 'u' (line 2) apparently addresses his advice personally to P, C constructs what he is saying as 'official' advice ('we recommend tha'chu use co:ndoms'), though once more made conditional by an 'if' format. As such, it is hearable as information-about-the-advice-we-give-in-this-clinic. Hence his 'u' can be heard as an 'indefinite reference' and the sequence can work as an AIS. Now the absence of any uptake from P in the possible turn-transition points on lines 3 and 6 need not have the damaging implications it would have in an unambiguous advice sequence.

The ability of Cs to maintain a multi-turn sequence about condom use without any response from Ps is also shown in Extract 8.26:

```
        Extract 8.26 (US2)
1   C:          thee o::nly::(hhh) (0.5) protection (0.5) that's
2               available at this point in histree:: (0.7) ah: is
3               the condom. (0.5) a::nd our recommendation is: (0.5)
4               la:tex only^ (0.9) ah:: preferably American made
5               (0.5) condoms which have some qualidy contro:l (1.0)
6               ah:: which: (1.1) the foreign imports: for the most
7               part do not have. there's a few (0.6) imports that
8               are very high qualidy, (.hhh)but it's:- (0.9) they
9               are an exception rather than the rule.
10              (1.4)
11  C:          .hhh the second recommendation is that (1.5) the lu-
12              condoms (.) should be lubricaded
```

Once again, P does not take up the available slots to acknowledge C's 'recommendation' – the 0.9 pause after 'only' (line 4); the 1.0 slot after 'contro:l' (line 5) and the 1.4 second pause after 'the rule.' (line 10). Nonetheless, given the ambiguity of the format, C proceeds to offer a 'second recommendation' (line 11).

This is because P can hear C's 'our recommendation is' (line 3) as indicating simply information about the kind of advice usually given in this clinic, i.e. as information delivery about advice rather than as pure advice-giving. Although the information delivery format is sustained by response-tokens, these can be delayed for long periods without endangering the stability of the format, e.g. where such delays are hearable as implying only that the information recipient is waiting for the completion of the information (see Chapter 3).

Alternatively, Cs sometimes go in search of a response token following an AIS, as below:

Extract 8.27 (US2)

```
1   C:      .hhh ah::we recommend that ah:: any kind of condoms
2           that you use for vaginal sex or anal sex Iunno f- if
3           you have anal sex on her. .hhh uh::m (0.7) then use
4           something with nonoxynol nine.
5           (0.9)
6   C:      okay?=
7   P:      =mmhmm=
8   C:      =NNoxynal nine is a spermicide.
9           (0.7)
10  P:      righ.=
```

In Extract 8.27, the 0.9 pause on line 5 can be heard as marking the completion of what C has to say about what 'we recommend' about condom use. When P does not take up that slot, C seeks some acknowledgment by her 'okay?' (line 6). This obtains an immediate 'mmhmm' from P. Now when C makes available another slot after a slight elaboration, P, having been coached, provides a further response token without being prompted ('righ.', line 10).

Note, however, that C's prompt ('okay?') is hearable as only seeking to establish that P is attending to what C is saying. Moreover, P's two response tokens can mark merely such attendance to information about what 'we recommend'. *Contra* Heritage and Sefi (1992), they need not be heard as implicit resistance to advice precisely because it is not clear that 'advice' is what is being communicated.

In the three 'condom' extracts above, we have seen an AIS set up using the following formats:

we recommend tha'chu use co:ndoms (Extract 8.25)
our recommendation is: (0.5) la:tex only^ (Extract 8.26)
we recommend that ah:: any kind of condoms that you use (Extract 8.27).

All these sequences depend upon an appeal to an impersonal voice ('we' or 'our'). As Watson (1987: 271) has shown, when such a voice is used by a single individual, that individual can be heard as 'speaking in an organizational capacity'. Our suggestion is that such a form of speech can construct any 'recommendations' that follow as simply information about the official line in this organization.

However, the data reveal other, more subtle, ways through which advice can be constructed as advice-as-information. Even advice couched in a personal voice ('I') can be made ambiguous, as Extract 8.28 will show:

Extract 8.28 (US2)

```
1   C:      um condoms come in all varieties and um in this day
2           and age, you know, I tell women that come through
3           here you know you are the one that is being put at
```

4		risk, and if your partner refuses to wear a condom
5		ah ah you know you're subjecting yourself to to the
6		risk and if necessary, you keep some for the
7		forgetful males, if it- say well I forgot to get any
8		or you know this that or something else, but
9		basically I you know it is for your protection and
10		you have to decide you know if you're going to keep
11		a supply of them.
		((More detailed transcription))
12		(0.4)
13	C:	i̲f you're going to keep any^, (1.0) ah: number one:,

Extract 8.28 apparently reveals unmistakably *personal* advice delivered by a personalized C ('I') to a P who is characterized (implicitly) as female and as 'you'. However, closer inspection shows the elegance of C's 'I tell women that come through here' (line 2). This creates a clear ambiguity. C can be heard now not to be *advising* P but to be *informing* her about the advice he gives to 'women' in general. Once more, the proof that C monitors the talk this way is demonstrated by the lack of turbulence after P's failure to use the first available slot (0.4 pause, line 12) to acknowledge C's 'telling'.

In Extract 8.28, C's introduction works as an elegant way of dressing up advice-giving as information delivery through embedding the advice in an account of a 'telling' (to 'women that come through here'). The implicit appeal to the form of a 'story' is made explicit in Extract 8.29:

Extract 8.29 (US2)

1	C:	MY:: (1.8) story on c̲o̲n̲d̲oms: that I give to people
2		is that .hhh there are:: a̲l̲l̲ ki:nds of them ou:t
3		there (.) a:nd when uh p̲e̲o̲ple well I don't like 'em,
4		they don't feel right. I say exp̲e̲riment with them
5		til you fi:nd some that (0.2) you know (0.5) work
6		for you because .hh there's enough vari:edy in
7		t̲h̲ickness sh:-
8		(1.0) ((closes drawer))
9	C:	SHA:pe(hh) si:ze (0.5) what have you that- (0.4) uh
10		there's going to be something that works for you.
11		(0.4)
12	P:	okay.

Note how C's 'advice' ('exp̲e̲riment' with condoms, line 4) is embedded in a narrative ('my story', line 1) about what he tells 'people' about condoms, the objections of such 'people'('well I don't like 'em, they don't feel right', lines 3–4) and what 'I say' (line 4) in response.

In Extract 8.29, the AIS works by constructing P as the recipient of a 'story'. Hence his 'okay' (line 12) serves to mark his receipt of the story rather than implying positive uptake of unambiguous personal advice.

Of course, as in earlier examples of the AIS, there is nothing to *prevent* Ps offering stronger acknowledgments. For instance, in Extract 8.30 below, a 'recommendation' about condoms evokes a 'newsworthiness' token ('ah ha'):[12]

Extract 8.30 (US2)

```
1   C:      (.hhh)AH: we do: recommend that you use co:ndoms
2           [in:-
3   P:      [ah ha
4   C:      ah:: ah:: (1.6) ah::m:
5           (1.0)
```

The point, however, is that AIS can tolerate a very broad range of responses (from marked acknowledgments, as above, to response tokens, to several turns with no client response). Conversely, unambiguous sequences of personal advice break down very speedily without marked acknowledgments.

Summary

By constructing advice sequences that can be heard as information delivery, counsellors manage to stabilize advice-giving. A function of maintaining an ambiguous communication format is that the counsellor does not have to cope with the difficult interactional problems of the failure of the patient to mark that what she is hearing is personalized advice and hence to offer more than a mere response-token in reply. For, as we saw in Chapter 3, information delivery can be co-operatively maintained simply by the client offering occasional response-tokens, like 'mm hmm'.

A second function of offering advice in this way is that it neatly handles many of the issues of delicacy that can arise in discussing sexual behaviour. First, the counsellor can be heard as making reference to what she tells 'anyone' so that this particular client need not feel singled out for attention about her private life. Second, because there is no step-by-step method of questioning, clients are not required to expand on their sexual practices with the kinds of hesitations we saw above. Third, setting up advice sequences that can be heard as information delivery shields the counsellor from some of the interactional difficulties of appearing to tell strangers what they should be doing in the most intimate aspects of their behaviour.

The US transcripts considered in this chapter reveal multiple forms through which counsellors avoid explicitly personalizing their advice. These forms include:

We would strongly encourage
>we would also< encourage
We would suggest
what we're- what we recommend
we recommend

(.hhh)we re:commen:d (1.0) use of a cond(h)om (0.2)
our recommendation is:
THE RECMMENdation is:
THE FIRST PREFerence: (.) is
the official recommendation is
I tell women that come through here
MY:: (1.8) story on condoms: that I give to people

Each form has subtle nuances, varying from a mere 'report' on policy ('THE RECMMENdation is:'; 'THE FIRST PREFerence: (.) is'; 'the official recommendation is'), to an account of what the professional usually does ('I tell women that come through here'; 'MY:: (1.8) story on condoms: that I give to people') to an impersonal recommendation in the voice of 'we'.

These forms play with devices such as an 'if' preface (the 'proposal of the situation' documented by Kinnell and Maynard, forthcoming), the 'oblique reference' (e.g. 'some people' as noted by Peyrot, 1987) and upon an appeal to an impersonal voice ('we' or 'our'), which, as Watson has shown, can allow professionals to be heard as 'speaking in an organizational capacity' (1987: 271).

These devices set up at least three dimensions of ambiguity, as set out in Table 8.1.

Table 8.1   *Three kinds of ambiguity*

Nature of ambiguity	Device	Example
Source of advice	Impersonal voice	'We', 'our'
Recipient of advice	Oblique reference	'Some people'
	Proposal of situation	'If you . . .'
Activity	Advice-as-information	'The recommendation is'[13]

It is beyond the scope of this chapter to address the different implications of each device, although it is worth observing an interesting feature of the 'impersonal voice', seen in the following extract:

```
        Extract 8.31 (US2)
    1  C:     o::m:: not (???) the (???) I've heard tha that the
    2         heavy duty plastic wrap ye know that stuff on the
    3         shelves that pink and blue they have like the
    4         microwave stuff not the saran wrap but the real
    5         heavy plastic.
    6  P:     Ah huh
    7  C:     ˆo::m:: the official recommendation is a dental dam.
    8         .hhh now where you can get a dental dam I don't
    9         know.
```

```
10              (1.6)
11   C:         do you know what a dental dam is?
```

As C embellishes his account of safer oral sex, he constructs an AIS using an 'impersonal voice' ('˚o::m:: the official recommendation is a dental dam.' line 7). Now C continues by appearing to undercut the practicality of the 'advice' he has just given ('.hhh now where you can get a dental dam I don't know.').

The fact that we do not hear a contradiction seems to arise by the way in which the utterance 'the official recommendation is ...' serves to distance a speaker from the very advice he is giving. This 'report' form serves as a neat device which allows professionals to do what is expected of them (i.e. report the 'official' view), while enabling them, if they wish, to depart from it. Like the AIS itself, the 'impersonal voice' functions by allowing an ambiguity in the interpretation of what is being said and hence a potential ambiguity about the meaning to be attached to P's response.

Conclusion

It must be stressed that we have not been concerned here with logical ambiguities of the kind that normative communication textbooks may criticize. Such ambiguities are usually identified without reference to sequential organization with the aim of 'getting language into shape'. Instead, we have followed Sacks's concern with what he calls 'sequential ambiguity'. As he puts it:

> Now when I talk of 'ambiguity', there's some special attention needed to the way I want to use it here. One tends to think about 'ambiguity' that, e.g. a word could mean this or that, or that it could mean this, that, or God only knows what else. The sort of ambiguity that I'm interested in specifically is 'sequentialized ambiguity', where the issue is what sort of thing should go next, turning on what this thing might have been. (Sacks, 1992: 671)

Following Sacks, we have been examining how clients can inspect what an utterance by a professional might mean in order to establish 'what sort of thing should go next'. In addition, we have shown how professionals might monitor that 'next' in producing a further turn. Unlike logicians or philosophers, these practical actors do not usually treat ambiguity as a 'problem' in need of a 'solution' (see Wittgenstein, 1969).

This method suggests that both students of communication and practitioners should avoid treating 'ambiguities' as problems in need of solutions. Instead, by playing with ambiguities, both practitioners and clients manage difficult interpersonal relations while displaying considerable interactional skills.

It may well be that pre-test counselling is ideally suited to the use of the AIS since 'the advice *cannot* unambiguously apply to the client until the test result is known' (Heritage, personal communication). Nevertheless, in many professional–client interactions, advice is expected to be delivered, often with little opportunity to elicit a client's perspective. Apt examples may be general practitioners expected to deliver health promotion messages or community lawyers giving legal 'advice'. In such cases, the AIS works as a neat device to shield both professional and client from some of the delicate implications of what they are doing.

Finally, however, it should be noted that the AIS is not a straightforward solution to communication problems. Like any such 'solution', it contains potential dangers or dysfunctions. For just as the ambiguity it serves to create may manage 'delicate' matters, it may create a further, less helpful ambiguity: are clients' minimal uptakes to be heard as acceptance or resistance to the advice they are given?

It seems that, without specific questions, counsellors will not know how their client is responding. But, of course, as Peräkylä (1995) shows, in the context of questions about future 'dreaded' situations, obtaining responses to certain questions is not always an easy matter!

Notes

1. Peyrot (1987) examines the use of terms like 'someone' in his discussion of the functions of 'oblique referencing' in psychotherapists' suggestions to their clients (see Kofmehl, 1992).

2. Readers will notice in this and other extracts the marker ((more detailed transcription)). I have not had access to the tapes so I am dependent on transcripts of varying standards. However, I have tried to focus largely on data which is transcribed in a more detailed way, i.e. according to standard conversation analytic conventions.

3. Hutchby (1995: 225) has noted how advice-givers on radio call-in programmes use such ambiguities to generalize the relevance of their advice to an overhearing audience.

4. Anssi Peräkylä (personal communication) has suggested that P's 'yeah' (line 17) may work as a pre-closing invitation, terminating the topic which was initiated by his question. In this case, the ensuing exchange of 'okays' between C and P can serve to accomplish such a closing in an orderly manner.

5. But note that the ambiguity of P's acknowledgment: '('at 'ould) definitely make sense' shows that P understands that this would be the 'sensible' thing to do but does not undertake to do it.

6. This extract closely follows the three-part sequence that Mehan (1979) has identified as distinctive of 'classroom' talk, i.e. question–answer–evaluation.

7. The topic of advice-closings was addressed in a talk by John Heritage at the Second Annual Qualitative Health Research Conference, University of Pennsylvania, June 1994.

8. This is presumably based upon Cs' assumption that the gay community are the most knowledgeable about HIV and AIDS.

9. Developing an argument from Silverman, Bor, Miller and Goldman (1992a), Kofmehl's (1992) concept of a 'proposal of the situation' device is quite close to what I describe as advice-as-information.

10. Another example of hypothetical 'advice' about what to do after a positive test is given below:

```
        (US2)
1   C:      okay, .hhh (0.6) if a person should test antibody
2           positive (0.4) what um:: we would certainly suggest
3           first off is that .hhh the person would seek (0.4)
4           medical attention. (0.9) particularly: physicians
```

```
5          working in infectious disease. (0.9) um because (0.8)
6          they are (0.8) f:ar more:: (0.3) up to date with
7          what's happening in the viral (1.0) situations.
8                 (0.2)
9    P:    okay.
```

As in Extract 8.22, C addresses her advice package to a 'person' to whom 'we would suggest' certain things. Therefore, this is another example of an AIS where C is hearable as talking about the advice that C *would* give to a seropositive person. Given the POTS character of this 'advice', response tokens, like P's 'okay' (line 9) serve to maintain rather than challenge the format.

11. There are exceptions to this rule. Some people present themselves for an HIV test at the request of their employers or insurance company. Also there are cases (see Extract 8.24 below), where people simply seek a test for peace of mind without any clear sense of risk.

12. The presence of this newsworthiness token may be related to the fact that an earlier question has elicited that P is contemplating his first sexual relationship and that he is therefore, unlike many clients at pre-test counselling, actively seeking advice.

13. Ambiguity deriving from the activity (i.e. is it 'information' or 'advice') is partly dependent and partly independent of the other two kinds of ambiguity. I am very grateful to Anssi Peräkylä for suggesting the presentation found in Table 8.1.

PART FIVE
CONCLUSION

This final part raises two general issues: politics and practice. In Chapter 9 we address the politics of counselling via a focus on the ways in which troubles – as socially constructed realities – are talked into being in two counselling settings: a UK haemophilia centre which counsels persons who have become HIV positive through the transfusion of infected blood products, and a family therapy centre in the United States.

Chapter 10 returns to the relevance of this research for the practice of HIV and AIDS counselling in relation to current counselling theories and training methods. It reprises many of the practical issues dealt with in earlier chapters.

9

Counselling as a Discourse of Enablement

This chapter has a rather broader focus and content than the rest of this book. First, it compares a US centre offering non-HIV-related, 'family therapy' counselling with the British Haemophilia Centre offering HIV counselling discussed by Peräkylä (1995). Second, it is a highly provisional attempt to focus on certain issues in relation to what might be called 'the politics of counselling'.

Given this focus, I ought at once to point out that such a political focus is not intended in a naively critical sense. For instance, in terms of its claims and its practices, my own profession of sociology has a set of political implications which are entirely the proper object of study. Indeed, I would be the first to criticize my colleagues who might try self-righteously to exempt themselves from the critiques they make of others.[1]

The specifically 'political' focus of this chapter is that it addresses the way in which counselling is a pervasive activity in contemporary institutional life. The particular topic taken up in this chapter is 'troubles talk', more especially the ways in which troubles – as socially constructed realities – are talked into being (Heritage, 1984) in counselling settings.

'Troubles talk' is treated as a major, and socially organized, aspect of counsellors' work (Gubrium, 1989, 1992; Miller, 1986, 1990). Through troubles talk, counsellors fulfil many of their most important professional responsibilities to their clients and colleagues. When we reflect upon the range of settings and issues in which counselling now takes place, we begin to see the outlines of a counselled society within which troubles are constructed, and made topics for public consideration.

The counselled society is a world that Foucault (1977, 1980) analyses as a site of power/knowledge. Foucault's approach to power is distinctive in its stress on how power is embedded in social relations and activities, and its 'productive' aspects. Power operates through the micro-political processes of social interactions, producing distinctive social realities and kinds of human subjects in the process. Power is not so much imposed from above, then, as built up through interactants' collaboration within concrete social settings. Knowledge is implicated in power relations because social interactions are arenas within which professional knowledge is applied to constitute individuals and groups as appropriate objects of institutional interest and action.

While maintaining a general concern for troubles talk in diverse counselling settings, two very different human service settings are analysed here. The first is a haemophilia centre located in a large hospital in London (UK5). The data are taken from counselling sessions with persons who suffer from haemophilia and have become HIV positive through the transfusion of infected blood products. Although the counsellors come from diverse professional backgrounds (social work and medicine), they all practise a theoretically based counselling method derived from family therapy (see Miller and Bor, 1988). The second setting is a family therapy centre in the United States to which clients bring a wide variety of troubles, including marriage dissolution, eating disorders, and problems in school. The therapists practise brief therapy, meaning that they emphasize finding solutions to their clients' troubles (not deep insight into their causes) in a minimum of sessions (Cade and O'Hanlon, 1993; de Shazer, 1982; Miller, G., 1987).

Several common interactional practices found in both settings are identified and discussed. These practices may be seen as aspects of a general institutional discourse (Miller, 1994) within which troubles talk is initiated and managed by counsellors and their clients. Thus, the analysis directs attention to both the distinctive (or situational) and trans-situational aspects of troubles talk in institutional settings.

Following Miller and Silverman (1995) the trans-situational aspects of the HIV counselling and family therapy settings are analysed as a discourse of enablement. Often associated with family therapy, this configuration of power/knowledge positions counsellors as facilitators who help clients develop new understandings about how their troubles might be managed. Such counsellors avoid telling clients how to respond to their troubles. Rather, they use various questioning tactics to elicit information (knowledge) about clients' lives, perspectives and troubles, and to guide clients towards mutually agreeable definitions of, and responses to, their troubles.

I analyse these questions as aspects of counsellors' professional knowledge, and 'productive' expressions of power. For example, in asking and responding to such questions, counsellors and clients produce distinctive types of power relations.

This approach to counselling as institutional discourse blends aspects of ethnomethodologists' concern for the reflexive social construction of social realities in social interactions with Foucault's (1973, 1977, 1980) interest in institutional gazes, power relations and social practices. We emphasize the common ground shared by the perspectives while recognizing that they are very different in other ways. Thus, while we focus on Foucauldian themes, our discussion remains informed by aspects of ethnomethodology, particularly by a concern for the ways in which institutionalized conversation practices are also locally organized and accomplished (Rawls, 1987; Drew and Heritage, 1992a). The blending of perspectives makes it possible to analyse how power relations are both embedded in institutional discourses, and constructed within social inter-actions (Molotch and Boden, 1985).

Troubles talk and conversation analysis

As I suggested in Chapter 2, conversation analysts have developed much of their distinctive approach to social interaction by explicating the distinctive aspects of 'ordinary conversation', the otherwise unremarkable interactions that predominate in everyday life. Such conversations are highly informal when compared with interactions in institutional settings. For example, speaker turns are not pre-allocated by formal rules – such as the rules that organize courtroom interrogations (Atkinson and Drew, 1976) – or managed by formally designated orchestrators of social interactions (Dingwall, 1980). Nor are participants in ordinary conversations bound to one or a limited number of topics, as they often are in institutional settings.

Indeed, so long as speakers adequately orient to prior talk and other salient aspects of social settings, they may pursue a variety of goals and issues within ordinary conversations. For example, a common form of topical organization is for a speaker to relate some event described in a previous turn to their own experience. Conversely, in institutional talk, one may not expect a professional to tell such 'second stories' about themselves (Sacks, 1992). It should not be surprising, then, that Jefferson (1988) reports that troubles talk in ordinary conversation is complex and varied, even 'disordered'. She analyses how interactants move from 'business as usual' discussions to troubles talk and back again in a variety of ways while attending to the local contingencies of particular situations. Jefferson and Lee (1992) elaborate on Jefferson's (1988) work by analysing how troubles talk in ordinary conversation may be altered by other interactants' different orientations to the interaction and/or by related interactional activities of setting members. Troubles talk is only one of a variety of potentially competing ways in which ordinary conversationalists may sustain their interactions.

While retaining their interest in ordinary conversation as a baseline for analysing institutional talk (see Maynard, 1991; Drew and Heritage, 1992b), conversation analysts stress the constraints and greater focus of institutional talk. Drew and Heritage (1992a) state, for example, that institutional interactions differ from ordinary conversations because the former orient to limited goals, and appeal to particular inferential frameworks. This is not to suggest, however, that institutional interaction patterns are imposed on interactants by abstract, macro-institutional forces. As ten Have (1991) shows in his analysis of asymmetries in UK, US and Dutch doctor–patient interactions, the patterns are interactional accomplishments of all setting participants.

Jefferson and Lee (1992) apply and elaborate on these themes in comparing and contrasting troubles talk in ordinary conversation and institutional service encounters. The latter interactions are distinctive in at least three major ways: (1) they include one or more professionals (2) to whom troubles-tellers orient as advice-givers, and (3) who express greater interest in troubles-tellers' problems than in their experiences with, or feelings about, their troubles. Thus, troubles talk in ordinary conversation and institutional settings may be analysed as occurring in different interactional domains (Miller and Holstein, 1995) involving different participant interests, expectations and opportunities.

Jefferson and Lee (1992) state that recipients of troubles-telling in ordinary conversation are frequently expected to express great concern for troubles-tellers' feelings and perceptions, and often find their advice ignored – if not openly rejected – by troubles-tellers reluctant to accept the lesser interactional status of advice recipient. In institutional settings, on the other hand, service providers often express indifference to troubles-tellers' feelings while insisting that others acquiesce in their preferred solutions. Jefferson and Lee state, for example, that callers to emergency ambulance services routinely found themselves confronted with what we are calling the 'cargo syndrome'. Specifically, the agency wanted certain information about the caller and did not want the same information about the sick or injured person, who was simply the item being transferred (Jefferson and Lee, 1992: 538).

In Chapter 3 I offered a complementary approach to troubles talk in institutional settings by analysing counselling interactions in terms of communication formats. The formats are typical role alignments taken by, and which link, counsellors and their clients. Such formats are interpretive and interactional domains that shape what, when and how utterances are expressed, and how they are received by others. This results in interactional 'patterns that are remarkably more uniform than those found in casual conversation' (Peräkylä and Silverman 1991a: 647).

Troubles talk as institutional discourse

Conversation analysis of troubles talk in institutional settings may be elaborated by treating the talk as embedded in institutional discourses which consist of the usual interpretive procedures used by setting members and their typical patterns of interaction (Miller, 1994). The discourses are both inferential and accountability frameworks to which setting members orient and may be held accountable. They structure, but do not determine, what may be said in social settings, how it may be said, and who may say it (Silverman, 1987).

Through these discourses, family 'troubles' are constituted as domestic 'reality' comes to be portrayed. Underlying this approach is 'the idea . . . that domestic reality . . . is produced in the very process of its designation' (Gubrium, 1992: 231). As Gubrium's ethnomethodologically informed ethnography shows, practitioners, like counsellors, cannot attend to the production of portraits of domestic order while engaged in producing it.[2]

Institutional discourses are conditions of possibility (Foucault, 1977) within which interactants formulate and express their practical interests in the issues at hand. The vocabularies, concerns and interactional practices that constitute institutional discourses may be assembled and articulated in a variety of ways to produce somewhat different forms of troubles talk, including different trouble-definitions and remedies (Emerson and Messinger, 1977). Thus, counsellors' and their clients' practical interests in troubles talk and the contexts of the talk are inextricably linked to the institutional discourses available to them in social settings. Continuities in troubles talk across institutional settings are related to continuities in the institutional discourses that are available within the settings, as Gubrium (1992) shows in his comparison of two family therapy clinics.

Institutional discourses are made available in social settings as members describe, negotiate and justify their preferred versions of social reality. While social settings may be analysed as providing their members with institutional discourses, the discourses only become available to setting members when they enter into and use the discourses to construct and sustain social settings. Setting members do so by using the vocabularies, orienting to the practical concerns, and interacting in ways provided by particular institutional discourses. For example, while many medical encounters may be organized to encourage biomedical troubles talk, the construction of biomedical troubles is contingent on setting members' ability and willingness to enter into a language of medical symptoms, disorders, causes and remedies.

Social interactions in institutional settings may be conducted under the auspices of several different institutional discourses, making it possible to construct both troubles and their social contexts in several different ways. It matters, then, which of the potentially available institutional discourses setting members enter. Consider, for example, Strong's (1979a) analysis of paediatrician–parent interactions as role formats. Each format provided setting members with resources for constructing distinctive types of clinical relationship, ranging from relationships that affirmed parents' claims to being caring and responsible persons whose children's health problems were unrelated to their parenting practices, to relationships that discredited parents' claims to being responsible and held them culpable for their children's health problems. Thus, social interactions that may be described as the same (medical interviews, for example) are not the same when they are conducted within different institutional discourses.

Further, not all interactants have equal opportunities to initiate entrance into institutional discourses or guide them in preferred ways. Some setting members may act as organizers or orchestrators (Dingwall, 1980) of social interactions. These social roles better position some interactants to strategically use available resources to achieve their practical interactional ends, while restricting others' strategic moves. For example, Jefferson and Lee's

(1992) discussion of the 'cargo syndrome' may be analysed as an institutional discourse made up of a transportation vocabulary that is provided to setting members within an interview format in which service providers direct the interactions by asking questions. It bears repeating, however, that entrance into this and other institutional discourses is a local and contingent accomplishment.

Our interest in institutional discourse and counselling practice may be stated in more explicitly Foucauldian (1980) terms by asking how trans-situational aspects of institutional discourse and power relations are discernible in different counselling sites. The question directs attention to the relationship between the micro- and macro-politics of troubles talk in institutional settings. For example, are counsellors' trouble-defining and remedy-seeking activities related to general professional strategies? If so, might the strategies be analysed as professional technologies for inciting troubles talk? Further, might the interactional patterns analysed by conversation analysts be aspects of general, troubles-telling technologies and power relations? We might also consider the related political question of when and how counsellors and/or their clients sometimes diverge from (even resist) typical institutional discourses and practices. We return to these issues later in the chapter after analysing the discursive practices of two different, but related, counselling sites.

Research sites

Our first empirical case involves counselling sessions with individuals who suffer from haemophilia and have become HIV positive through the transfusion of infected blood products. Counselling is provided free of charge within the British National Health Service (NHS) although the hospital itself is an autonomous NHS Trust. Haemophilia is a genetically determined blood disorder which affects only males, usually diagnosed in the very early stages of life. The centre (UK5) had provided counselling for haemophiliacs and their families for many years before the HIV epidemic was identified. Counselling was part of clients' routine visits to the centre for assessment and treatment of haemophilia. Some clients represented in our data had been coming for counselling at the centre for twenty or more years. Although the counsellors come from diverse professional backgrounds (social work, medicine and psychology), they all practise a theoretically based counselling method derived from family therapy (see Bor et al., 1992; Peräkylä, 1995).

Clients were expressly invited to include their 'significant others' in counselling sessions. Depending on clients' age, their significant others might be parents, partners and/or friends. While there were always at least two counsellors present, one counsellor always took the leading role in counselling sessions. The other counsellors only asked questions through the lead counsellor. Most counselling sessions lasted between 45 minutes and one hour. Advice from counsellors was only delivered after long sequences of questioning or avoided altogether in favour of an attempt to get clients to formulate the advice implied in a particular sequence of hypothetical questions (see Chapter 6, pp. 121–4).

The other case considered in this chapter involves family therapy sessions conducted in a private clinic to which clients brought a wide variety of complaints, including marriage break-up, eating disorders and various educational problems (US3). The clinic staff offered services to an economically and culturally diverse clientele, including voluntary clients who complained of various troubles (not just those typically associated with family therapy), and clients referred by area courts and human service agencies. The therapists practised 'brief therapy', meaning that they emphasized finding solutions to their clients' troubles (not deep insight into their causes) in a minimum of sessions (Cade and O'Hanlon, 1993; de Shazer, 1982). The therapists stated that effective therapy involves defining solvable troubles (Miller, G., 1987). Such definitions are concrete, focusing on behaviours or conditions that are observable and changeable. Thus, clients who complained of troubles that might be classifed and treated as the same were allowed to define them as different and identify different remedies for them. The critical issue for the therapists was whether clients could identify concrete solutions to their troubles, however they might be defined.

The therapists described their approach to family therapy as positive, because they emphasized clients' skills in solving their troubles. They explained that most of the time their clients were quite effective at managing their lives but sometimes clients became 'stuck' or stymied by one or a few troubles (Miller, G., 1987). From this standpoint, then, the therapists' primary professional responsibility involved helping their clients become 'unstuck' so that they might return to their normal problem-solving activities. The therapists further argued that the best way to help their clients become unstuck was to focus on concrete and limited changes in clients' lives. They explained that once such changes are initiated, other – perhaps more dramatic – changes will follow.

The therapists implemented the brief model by use of the therapeutic team. Clients met with a therapist in an interviewing room and one or more therapists (the team) observed from an adjoining observation room. Team members could and occasionally did communicate with the interviewer by means of an in-house telephone system. Typically, their communications consisted of requests for further information from clients or a recommendation that the interviewer utilize a different interviewing strategy. Most of the session was taken up with a therapeutic interview that involved approximately two-thirds of a typical 50- to 60-minute session. The interviews focused on clients' reasons for seeking therapy, the establishment of therapeutic goals, and whether clients were achieving their goals. Like the HIV counsellors, the therapists rarely told their clients how to define their troubles. Rather, they used indirect strategies to encourage clients to alter troublesome behaviour patterns and/or think about their lives in new – more positive – ways.

Comparing the sites

Two major differences between the sites are especially relevant for the analysis. The first involves the focus in the haemophilia centre on clients' status as persons having been diagnosed as HIV positive. While the counsellors talked with clients about wide-ranging issues and concerns, the counsellors' questions centred on how clients might manage, or were managing, their lives in the context of HIV (see Peräkylä, 1995). Interviews in the family therapy centre, on the other hand, had no such topical focus. Second, the haemophilia centre offered continuing, indeed lifetime, care and support to its patients. This meant that counsellors and clients grew very familiar with one another; indeed some of the counsellors were the very doctors who were treating clients for their medical conditions. Conversely, the family therapy centre offered a limited number of sessions to clients previously unknown to the centre.

A major similarity between the two centres was the use of methods derived from the systemic model of family therapy (Goldenberg and Goldenberg, 1991). This meant that counsellors avoided preconceived definitions of (and solutions to) their clients' troubles. Instead, they sought to elicit how clients perceived their own troubles (particularly in the context of their significant others) and clients' own past solutions to such troubles. The emphasis was always supposed to be on building clients' own skills rather than on providing Olympian solutions. To that end, counsellors in both settings took a non-judgmental attitude towards their clients' troubles and concerns. The attitude partly involves 'using a neutral tone of voice which does not necessarily convey surprise, astonishment, agreement or anger' (Miller and Bor, 1988: 18).

The systemic model of family therapy also emphasizes how personal troubles are embedded in family and other social systems. Viewed from this standpoint, personal troubles emerge, and are sustained by, the inter-pretive, behavioural and relational patterns that structure system members' lives. Effective intervention, then, involves asking circular questions (Lipchik, 1988) which focus on clients' and their significant others' distinctive perspectives, and on how family members' behaviour and perspectives are related to other system members' actions and interpre-tations. Systemic counsellors also ask hypothetical questions which en-courage clients to discuss 'dreaded' issues and/or future circumstances in which their troubles are solved (Peräkylä, 1995).

A second similarity between the settings was the availability of coun-selling teams to assist the interviewers. When available, team members' questions and advice would be directed to the interviewers who orchestrated (Dingwall, 1980) the counselling sessions by asking clients questions and suggesting ways in which clients might deal with their troubles. The interviewers indicated to clients when they might speak and the topics about which they might speak. Thus, an important continuity in troubles talk across the settings was the discursive positions of the professionals and their clients.

Counselling as a discourse of enablement

While recognizing their differences, we focus our analysis of troubles talk in these settings on their similarities. Of particular significance is the influence in both settings of a professional model that stresses the use of indirect methods in defining and treating clients' troubles as systemic problems. We analyse this approach and the counselling practices through which it is organized and implemented in counselling sessions as a *discourse of enablement*, which is a professional strategy for inciting preferred forms of troubles talk and encouraging preferred forms of change in clients' lives. It is also a vocabulary and theory about troubles, their social contexts, and how they are best remedied.

The discourse of enablement is a distinctive configuration of power/ knowledge that positions counsellors as facilitators who help clients develop new understandings about how their troubles might be managed. Within this discourse, counsellors avoid telling clients how to respond to their troubles because clients are constructed as 'free to choose' how to remedy their troubles. Rather, the counsellors use various questioning tactics to elicit information about clients' lives, perspectives and troubles and to guide clients towards mutually agreeable definitions of, and responses to, their troubles. The assumptions of the discourse of enablement, then, are inextricably intertwined with the concrete, local and contingent practices of counsellors and others involved in counselling sessions. It is through such practices that interactants socially construct clients as troubled persons who are embedded in describable social systems and justify practical actions intended to better manage clients' troubles.

Counselling practices

There were three major topical and interactional continuities in the troubles talk associated with the settings. They involve discursive practices concerned with trouble definitions, trouble remedies, and the social contexts of clients' troubles. We discuss the practices through which these issues were formulated and discussed in the next three sections. It bears noting, however, that while we discuss them as discrete aspects of professional–client interactions, the practices are interconnected features of the interactions. Talk of troubles contexts, definitions and remedies are recurring and shifting topics in counsellor–client interactions. Counsellors and clients might, for example, discuss one topic, shift to another, only to return to the first, and move on to yet another one as their interactions proceed. In this way, they combined and linked the topics in various ways to produce distinctively local forms of troubles talk and client–counsellor relationship.

Contextualizing practices

While troubles may be located within a variety of contexts and constructed through various discursive practices, the counsellors and therapists shared a strong preference for constructing family contexts for their clients' troubles. Counsellors at both centres asked questions about the various ways in which family members were connected, their perceptions of one another's behaviour, feelings about the troubles at hand, and how other family members might respond to possible future changes. Taken together, these questions may be analysed as procedures for constructing family systems as the primary contexts for defining clients' troubles and identifying appropriate remedies to them. The questions are conditions of possibility within which various (but not unlimited) trouble definitions might be constructed.

One kind of question used by the counsellors asked clients and their significant others to report on their lives and troubles. Such questions were usually asked at the outset of the interactions, with the aim of eliciting one person's assessment of clients' troubles. The therapists asked, for example, 'So, how have things been?' and HIV counsellors asked, 'How have things been between you, in your view?' Often, the therapists modified the question by focusing on changes in clients' lives and family systems by asking, 'How are things better?' Or, at the end of an interview, an HIV counsellor would ask 'Do you think what you've heard today is going to make any difference to how you carry on?'

The counsellors also asked circular questions (Lipchik, 1988). These questions focused on connections between clients and their significant others, and sometimes involved multiple voices. The questions recast the troubles at hand as aspects of family systems which might involve complex patterns of interrelation and/or diverse perspectives. The questions also potentially increased the number of issues to which counsellors might attend in defining and remedying clients' troubles, such as satisfactorily responding to the different concerns and perspectives of family members. Consider, for example, the following exchange which occurred during an HIV counselling session. It begins when Counsellor 2 (C2) asks the client (Keith) if he fears that his sexual relationship with his wife (Mary) might deteriorate in the future:

Extract 9.1 (UK5)
1   C2:   Would it have any effect?
2   Keith: Ye:s I think it would. (1.3)
3   C1:   hhh (0.4) Well I think we need to check up if Mary

4		has the same view: as Keith=I mean may have a
5		diff- she may have a different view:. (1.0)
6	Mary:	I don't ha- well I think that first I think I have a
7		slightly different view.=I mean I don't
8		regard it as being .hhhh (1.3) I don't regard it
9		as being an insuperable problem pu(h)t i(h)t that
10		way. (.) [hhh .hhhhh=
11	C1:	[Okay.

Extract 9.1 shows how circular questioning was used to construct hypothetical circumstances to which clients and their families might respond in several different ways. Notice here how C1 refers the client's answer to his wife for her own assessment (lines 3–5). The counsellors used such circular questions to explore the connections between family members by having setting members assess others' perceptions of, feelings about and/or responses to clients' troubles. They did so by asking clients or other setting members to assess how others do or might perceive, react to and/or feel about an issue. The counsellors treated clients' and significant others' responses to circular questions as information about their understandings of their family systems, not objective reports on how the systems 'really' worked. Thus, they often asked clients to speculate on the feelings of other family members in their absence.

Extract 9.2 below begins in this way as a family therapist (C) asks a patient (P) to assess her husband's wants:

Extract 9.2 (US3)

1	P:	I'm not sure what he wants. (1.0) He says he wants
2		to be happier. He thinks that maybe we should
3		separate but he doesn't- (.8). He does love me but,
4		(.5) I mean, his life is derailed in what he- (2.3),
5		and I and the children have been a focus for a lot
6		of the anger. (6.3) He doesn't want to lose us, but
7		he also doesn't (4.7), I can't speak for him, the
8		way I interpret his anger is that he doesn't know
9		(.3) what to think.
10	C:	Uh, hum, do you know what he would say if he were
11		here? (5.7) I mean can you guess?

In addition to illustrating the family therapists' interest in constructing clients' troubles within family contexts, this exchange displays how clients sometimes answered therapists' questions by downgrading their assessments of others' attitudes and behaviour. As Peräkylä and Silverman (1991b) have observed, such downgrades are interactional devices which attend to members' limited access to each other's experiences. In the above exchange, the client downgrades her assessments at two points. First, she says 'I'm not sure what he wants' (line 1). Then she points out 'I can't speak for him' (line 7). Only in the final turn (line 11) does the therapist attend to the downgrade by asking, 'I mean can you guess?' It is a hypothetical question that invites the client to say more about her husband's possible desires.

The same form of hypothetical questioning about others' feelings is found in the HIV counselling data. In Extract 9.3 below, a hypothetical question is once again followed by a downgrade ('hhhhh (0.3) It's a difficult one.', line 3):

> Extract 9.3 (UK5)
> 1   C: How do you think she: and the family where you are
> 2   would react if they knew you had HIV. (1.2)
> 3   P: hhhhh (0.3) It's a difficult one. .h Uhm (0.8) you
> 4   know they're: a very (.) very broad scoped family.
> 5   C: Mm:
> 6   P: Very broad scoped. (0.5) Uh::m (0.9) her father
> 7   (which let her outside)
> 8   C: Mm:
> 9   P: hhh he:: is (0.3) the one with the very broad
> 10   mind.=[Out of all of them. (0.5)

This exchange differs from Extract 9.2 in two important ways. First, the counsellor 'invites' the client to elaborate on his downgrade by offering minimal responses ('Mm') in lines 5 and 8. The responses meet the counsellor's obligations in the interactional sequences while maintaining their focus on the client's emergent answer to the earlier hypothetical, circular question. Second, we see here a client delivering a version of the social context of others' feelings ('a very (.) very broad scoped family.') which approximates to the very systemic model that the counsellor herself is using. Rather than being a deviant case, such adoption by clients of the professionals' rhetoric is common at the HIV counselling centre. We will later return to the bases and implications of this phenomenon.

Suffice it to say at this point that, in adopting the counsellors' rhetoric, clients signalled their entry into an institutional discourse of systemic relationships and remedies. Indeed, perhaps the very notion of 'personal troubles' invites expert assessments. As Gubrium notes:

> Personal troubles bring domestic order within the purview of interpretive experts, transforming troubles and the related privacies of the home into public concerns' (Gubrium, 1992: 224)

Emerson and Messinger (1977) analyse the construction of family systems and similar trouble contexts as integral to the definition of people's troubles as relational issues. This definition locates people's troubles in ongoing interpersonal relationships, and justifies remedies that draw on resources that are intrinsic to the troubled relationships. Thus, the contextualizing practices analysed in this section have practical implications for clients and counsellors alike.

The practices focused clients' concerns on limited aspects of their lives and provided them with interpretive frameworks for understanding and responding to their concerns. The efforts were of practical significance for the counsellors because they provided interactants with resources for interpreting the issues at hand in professionally approved ways. Defined as 'systemic' problems, clients' troubles might be contrasted with psychoanalytic and biomedical troubles, the two major alternative accounts available to clients. Eliciting systemic answers from clients and others, then, was integral to the counsellors' fulfilment of their professional responsibility.

Trouble-defining practices

A related aspect of counselling work is eliciting troubles talk from clients. Without troubles, counsellors have no reason to intervene in their clients' lives. This was especially problematic for the family therapists who dealt with a wide variety of clients' complaints. Thus, the therapists tried to elicit trouble descriptions from their clients early in their initial meetings, usually asking some version of the following questions: 'OK, well, what kind of a problem do you have that you need some help with?' or 'So, what brings you to us?'

The counsellors in the HIV counselling centre, on the other hand, knew from the outset that a potential issue for all their clients was the management of their own and others' vulnerability to HIV. But the clients' current concerns about haemophilia and HIV were not known in advance by the counsellors. For example, some clients expressed great concerns about how the virus might be transmitted through sexual intercourse, whereas others emphasized their concerns about bleeding in non-sexual encounters. Each such formulation of clients' most pressing troubles called for a somewhat different response from the counsellors.

Both types of counsellor shared a practical interest in eliciting detailed troubles talk from their clients. They pursued this interest by engaging in two similar trouble-defining practices. First, they asked questions which focused on clients' fears and/or major concerns about their present and future circumstances, as well as those of other members of their family systems. This practice is consistent with Miller and Bor's approach to dreaded issues. They state:

> loss, disfigurement, death and dying can be approached in a way that encourages the patient to talk about them. It is also an indication that the counsellor is not afraid to address these issues with the patient. (Miller and Bor, 1988: 17).

We see a successful attempt to elicit a dreaded issue (informing a partner of one's HIV status) in Extract 9.4 below:

Extract 9.4 (UK5)
1 C: What's your greatest fear of telling her. (0.9)
2 P: er The greatest fear:?
3 C: Mm (0.6)

```
 4   P:    Uh:m (0.2) Probably s:splitting u:p,
 5   C:    Mm:
 6   P:    splitting up probably. (.)
 7   C:    Mm: (2.7) What do you think (.) if you did decide
 8         to go ahead and (0.5) really have a permanent
 9         relationship with your girlfriend what do you see as
10         the greatest problems there.(0.8)
11         [For the future. If she knew the moment you=
12   P:    [Uh:m
13   C:    =decided to (1.3)
14   P:    er The greatest problem I suppose would be to make
15         sure that she didn't get infected.
```

This exchange shows how the HIV counsellors and family therapists sometimes asked dreaded questions in series, one dreaded question (line 1) followed by others (line 7) (see Peräkylä, 1995). However, as we shall see later, the counsellors' attempts to elicit talk of dreaded issues were sometimes successfully resisted by clients and their significant others. The counsellors also raised dreaded issues by asking circular questions which invited assessments of others' fears and concerns. The counsellors used the answers simultaneously to construct contexts for, and definitions of, clients' troubles.

The second trouble-defining practice found in both settings was scaling questions. That is, the counsellors asked clients and significant others to rank the severity, persistence and/or their own and others' fears about clients' troubles. HIV counsellors asked the question as a comparison of two or more fears about clients' circumstances, inviting others to specify which of clients' several troubles most concerned them. This is evident in Extract 9.5:

```
     Extract 9.5 (UK5)
 1   C:    Can I just ask Mary what she thinks: (.) having heard
 2         some of the things today Keith's greatest
 3         fears are.
 4         (1.1)
 5   C:    Or: what is .h uh maybe top of his mi:nd.
 6         (0.4)
 7   C:    His greatest worry or his greatest fear.
```

The therapists, on the other hand, asked their clients to rank their troubles on a 10-point scale, usually asking clients to rank their troubles from 'one through ten with one being the worst it has ever been and ten being the best that things could be'. The therapists used the question to define clients' perceptions of the seriousness of their troubles, to assess whether clients believed their troubles were getting better or worse, and to elicit information about clients' orientations to possible responses to their troubles. Like dreaded questions, scaling questions were sometimes asked as circular questions and in a series. Extract 9.6, from a family therapy interview, is an example of how the therapists used dreaded questions to define clients' troubles:

Extract 9.6 (US3)

1	C:	Well, taking all that into account then how, at what
2		number would you rate this marriage as-, as-, as
3		marriages go, that you would consider needing it?
4		(3.1) Is it a seven: or is it a four: or is it a
5		nine:, or (.) (1.9)
6	P:	It's certainly on the bottom half of the scale.
7	C:	Uh, huh, uh, hum.
8		(1.2)
9	P:	And I would say a four or so=
10	C:	=And at what point, how long do you think it would
11		have to go for you to say this is impossible, I
12		cannot stand it?

This exchange also shows how the therapists' scaling questions about clients' troubles might include assessments of possible solutions to the troubles at hand. In this case, the therapist follows her trouble-defining question with a scaling question about the circumstances in which the client would consider divorce as an appropriate solution to her troubled marriage.

Scaling questions and questions about dreaded issues were interrelated aspects of HIV and family therapy interviews. Both types of counsellor used the questions to orchestrate interviews, asking about one party's perceptions and concerns, and then turning to another member of the client's family system. In so doing, they collaboratively constructed various definitions of clients' troubles and family systems to which they might attend in recommending remedies to clients' troubles. As C2's questions in the following HIV counselling interview show, the counsellors and therapists also used significant others' answers to such questions to lead the discussion in the direction of professionally preferred understandings of, and responses to, clients' troubles.

Extract 9.7 (UK5) [Extract 9.5 continued]

1	C1:	Can I just ask Mary what she thinks: (.) having
2		heard some of the things today Keith's
3		greatest fears are. (1.1) Or: what is .h uh
4		maybe top of his mi:nd. (0.4) His greatest
5		worry or his greatest fear. (0.8)
6	Mary:	Well I think his greatest fear is- is er (0.8) going
7		on to develop more: (0.3) AIDS related
8		symptoms, and to pass er (then) something on to me:.
9	(?):	.hhh[hh
10	C1:	[I see. (1.5) Which do you think are the
11	Mary:	Well I don't know which order to put those i:n.

```
12                  (1.0)
13   C1:            Uh:m: (0.9)
14   Mary:          I think he- I think there is a big fear about- about
15                  transmit- about transmitting.=
16   C1:            =Would you agree with what she's just said?
17   Keith:         Mm: (0.5)
18   C1:            Which of those two are you more worried about.
19                  (2.0)
20   Keith:         It's difficult to put them in an or:der but (0.2) I
21                  suppo:se if abslu- absolutely pu:shed and that
22                  doesn't mean to say=
23   C1:            =Mm[:
24   Keith:            [it's at the top  [of my mind [all the time=
25   C1:                                [No.         [No no.
26   Keith:         =but .hh a- (0.6) fear of transmitting i:t. (0.6)
27                  [Is my- is the fir:st
28   C1:            [              [   ) about the=
29   Keith:         ( )-           [concer::n
30   C1:            =transmitting (      [   ).
31   C2:                                 [Do you: (1.2) I mean do you-
32                  y- you obviously know: how this
33                  [(er)- virus is tra[nsmitted. .h=
34   Keith:         [Ye:s              [Ye:s.
35   C2:            =Wha- (0.2) wha:t (0.7) what- what precautions (.)
36                  do you take at the moment. To- to stop that
37                  happening. (1.0)
38   Keith:         We use condoms.=
39   C2:            =Mm
```

In Extract 9.7, troubles are elicited from clients in a set of related sequences. First, in lines 1–5 a family system is constructed by asking Keith's wife (Mary) to construct her husband's fears by means of a scaled dreaded issues question. Second, in lines 6–15, C1 and Mary collaborate in a further scaling exercise. Third, using the method of circular questioning, the wife's answer is passed on for comment to her husband (line 16), who offers a scaling response of his own (lines 20–9). Finally, C2 uses the previously elicited dreaded issue to ask about the precautions taken by the client to protect others. Notice, however, that while the question moves the interaction towards solution talk, C2 avoids offering direct advice to the client.

In sum, the social construction of trouble definitions in these settings was inextricably linked to the professionals' and clients' contextualizing practices, which usually cast clients' circumstances as family troubles, and their interests in identifying 'appropriate' – preferably client-initiated – remedies to the troubles. The latter issue is considered in the next section.

Remedy-identifying practices

Unlike the family therapy centre, the focus on HIV-associated troubles at the haemophilia centre meant that counsellors pursued a public health orientation, encouraging their clients to inform other people involved in their lives about their infection and to take precautions whenever the clients believed that they might infect others. The counsellors emphasized clients' responsibility to inform fully their sex partners, and to use condoms during sex. However, counsellors in both centres avoided, where possible, adopting the role of the advice-giver. The HIV counsellors did so by asking leading questions of clients rather than directly advising their clients about the importance of informing others and taking precautions.

Similarly, the therapists asked questions intended to 'lead' clients to re-think aspects of their lives that the therapists considered troublesome. For example, clients who came to therapy complaining of family conflicts were sometimes encouraged to think about their alcohol or other drug use as a related family trouble.

While they had different practical interests in identifying appropriate remedies to their clients' troubles, some of the strategies used by the HIV counsellors and family therapists were similar. Two deserve special note. The first involved asking clients to imagine future states when their lives would be less troubled, and/or they would be better managing their troubles. The counsellors did so by asking hypothetical qustions about how others in clients' social worlds would respond to possible remedies to clients' troubles. Consider the following interaction in which an HIV coun-sellor and client are discussing how the client might inform others of his HIV status. Note how the sequence begins with a hypothetical question from C:

```
        Extract 9.8 (UK5)
 1   C:      I mea:n (0.5) say you decided after talking to us
 2           toda:y (0.4) to tell them. (0.3)
 3           How do you think (0.2) what effect would it have on
 4           you staying there do you think?
 5   P:      Uh:m (0.5) so long as it was explained to them
 6           correctly (0.6) I don't think there really
 7           would be any. So long as it was explained the
 8           ri[ght way. But I think the best idea would to=
 9   C:        [Mm:
10   P:      =be: (0.4) when the time came to explain to them
11           bring them all here:[and have (0.5) your people=
12   C:                          [Yes.
13   P:      =to explain to [them better than what I=
14   C:                     [Well we'd be-
15   P:      =could. [(              )-
16   C:              [Well I'd like to say that if that's
```

17   something you wanted to do: and you wanted to do (.)
18   with them here [.hhh then we'd be very happy=

Notice how the counsellor's questions treat the solution to the client's troubles as embedded in his social worlds (particularly in his family system), and as a matter of explaining to others about his infection. The client collaborates in the process by stating that his problems can be resolved by explaining things correctly (line 6). He then underlines this collaboration by inviting the counsellor to help in the explanatory enterprise (lines 10–15). This now becomes the basis for the development of a plan in which the counsellor would help the client explain his circumstances to others in his social world (lines 16–18).

The therapists used future-oriented, hypothetical questions to gain insight into their clients' hopes for their lives. They asked clients to identify concretely how they wished their lives to change based on the therapy experience, and/or how their lives would be different if their most pressing troubles suddenly disappeared. Consider, for example, Extract 9.9:

Extract 9.9 (US3)
1 C: Uh, hum, can you see yourself- can you imagine
2   yourself- away from the relationship?
3 P: Uh, hum. (1.6)
4 C: Alright. (2.8) In that, if you can imagine yourself
5   away from that, what are the-, what are
6   the things that you feel best about?
7   (8.9)
8 P: Well:, when I'm away from it for any length of
9   time.=
10 C: Oh I don't mean, I mean can you project yourself
11   (.3) divorced or away from it (.5) totally living
12   separately from your husband so you will be out of
13   this relationship and that (3.4) it would be a great
14   loss to you?
15 P: Yeah.
16 C: So now if we project ourselves into the future (.7)
17   and you're, (1.5) you're, uh, you're away from it,
18   (3.7) what would be the greatest losses and what
19   would be the things you are feeling best about?

The therapist accomplishes two major ends in this exchange. First, she raises the possibility of separation (even divorce) as a solution to the client's troubles without advocating it. The therapist asks 'can you imagine yourself-away from the relationship?' (lines 1–2), not 'have you thought about divorce?' or some other more direct question. The therapist's hypothetical questions also invite information about the client's orientation to separation as a possible remedy, both whether she can imagine it and, if so, what its practical implications for her life might be. The therapists treated clients' answers as revealing the depth of clients' concerns about their troubles, and as potentially useful in future sessions if other, less 'extreme' remedies proved to be unsatisfactory to clients.

The second common way in which the HIV counsellors and therapists identified preferred remedies to their clients' troubles involved formulating the gist of the clients' positions and agreeing with them. They used this strategy to suggest to clients ways in which they might manage their troubles in ways preferred by the counsellors. Sometimes this meant that the counsellors highlighted one or two client statements during the interview, and elaborated on how the clients might implement them. Unlike the HIV counsellors, however, the therapists sometimes formulated the gist of clients' statements, agreed with them, and then handed the trouble back to clients by stating that they were not sure how clients might implement their insights. Consider, in Extract 9.10 below, the intervention message given to a client who is planning to divorce her husband:

```
        Extract 9.10 (US3)
 1   C:        hhhhh. You certainly have come up with some good
 2             ideas with what to te:ll, uh, the kids and what not
 3             to te:ll them, (2.5) and, uh, (1.4) you know, to
 4             tell them in an honest and truthful ma:nner.
 5             (2.2)
 6   C:        And we agree:, uh, with what you've come up (.8)
 7             with so far, (2.3) and we agree that there's no need
 8             to tell them anything mor:e than they can
 9             understand, (2.3) hhh we don't know when you
10             should tell the kids.
11             (3.6)
12   C:        You'll have to be the judge of that.
13             (3.5)
14   C:        And we don't know if (.) telling them is going to
15             make it any easier for anybody.
16             (3.1)
17   C:        This is just going to be a tough period of time.
18             (3.1)
```

As Extract 9.10 shows, the therapist's expression of agreement included compliments for clients about their insights into their difficulties (lines 1–4) as well as direct statements of agreement (lines 6–9). These moves served several of the therapists' practical interests. First, their expressions of agreement signalled their alignment with the clients, that they were on the 'clients' side'. Second, the therapists' formulation of the clients' troubles conveyed a sense that the therapists understood their complaints. Finally, the therapists used this move to allocate primary responsibility for solving the clients' troubles to the clients, insisting that they use their judgement in deciding how to proceed (line 12).

In contrast, the HIV counsellors were more directive about remedies, using gist formulations to point clients in institutionally approved directions. Consider the statement made by a counsellor in Extract 9.11 below. The client has just said that he does not feel that his relationship with a woman is sufficiently serious to necessitate telling her about his infection. The counsellor agrees, but also stresses the importance of taking precautions against spreading the infection, and suggests that the client should think about how he might inform his friend should the relationship become more serious.

Extract 9.11 (UK5)
```
1   C:    .hh I mean (.) if you: (0.2) take the necessary
2         precautions in your li:fe (0.5) then I agree with
3         you nobody needs to know. (0.7) Except if you
4         develop a very strong relationship with someone. .hh
5         Which a lot of our boys do:, .hh (.) then: (0.2)
6         it's just (.) you would have to find way:s over time
7         of telling someone (0.8) (you were actually
8         going)-(0.2) we:ll that would be one of other issue-
9         one of the people who you might want to tell. (1.4)
10        But otherwise (2.0) any questions you'd want to a:sk
11        at this point.
```

Extract 9.11 shows a directive strategy which makes it clear to the client that 'telling someone' (line 7), who is a potential sexual partner, about your HIV status is a proper thing to do. Nonetheless, note how the counsellor couches her 'advice' within a professional ideology which emphasizes choice, i.e. such a person would be 'one of the people who you might want to tell' (line 9). At the haemophilia counselling centre, we see this combination of professional direction and apparent client autonomy most clearly when counsellors ask about clients' knowledge. Such a question arises in Extract 9.12 below, immediately after the client has raised the issue of infecting his girlfriend:

Extract 9.12 (UK5)
```
1   P:    er The greatest problem I suppose would be to make
2         sure that she didn't get infected.
3   C:    Mm (0.3) What are the ways that you know you can do
4         that?
5   P:    Uh:m (1.1) Obviously not mak- making sure she has no
6         cuts when I do:, (0.2) coming into contact with
7         blood.
```

Here the counsellor has established a 'teaching' format (Mehan, 1979) where, as in schools, teachers ask questions in order to set up the possibility of an answer-evaluation as the final turn of a three-part sequence. The family therapists were less likely to ask questions of this type. Two factors may be associated with this difference. First, the HIV counselling centre (UK5) served clients of school age – notice the counsellor's reference to 'our boys' in Extract 9.11, line 5. Second, it was regularly concerned with serious public health issues (the spread of infectious diseases) that counsellors could use to justify more evaluative responses to clients' accounts. The therapists did occasionally enter into similiar format, usually in dealing with clients who complained of being physically abused. The therapists stated that these cases were different, because the therapists had legal and moral obligations to these clients to help them protect themselves from further abuse.

Earlier I argued that our interest in institutional discourse and counselling practice may be stated in more explicitly Foucauldian (1980) terms by asking how trans-situational aspects of knowledge/power relations are discernible in the counselling sites. I examine how this study bears on this issue next.

Counselling, troubles and enablement

Perhaps the most obvious similarity found in both settings is the dominance of a discourse of enablement within which clients were constructed as subjects who are 'free to choose'. This is evident in the family therapists' general lack of interest in specifying trouble definitions or remedies for their clients, so long as clients' definitions fit within the therapists' notion of solvable problems. Even the more directive strategies of the HIV counsellors co-exist with the construction of clients who are free to choose how to remedy their troubles. We saw this in Extract 9.11 where a public health message was incorporated in an appeal to whom the client might 'want' to tell. Similarly, the 'educational' question that the counsellor asked in Extract 9.12 was embedded in a proposed course of action that the client had apparently volunteered.

Foucault (1977, 1980) argues that institutionalized discourses – such as the discourse of enablement – are sites of power and discipline. Power is more than a simple, hierarchical structure. It is an aspect of the social processes through which embodied actors act in, and shape, their social worlds. It is a collaborative process involving counsellors, clients and significant others, all of whom act within available institutional discourses to define, contextualize and remedy clients' troubles.

This collaboration may be seen in Extract 9.6 (p. 199) in which the client responds to the therapist's scaling question by stating that she would rate her marriage as in the 'bottom half of the scale' (line 6), and then elaborates with: 'And I would say a 4' (line 9).

Power moved through many voices and implicated several different sources of knowledge in these settings, making it possible to elaborate the conditions of possibility embedded in the dominant discourse in varied, and sometimes complex, ways. Consider the following excerpt from a family therapy session concerned with the times when the client had satisfactorily managed her life. The therapists used this strategy to identify personal and social resources that clients might use to better manage their troubles.

Extract 9.13 (US3) [FAM=family member]
```
1  C:     Were there any other periods in your life since then
2         that you really felt very good like that?
3  P:     Um. (1.4)
4  FAM:   You were pretty good in California, [weren't you?
5  P:                                         [Yeah, I wasn't
6         bad in California. I enjoyed my job there-.
7  C:     Why was that?
```

In Extract 9.13, we see how counsellors implicate clients' significant others in eliciting information about clients' lives and troubles. Not only are they interested in clients' social systems, but they also invite members of the systems to speak on their own behalf. In counselling sessions that included clients' significant others, then, the social systems were more than contexts for clients' troubles. They were also embodied gazes and voices for socially constructing clients' troubles, a subject about which the significant others might claim to be as knowledgeable as the clients. A major practical implication of the counsellors' systemic emphasis was to construct social conditions for inciting troubles talk from a variety of others.[3]

Foucault also shows how power can work by constructing subjects who discipline themselves apparently of their own free will. Two earlier extracts allowed us to catch sight of this process. In Extract 9.8, a client invites the counsellor to include further members of his family network within her disciplinary gaze: 'I think the best idea would to be: (0.4) when the time came to explain to them bring them all here: and have (0.5) your people to explain to them better than what I could.' In Extract 9.3, another client actually proposes his own systemic view of his family network: 'you know they're: a very (.) very broad scoped family.'

Rather than being a deviant case, such adoption by clients of the professionals' rhetoric was common at the HIV counselling centre. It was also evident in later family therapy sessions with long-term clients, and with clients who had tried other forms of therapy prior to coming to the therapy centre. In these situations, but particularly with the haemophilia clients who have been counselled over their whole lives, we see writ large the micro-politics of counselling as a preferred solution to personal problems. Instructed by counsellors (magazines, talk shows and university professors), people's gaze turns on themselves and their partners to produce a veritable counselled society.

Following Foucault, the incitement to troubles talk offered to subjects constructed as free to choose is double-edged. Predictably, our data show resistance to, as well as compliance with, institutionally preferred discourses. For instance, while Extracts 9.4, 9.5 and 9.7 revealed client compliance with counsellors' attempts to evoke dreaded issues, resistance to this tactic also occurs (see also Peräkylä, 1993, 1995).

We see such resistance in Extract 9.14:

Extract 9.14 (UK5)

1	C1:	And if Doctor Langer: if more symptoms developed
2		what would Mister Keith's greatest fear be
3		about that.
4		(1.4)
5	C1:	er what would be most difficult for him.
6		(1.5)
7	P:	I don't know I haven't thought about that. (1.2)
8	C2:	Can I a:sk (.) one final (0.3)

In Extract 9.14, asking her question via C2, C1 raises a potential dreaded issue for her client (lines 1–3). Hearing resistance in the client's failure to take the 1.4 second slot available at line 4, C1 elaborates her question (line 5). Now, after a further long pause, when the client refuses to produce the proposed dreaded issue (line 7), C2 enters to change the topic. So resistance, just as much as compliance, is to be expected among free, speaking subjects. Indeed, one part of the counsellors' work within this discourse involves recognizing and effectively responding to such client moves. A strategy used by counsellors in both settings was to change the interactional focus by asking a different kind of question, although the family therapists often returned to such 'dropped' issues later in the interactions.

A less common and more challenging circumstance sometimes emerged in family therapy interviews when clients refused to acknowledge that they had any problems, or that their lives needed to change in any way. Clients who were ordered to enter therapy by the courts sometimes argued that they had done nothing to warrant either the court's attention or therapeutic intervention. The therapists responded by questioning clients about aspects of their lives (particularly those aspects that most interested the courts), asking if any of these issues might be problems for clients. When this strategy failed to produce problems, the therapists asked if the courts might be a problem for clients. For example, 'Is your real problem how to get the judge off your back?' When clients persisted in arguing that they had no problems, the therapists stated that they could not continue to meet with the clients. The therapists explained that their jobs involved helping clients solve their problems. If clients had no problems, then the therapists could not justify meeting with them.

In addition to displaying how therapy clients sometimes resisted invitations to troubles talk, this points to aspects of the discontinuity between the therapeutic discourse of enablement and the law's stress on personal accountability. The former discourse assumes that clients are free to choose whether they have troubles, whereas the latter assumes that clients are troubled regardless of their perspectives and preferences. The discourse of enablement, then, operates in a world that includes a variety of other institutional discourses, some of which may impinge upon the counselling society in very practical ways.

Finally, while I have focused the analysis on continuities in the HIV counselling and family therapy settings, I emphasize that they are also different. The discourse of enablement may be adapted and applied in a variety of ways in concrete situations. This is evident, for example, in the HIV counsellors' greater readiness than the therapists to offer direction to their clients, suggesting whom they should inform of their infection, and how. Institutional discourses, then, are textured by the various situational contingencies and practices of specific settings.

Sociological implications

It has recently been remarked (e.g. Atkinson, 1995; Clavarino et al., 1995) that one of the major problems which besets sociological analysis is our apparent preference for erecting strong boundaries between research paradigms. This chapter is an initial attempt to pull together strands of ethnographic, Foucauldian and conversation analytic work at an empirical, rather than purely theoretical, level.

Of course, this enterprise is not without its dangers. It can encourage an uneconomical use of surplus concepts – such that the argument skips around between different paradigms without the rigorous analysis demanded by a single paradigm. Moreover, paradigm-crossing can be promiscuous; crucial elements found in a particular perspective can be forgotten, as Schegloff (1991) persuasively argues about attempts to combine conversation analysis with the analysis of apparently 'structural' variables.

Whatever its perils, following Miller and Silverman (1995), I believe that the journey is worth making. Attempts at syntheses in the contexts of grand theories, like those of Talcott Parsons and Anthony Giddens, only take us so far. Ultimately, the best test of whether such syntheses work is to be found in the tough arena of field research. To further that end, the chapter concludes by discussing three issues of relevance to future studies of troubles talk and institutional discourse.

The first issue involves the relationship between the so-called macro- and micro-aspects of discourses about troubles. We have previously described them as 'top-down' and 'bottom-up' approaches and noted how Foucauldian and conversation analytic perspectives differ in this area. Foucault focuses on the ways in which general and formalized discourses emerge in particular historical periods and then permeate concrete social settings, rearranging their discursive possibilities in the process. Conversation analysts, on the other hand, begin with talk in social interaction and then explore how the talk is related to general cultural practices.

This analysis does not resolve or transcend these tensions, but it does offer a practical approach to managing them. We started with empirical data (transcripts and observations of numerous counselling sessions) and analysed them by comparing practices. While my analysis was informed by Foucauldian concerns from the outset, we did not assume that ideological continuities in the professional literature on HIV counselling and brief family therapy were guarantees that the *in situ* practices of counsellors would be the same. The analysis both affirms the significance of Foucault's (1973, 1977) studies for field research on troubles talk in institutional settings and shows how the talk is locally produced and managed. Following Gubrium (1992: 237), I have shown how each centre offers an institutionalized incitement to speak structured according to its own practical theories.

A second and related issue involves the distinctiveness of the discursive practices analysed here and those associated with the interaction order (Rawls, 1987). The issue turns on whether the counsellors' practices are unique to the discourse of enablement or modifications of generally shared interactional devices for inciting preferred forms of troubles talk. Following Miller and Silverman (1995), I see this as an empirical question that warrants study in its own right. It should also be noted, however, that empirical demonstrations that counsellors trade on general troubles-telling strategies and devices are not adequate grounds for abandoning the study of troubles talk as an institutional discourse. Institutional discourses are complex and varied configurations that include both distinctive and shared elements. Further, the organization and practical implications of troubles talk in institutional discourses and settings are quite different from those of troubles talk in ordinary conversation, even when similar devices are used to elicit the talk.

Finally, I turn to power as an ever-present aspect of social interaction and relationships. This chapter analyses one of a variety of institutional discourses within which power moves and people may be constructed as objects of power. The analysis focuses on power as practical activity, as the socially organized work of counsellors in collaboration with others. It shows how the movement of power within institutional settings may be empirically studied by attending to the mundane details of the talk through which service providers fulfil many of their professional responsibilities.

This brings us back to my prior point about analysing institutional discourses from the bottom up. While power and resistance may be ubiquitous in everyday life, their concrete form and practical implications are locally contingent matters that cannot be fully anticipated by looking only at the formal strategies of the professional literature.

Notes

1. A very good autocritique of the imperialist ambitions of sociology is offered by Strong (1979b).

2. Gubrium identifies three rules used in these settings to depict domestic reality. Each rule shows how what he calls 'constitutive work' is unavailable to the practitioner. These rules are:

1 Ignore the constitutive work that constitutes domestic reality i.e. treat it as a feature of the home.
2 Identify those features of the home that have supposedly produced particular features of domestic life.

210 Discourses of Counselling

3   Use practical reasoning to identify some feature as an instance of some institutionally based theory: e.g. how family seat themselves only matters where they are able to determine seating arrangements themselves. (Gubrium, 1992: 232–5)

3. As Peräkylä (1995) points out, the systemic method of first inviting a partner to offer a version of a client's experience is a nice way of inciting clients to talk about 'dreaded issues' – as a correction or amplification of their partner's version.

10

Implications for Practice

Practitioners and researchers do not necessarily have an easy relationship. In the UK public sector, where, largely due to economic stringencies, the fashionable management phrases are 'audit' and 'efficiency savings', practitioners often identify research with reduced conditions of service or even job cuts. Equally, within all Western societies, in the varied conditions of private practice it is not easy to convince practitioners of the relevance of research to their individual circumstances.

Counsellors and related professionals are not exempt from these conditions. For instance, in psychotherapy, with its strong private practice, practitioners often deny the applicability of research findings to their own practice. One US study of the utilization of therapy research by practising psychotherapists noted many criticisms of such research. A selection of these criticisms is set out in Table 10.1.

Table 10.1   *Practitioner criticisms of research*

1. Studies designed to incorporate the complexities of psychotherapy are rarely done.
2. In an effort to make studying psychotherapy more manageable, researchers often ignore important variables.
3. Often researchers focus on specific techniques while ignoring the importance of the relationship between therapist and client.
4. Traditional research methodologies . . . derived from the physical sciences, are not for the most part appropriate for the investigation of psychotherapy.

Source: Morrow-Bradley and Elliott, 1986: adapted from McLeod, 1994: 182–5

Now I certainly do not want to imply that practitioners who question research in these terms are self-interested reactionaries. On the contrary, as I suggested above, in the economic conditions in which we live, it is quite sensible for practitioners to be resistant to much of what counts as 'research'. Again, in both private and public practice, it is quite proper for practitioners to cast doubt on the relevance of research to the special constraints under which they maintain their own practice.

However, I do argue that, in the research discussed in this book, I can offer what is, I hope, a reasonably convincing response to each of the criticisms listed above, as shown in Table 10.2.

I developed these methodological issues in Chapter 2 and I do not want to dwell further upon them now. Ultimately, in my view, most counsellors and

Table 10.2   *This study's response to methodological criticisms*

---

1. By detailed transcription of audio-recordings, many of the complexities of counselling are made visible.
2. Using largely qualitative methods, without pre-defined variables, most of the important practical issues that actually confront practitioners are addressed.
3. No normative position on the efficacy of particular techniques is adopted. Instead, close attention is paid to how the client-practitioner relationship is actually organized.
4. The type of qualitative methodology used – conversation analysis – is highly appropriate to investigate many of the real-time features of counselling interviews.

AIDS professionals will be less interested in how I got to my findings than in their possible implications for their practice.

My preference is to identify specific counselling practices in the details of talk. Practical issues can then be immediately confronted as we examine the local consequences of the particular form of any given practice. For example, in Chapter 3 we discussed some consequences of counsellors asking a string of questions (the Interview Format, as we called it) versus delivering information (the Information Delivery Format).

As a sociologist rather than a counsellor, it is not for me to take a position on the therapeutic or health promotion implications of the practices I have identified. However, this is not to wash my hands of such practical matters. Instead, in the many workshops that have followed this research, my transcripts and findings have been offered to practitioners as a means to establish a dialogue about their practice and the constraints under which it operates.

The pages that follow summarize the main issues involved. However, I can best indicate the direction I have followed by referring to the research of my colleague, Anssi Peräkylä, on the 'Family Systems' method of counselling used by Bor, Miller and Goldman (1992) in relation to HIV, AIDS and haemophilia at the Royal Free Hospital, London. Although the counselling Peräkylä studied was much more 'theory driven' than most of the HIV counselling discussed in this book, Peräkylä and I both gathered and analysed data in the same way. Part of the conclusion to Peräkylä's book nicely indicates the version of the relationship between research and practice which we share:

> The most fundamental implication of this study for counselling practice is to have shown that the Family Systems Theory based techniques can be successfully adopted in the counselling with HIV positive patients. Throughout the various chapters, we have seen that Family Systems Theory based AIDS counselling 'works': the counsellors and their clients produce unique interaction scenes and episodes which are unlike ordinary conversation and probably also unlike any other type of counselling or therapy. Conversation Analytical study cannot make any claims regarding the therapeutic effectiveness of these interactions – but what we have demonstrated is that Family Systems Theory is most effective in shaping, in a controlled and conscious fashion, the way that people interact with one another in the counselling setting. (Peräkylä, 1995: 332)

At one level, Peräkylä's research served to demonstrate, as he claims, that the theory which these counsellors preached did have many of the interactional consequences that it claimed. However, as Peräkylä points out, this demonstration is confined to the counselling interview itself – the author does not take a position on what he calls 'the therapeutic effectiveness' of such counselling practice.

But Peräkylä's research was not simply a welcome pat on the back for the counsellors concerned. Instead, his research revealed facets of their practice of which they were unaware. An example of this is found in Peräkylä's discussion of how counsellors encouraged their clients to talk about their fears for the future by asking hypothetical questions. On this topic, Peräkylä suggests:

> our analysis has emphasized the importance of *preparatory work* before 'hypothetical questions' are asked. The counsellors' own theoretical statements concerning talk about the future focus almost exclusively on 'hypothetical questions'. *Here the counsellors' own practice is even more sophisticated than their theory*: in a most systematic way, they prepare their clients for hypothetical questions concerning the future, through careful means of topic elicitation and topic development. The importance of this preparatory work could possibly be given specific attention in the teaching of counselling skills. (ibid.: 333; my emphasis).

We can glean two relevant points from Peräkylä's comment above. First, this kind of detailed work on actual counselling episodes, as Peräkylä argues, has an immediate relevance for the training of counsellors. Second, such work is able to reveal the limits of purely theoretical accounts of counselling. Sometimes this will mean showing how the practice falls short of the theory. This is a common concern of many research studies which seek to evaluate counselling. Sometimes, however, as here, Peräkylä's kind of detailed, turn-by-turn analysis can show how counselling practice is 'more sophisticated' even than its own theory.

We have largely dealt here with far less theoretically driven practices of HIV counselling. Sometimes, indeed, we have confronted activities by counsellors that would be frowned upon both in the textbooks and by fellow practitioners. The delay in the delivery of HIV test results, discussed in Chapter 5, may be an apposite example of this.

Nevertheless, Peräkylä's conclusions are highly relevant to my own. In the pages that follow, as I draw together the practical implications of my research, the implicit message is the same: 'treat counsellors neither as dopes nor as geniuses: instead try to understand the local or structural exigencies in relation to which they construct their activities'.

Having reviewed the philosophy of this research, I now summarize the major findings and their implications for HIV counsellors. The chapter (and the book) will conclude by addressing the contentious topic of the relevance of research on work in the area of HIV and AIDS to counsellors in other areas.

If you have taken the worthy route of reading this book from beginning to end, I am afraid that you may well find parts of this chapter repetitious. However, I am aware that some from among my busy, practitioner audience may, quite reasonably, have skipped the data analysis chapters in order to get at the 'meat' of the book. So here it is – and I hope that you do not find it too bloodless!

Implications for HIV counselling

The functions (and dysfunctions) of communication formats

In Chapter 3, I described how talk in HIV counselling moves between two different communication formats. In the information delivery format (ID), counsellors (Cs) deliver information which their clients or patients (Ps) acknowledge with 'response-tokens' such as 'mm' and 'yeah'. In the Interview Format (IV), Cs ask questions to which Ps provide answers. Although other communication formats occur, for instance clients asking questions and delivering information, they are unstable and quickly dissolve into one of the two 'home-base' formats.

The stability of IV and ID formats was shown to arise for two main reasons. First, because of the way in which questions and answers (IV) or information and receipts (ID) allow the maintenance of particular conversational rights over long stretches of talk, potentially involving multiple topics. Second, because these formats, by providing for the leading role of the counsellor (and the passive and responsive role of the client), work well given the relative opacity to clients of counselling as an activity as well as the 'delicacy' of the topics addressed.

By analysing comparative material from different centres and countries, we saw how communication in HIV counselling can take distinctly different shapes, despite the predominance of the two home-base formats. In some clinics, the counselling practices favour one format, and in others, another format.

Our study supports Green's (1989: 9) assertion that most HIV counsellors have adopted a largely pragmatic approach. At some British and US centres, particularly where counsellors are trained in methods deriving from family therapy, we find that Cs only move into ID after extensive questioning of clients (see also Peräkylä, 1995). Conversely, at many British testing centres, given the huge agenda of pre-test counselling, Cs seem to focus on health promotion as a set of truncated sequences of C-initiated information or advice. Yet even the most directive Cs do set up IV communication formats, most notably at the start of an interview or when P resistance to a specific piece of advice or information becomes manifest (see Chapters 3 and 8).

The fact that either format may be used as a home base suggests the specific functions that each serves. The interview format has the major advantage that, because of the nature of question–answer adjacency pairs, Ps are required to speak. This is particularly important in relation to topics like safer sex or the medical aspects of HIV and the HIV test. As all research shows (see Nelkin, 1987; Aggleton, 1989), the lack of impact of information alone on behavioural change suggests that to rely solely upon the use of an information delivery format for the discussion of safer sex is probably inadequate. Regarding talk about 'dreaded issues' (Chapter 3, pp. 53–6), the benefit of the IV format is that it gives Ps an opportunity to express their own concerns and fears about the future.

In comparison with the interview, the information delivery format is far less complicated for Cs. Although multi-unit turns of information delivery are a joint achievement, the contribution required from Ps is of a smaller scale than in an IV format. This has two advantages for hard-pressed Cs: the C can deliver pre-designed information packages without much reflection, and a similar range of issues can be covered within a shorter period of time.

However, much depends on the sequence in which formats are placed. In our material, Cs using the interview format to discuss safer sex do quite often also offer Ps their own views on the topic. But that happens only after a long sequence of questions and answers and is grounded in the P's own account of what they are thinking and doing. This suggests that favouring an IV format is not incompatible with giving the Ps the latest expert information – indeed it is highly compatible with delivering that information in a way specifically designed for its recipient, following a long question–answer sequence in the IV format.

Formats and the management of 'delicacy'

The special character of HIV counselling as a communication structure entails much more than the deployment of the two home-base communication formats discussed above. Most notably, acting as a 'counsellor' or as a 'client' seems to be related to the organization of talk about 'delicate matters' which may possibly include sexual orientation and behaviour, use of illegal substances and Ps' fears about a potentially threatening future (see Chapter 4). However, the consistent use of the stable communication formats, with the initiatory role they give to Cs, appears to be a central precondition for achieving these more specific 'counselling' tasks.

In this chapter, I have already pointed out the possible functionality of the two home-base communication formats for the management of talk about 'delicate' issues. Peräkylä has developed this point very clearly, observing that:

> the presence of delicate issues may encourage the clients to remain in a responsive position. During much of the time in counselling sessions, the participants are talking about the clients' sexual practices and about their fears concerning the future. The etiquette of addressing topics like those is very complex in ordinary conversation (cf. Jefferson, 1980). The counsellors, however, direct the talk – sometimes persistently – towards these issues. . . . *Clients can embody their expressive caution in a strategy where they talk about delicate matters only as much as the counsellors, through their questions, create special space for such talk.* (Peräkylä, 1995: 99–100; my emphasis)

As Peräkylä implies, the IV format can be an effective vehicle for encouraging Ps to talk about potentially delicate matters. We need add only two riders to this observation. First, as Chapter 4 demonstrated (and as

Peräkylä himself shows), it is not just 'through their questions' that Cs 'create special space for such talk'. For instance, Cs who remain silent during a possible turn-transition point or who offer only the most minimal response-token *may* be able to encourage Ps to tell more.[1] In this way, in the terms of Chapter 9, counselling may turn on the 'incitement to speak'.

The second point is that, as Chapter 4 argues, there are no intrinsically 'delicate' matters. For instance, where parties are routinely or professionally concerned with matters related to sexuality or death (e.g. in case conferences of surgeons treating transexual people or discussion between workers in funeral parlours), one need not expect to find delicacy markers. As it turns out, what is a 'delicate' matter is something that is locally produced and managed as participants themselves assemble some context for their talk.

The demonstrably 'local' character of delicacy relates, I believe, to the issue of 'empathy'. Because this issue, as well as inciting clients to speak, seems to relate to matters of concern to all counsellors extending beyond the field of HIV and AIDS, I will return to these matters in the appropriate section below. For the moment, I will move to the issue of advice-giving in HIV counselling.

Advice-giving

For many counsellors, counselling is essentially non-directive (see Feltham, 1995). One of the features of our data that may shock counsellors working in other areas is the regular presence of advice-giving. I later discuss two issues that arise from this. First, the 'institutional mandate' (Maynard, 1988) that makes HIV counsellors deliver advice, and, second, whether this means that our data is not about 'counselling' but about other activities such as 'information-giving' or 'health promotion'.

For the moment, however, I want to delay these important issues in order to focus simply on the implications of our research for the mechanics of advice-giving and advice reception. As Chapter 6 showed, clients' reception of advice is affected by the conversational environment in which the advice is actually delivered. Attempts to elicit Ps' perspectives prior to the delivery of advice (which advice can therefore be recipient-designed) is strongly correlated with marked acknowledgments of that advice by Ps. Conversely, Ps typically offer minimal acknowledgments to advice which arrives 'out of the blue' without any attempt to elicit their perspective or concerns.

For instance, Chapter 7 shows how P resistance to advice can be minimized, either by packaging a piece of advice as a question about P's perspective (Chapter 7, Extract 7.12, p. 147) or by C offering a candidate formulation of P's perspective to him (as in Extract 7.13, p. 148). On both these occasions, we see the way in which perspective display devices (Maynard, 1991) may align clients to an upcoming piece of advice or, presumably, allow that advice never to be explicitly offered.

In line with Bor, Miller and Goldman's (1992) text on HIV/AIDS counselling, my research has revealed the nature and effectiveness of step-by-step methods of counselling based on the question–answer sequences of the IV format rather than on the delivery of information. Through such methods, clients do indeed learn *relevant* information. More important, following Stoller and Rutherford (1989: S294), they learn the skills to determine what is appropriate for themselves and their partners.

Nonetheless, as shown in Chapters 7 and 8, in contexts like the HIV test, where clients do not necessarily present with a 'problem', personalized advice-giving remains a potentially difficult activity, in part because obtaining the client's perspective can be a slow procedure. Along this line, Chapter 8 examined the *functions* of truncated, information-based ways of delivering advice. Once again, we come to the conclusion that devices which may function well for counsellors' purposes depend upon the kind of leisurely interview which circumstances do not always allow.

Lest readers throw up their hands at my apparent 'support' for what may appear to them to be, in normative terms, 'bad' counselling practice, earlier chapters have shown that I am very aware of the 'dysfunctions' of the professional-centred style of counselling. Not only is there no exploration of the patient's perspective but Ps' minimal responses mean that Cs never know how far Ps are aligned to their information. This lack of patient uptake fails to create an environment in which people might re-examine their own behaviour – a practice demanded in most normative accounts of counselling (e.g. Bor et al., 1992).

Equally, however, apparently 'good' counselling practice, based on extensive elicitation of Ps' perspectives, is fraught with interactional traps (see Peräkylä, 1995). The point is not to adopt a normative position but to examine the gains and losses of any method.

Two possible solutions suggest themselves from the data analysed by this study (see also Silverman et al., 1992a). First, avoiding necessarily 'delicate' and unstable advice sequences but encouraging patients to draw their own conclusions from a particular line of questioning (see Chapter 6, Extract 6.6, p. 121). Second, since both this method and step-by-step advice-giving take considerable time, finding ways of making more time available for what fellow counsellors may see as more effective counselling.

Telling the HIV test result

In Chapter 5 we saw how any delay in delivering the HIV test result in post-test counselling can be analysed by a P to suggest that C is about to deliver a 'positive' result. So while offering the agenda to the P may, in other circumstances, be normatively defined as 'client-centred', in the context of post-test counselling it can create a series of culs-de-sac. In particular, as Maynard (1996) has suggested, the P can hear the C to be 'stalling', leading to misapprehension about the nature of the P's test result.

As I noted in Chapter 5, referring to the comments of a volunteer counsellor, some Cs may delay delivery of the test result in order to keep the attention of their Ps. As Sheon comments:

many clients are tense and ready to bolt out the door as soon as they hear the result, and, even if they don't leave straight away, they are not really mentally present. Because it is a challenge to keep a client for a post-test, *it is sometimes tempting to use the delay of the result as a way to get the client to talk.* (Sheon, personal correspondence; my emphasis)

However, this can lead to extra strain on both C and P as C tries to extricate himself from P's assumption that C's apparent 'stalling' implies the 'bad news' of a positive test result. So Sheon writes:

the strategy of the good counsellor is to siphon off this tension as quickly as possible because the longer you delay disclosure, the tension mounts exponentially and counselling becomes impossible. (ibid.)

As we saw in Chapter 5, Sheon suggests that such a strategy can be deployed simply by C asking: 'Do you have any questions or would you like to get right to the result?' Following this disclosure, health promotion issues can properly be addressed by now asking: 'What originally brought you in for the test?'

Constraints on HIV test counsellors

Throughout this book I have consistently argued that normative questions about what counselling 'is' or 'should be' are, at best, political and, at worst, deflect counsellors from inspecting their experience and researchers from inspecting their data. This implies that the question of 'effective' HIV counselling and 'effective' HIV counsellors can only be addressed in the context of the management of the interactional and practical constraints on counselling practice. There are no simple normative solutions to these constraints – although, as I suggest below, my experience running workshops for such counsellors suggests the value of these kinds of detailed transcript in in-service training provision.

In Chapter 6, I suggested that counselling prior to the HIV-antibody test occurs within at least two major constraints: variable patient flow and the many medical, legal and even economic topics that pre-test counselling is expected to cover. To understand properly the (sometimes perplexing) activities of HIV counsellors described in this volume we must never forget these constraints which relate not just to time and resources but also to the officially defined role of such counsellors or Maynard's (1988) 'institutional mandate'.

For instance, Kinnell and Maynard (1996: 430) note that US HIV counsellors are taught 'that it was important to relay information to the community through their clients'. As they note: 'Counselors' orientations to such goals may explain why they persist in providing recommendations when clients are resistive or even when clients state that advice is irrelevant' (ibid.).

Kinnell and Maynard's observation helpfully explains the apparently perplexing activities of Cs who persist in delivering repetitive chunks of information (as in Chapter 6, Extract 6.3, p. 113) or who encounter resistance from their clients (as in Chapter 7). Like Kinnell and Maynard we have tried to understand 'the concrete difficulties of the counseling task' (Kinnell and Maynard, 1996: 432). Like them, we have demonstrated: 'how counselors presently are embedded in a dilemma that results in impersonal, informational counseling' (ibid.).[2]

The dilemma referred to here also arises where testing centres have to adjust their communication methods to such apparently helpful developments as giving test results on the same day as the test itself. A pilot study which I carried out in such a clinic suggested that the shorter time available for pre-test counselling meant that Cs tended to make an early shift away from the Interview Format (which they had favoured in other clinics) and moved into the rapid coverage of multiple topics through Information Delivery.

This suggests that organizational structures (like same-day test result delivery) have a clear impact on communication. Therefore, focusing on communication techniques alone can be minimal or even harmful. For instance, encouraging patient uptake will usually involve longer counselling sessions. Experienced counsellors will tell you that if they take so long with one client the waiting period for others increases and some clients will simply walk out – and hence may continue their risky behaviour without learning their HIV status.

One possibility that British centres might consider is the US model of group pre-test counselling combined with the completion by patients of individual, confidential questionnaires about their reasons for wanting an HIV test. This is followed by lengthy one-to-one counselling at the *post-test* stage. A second possibility is to retain pre-test individual counselling but to make more use of the time while patients are waiting. Interactive videos, although costly in the short run, might well turn out to be cost-efficient in terms of covering a lot of the ground currently taken up by information delivery by the counsellor. Not only would this allow each counselling session to be more structured to the needs of individual patients but it would also make pre-test counselling far less repetitive and far less boring for the counsellor.

Implications for all counsellors

I have already discussed at length (notably in Chapter 1) the debate in the counselling literature about whether advice-giving is compatible with counselling. Following Feltham (1995), I showed, especially in Chapter 9, how even apparently 'non-directive' styles of counselling, based on the IV format, may imply a piece of professionally defined advice.

Overall, however, I am agnostic about whether the data discussed here are or are not 'counselling'. As Maynard (personal communication) has suggested, if practitioners define themselves as 'counsellors', then that is good enough for the sociologist!

Even if the definition of 'counselling' is, ultimately, a politically contentious but logically empty conceptual puzzle, let me face this issue head on by
beginning with the issue of advice-giving.

Advising and/or counselling

According to one recent text fearlessly called *What is Counselling?* (Feltham, 1995), the dividing line between counselling and advice-giving may be
slightly wobbly. First, 'it would be foolish, if not unethical, to withhold
crucial information or advice when the client is vulnerable or confused'
(Feltham, 1995: 18). Feltham also notes a range of counselling practices
which are highly advice-implicative. For instance:

> 'You might want to consider the advantages of doing X.'
> 'If you want to achieve your goals, then you had better do X.'
> 'I don't want to withhold my opinion sadistically, but I think it's more valuable if
> you find your own solution'.
> (ibid.: 18).

Although, as Feltham notes, such formulations may, in principle, avoid 'the
tyranny of the should', nonetheless, in practice they involve covert advice-
giving. He goes on to point out that a number of influential writers acknowledge that 'persuasion and influence generally is a feature of counselling'
(ibid.: 19). In looking at examples of 'hypothetical questioning' in this book
and elsewhere (notably Peräkylä, 1995), it is difficult to deny that such
apparently 'non-directive' methods involve subtle forms of persuasion.[3]

Whether we talk about 'persuasion', 'advice-giving' or 'leading in a particular direction', this research carries a very clear message about the local
circumstances in which Ps display uptake of Cs' 'messages'. More specifically, in Chapter 6 I showed how Ps are far more likely to demonstrate
'marked acknowledgments' of Cs' advice where that advice is geared to a
problem raised by the P or generated by means of Cs' questions within the
IV format. Conversely, minimal acknowledgments are usually found when
Cs simply deliver information or advice that has an unknown relationship to
Ps' concerns and perspectives. This finding is totally in line with Heritage
and Sefi's (1992) work on British health visitors. Moreover, it fits with
Maynard's (1991) more generally applicable observation that communication tends to work most effectively when tied to a perspective actively
elicited from a client.

Of course, these arguments are not only intuitively predictable but also fit
the client-centredness implied in most accounts of counselling. For instance,
Feltham and Dryden's *Dictionary of Counselling* defines counselling as:

> a principled relationship characterized by the application of one or more psycho-
> logical theories and a recognized set of communication skills, modified by experi-
> ence, intuition and other interpersonal factors, to *clients' intimate concerns,
> problems or aspirations.* (quoted by Feltham, 1995: 8, my emphasis)

So my analysis of advice-giving and advice reception in HIV counselling may be of interest to counsellors not concerned with AIDS or health promotion precisely because it raises relevant general issues about how clients may be involved in the counselling interview.

Counselling and empathy

'Empathy' between professional and client is a central concern of counselling texts. Carl Rogers (1975: 4) has offered a highly respected definition:

> [empathy] means entering the private perceptual world of the other and becoming thoroughly at home in it. It involves being sensitive, moment to moment, to the changing felt meanings which flow in the other person. . . . To be with another in this way means that, for the time being, you lay aside the views and values you hold for yourself in order to enter another's world without prejudice.

A technique held to embody this empathy is for counsellors to use their turns at talk to offer regular *paraphrases* of clients' utterances (Rogers, 1975; Nelson-Jones, 1988), as we saw in Chapter 4, Extract 4.11 (p. 85) and Chapter 6, Extract 6.6 (p. 121).

Such examples give us an interesting contrast with most accounts of empathy. Exemplified by Rogers's definition above (but also see Nelson-Jones, 1982: 212–14), they imply a view of communication as a public process building a bridge between two *private* consciousnesses. This leads to research which treats different verbal and non-verbal modes of action as indications of the underlying characteristics of empathic orientation between the participants (see Ellickson, 1983; Maurer and Tindall, 1983; Barkham and Shapiro, 1986).

The problem with these studies is their unacknowledged leap from public to private, and vice versa.[4] Contrary to these approaches (and to common sense), the above analysis suggests an approach to empathy less as the psychological propensity to attune to the private meanings of the client and more as the social ability to pick up the behavioural cues present in what clients are saying and doing. The core of this process is not the interplay of two private selves, but the interplay of actions making use of publicly available apparatuses of description.

It is evident that, in this perspective, there are no *a priori* right or wrong ways of responding to clients. What works has to be interactionally devised on each occasion. This suggests a revision of the conceptions we have about counselling (and indeed about any profession involved in communicating with clients). The skills of the counsellors we have examined in these extracts are not primarily based on owning a special (professional) body of knowledge. Instead, such skills depend upon an apparatus of description that is publicly available to everyone – including clients, as the extracts above have graphically shown.

The distinctive character of counselling arises in the systematic deployment of this apparatus in encouraging the client to talk.[5]

Counselling 'techniques'?

My discussion above of the limits of identifying 'empathy' with a professional 'technique' is part of a more general argument. Throughout this
book I have argued that we can develop the practical pay-off of counselling
research by avoiding the language of 'communication problems' (which
implies that professionals are bad at their job) and instead examine the
functions of communication sequences in a particular institutional context.
Let me illustrate this point with two different examples already discussed in
this book.

In Chapter 8, I discussed how HIV counsellors sometimes manage to skirt
around some of the problems of personalized advice-giving by designing
what they are saying as potentially hearable as general information. I called
this the Advice-as-Information Sequence, or AIS (see also Kinnell and
Maynard, 1996: 421–2). However I also noted that the AIS is not a
straightforward solution to communication problems. Like any such
'solution', it contains potential dangers or dysfunctions. For just as the
ambiguity it serves to create may manage 'delicate' matters, it may create a
further, less helpful ambiguity: are clients' minimal uptakes to be heard as
acceptance or resistance to the advice they are given?

It seems that, without specific questions, Cs will not know how their client
is responding. But, of course, as we saw in Chapter 4 (and as Peräkylä, 1995
shows in regard to 'dreaded issues') considerable work is often required by
Cs to elicit Ps' talk.

The lesson of the AIS sequence is clear: students of communication and
practitioners should avoid treating 'ambiguities' as problems in need of
solution. Instead, by playing with ambiguities, both Cs and Ps manage
difficult interpersonal relations while displaying considerable interactional
skills.

Many such skills are to be found in what we do in everyday talk. It follows
that attempts at normative definition of counselling 'skills' when abstracted
from the skills (and complexities) of everyday talk can be lopsided.

A second case in point is my discussion of the delayed delivery of an HIV
test result, considered in Chapter 5. As I have already implied, it is
misleading to see the counsellor involved as simply 'mistaken' or 'badly
trained'. First, by pursuing the utterances of his clients in the way that he
does, he is recognizably doing counselling in the way that we have seen other
counsellors fulfil their role (namely, asking questions and delivering
information). Moreover, in making his agenda-offer, he is seeking to align
himself to his client, using a tactic from a range used by apparently 'listening'
or 'non-directive' professionals.[6]

I do not wish to deny that, in post-test counselling, the agenda-offer,
positioned *before* the telling of the result, can create problems for both
clients and counsellors. What is at issue here is simply the *timing* of a tactic
which, when placed elsewhere, may be helpful to all parties. The importance

of this example is simply to remind ourselves that mechanical application of communication 'techniques', without regard to their local relevance, can create confusion rather than mutual understanding.

Training

Feltham (1995) has noted the multiple versions of 'counselling' currently on offer. As I suggested in Chapter 2, the weakness in purely normative versions of counselling is due both to the varying contexts of practice and to the limits of textbook definitions of 'counselling'. For instance, even Bor, Miller and Goldman's (1992) otherwise exemplary text uses 'tidied up' extracts from HIV counselling interviews as well as invented examples.

In the context of such issues, Feltham has suggested that

> training courses will need to pay more attention to these issues, for example by challenging the idea of pure, core, theoretical models and by taking research and critiques of counselling more seriously. (Feltham, 1995: 163)

Following Feltham, I have argued that the limits of normative versions of counselling not based on analysis of real-time counselling interviews are seen most clearly in the training of counsellors.

Conventional training courses seek to impart many of the following skills noted by Feltham:

> attentive listening, accurate understanding, an ability to articulate what one has heard and understood and to know how to paraphrase and to summarize another's concerns expressed through conversation, an ability to engage emotionally with others and so on. (Feltham, 1995: 23)

However, in teaching such skills through normative instruction or role-plays, one can easily miss some of the complexities of actual counselling practice – both the problems that counsellors encounter and the practical solutions they find in the constraints of routine counselling practice.

In this book, I have argued that the theoretically guided analysis of detailed transcripts of actual counselling interviews can make a significant contribution to counselling practice.[7] The implication is that effective training begins from a close analysis of the skills of counsellors and their clients revealed in careful research rather than from normative standards of good practice.

As our workshops with counsellors show, professionals respond to research which seeks to document the fine detail of their practice, while acknowledging the structural constraints to which they must respond. Put another way, this means that we should aim to identify the interactional skills of the participants rather than their failings. Although the researcher cannot tell practitioners how they should behave, understanding the intended and unintended consequences of actions can provide the basis for a fruitful dialogue.

Counselling as troubles talk

Counselling is a pervasive activity in contemporary institutional life. It is, for example, an aspect of such diverse institutions as religious organizations, schools, businesses, hospitals, prisons, the military, and human service agencies. As we have seen in this book, following Peräkylä (1995), a central plank of counselling activity consists of counsellors asking questions. In the case of 'systemic' or 'family therapy' counselling, questions often serve to elicit what Miller and I have called 'troubles' (Miller and Silverman, 1995).

As defined in Chapter 9, troubles talk consists of portrayals of (and interactions about) aspects of people's lives as undesired and, perhaps, warranting change in behaviour or perspectives. Troubles talk can range from portrayals of people's life experiences as serious problems that necessitate professional intervention to portrayals of undesired circumstances as mildly irksome, to denials of the existence of any trouble. However, in every instance, I argue that the description of a trouble is co-operatively achieved through the ways counsellors and clients monitor and respond to each other's talk.

Through troubles talk, counsellors fulfil many of their most important professional responsibilities to their clients and colleagues. At the same time, by inciting clients to speak, counsellors take their place not only among the caring professions but also, to some extent, within a society in which the 'confessional' is a central technique of tabloid newspapers and television chat shows (see also Silverman and Atkinson, forthcoming). Not only do clients 'confess' but, over time, they can come to adopt counsellors' own rheoric. This was true in US family therapy sessions with long-term clients and in UK counselling with haemophilia clients.

In focusing on people who have been counselled over many years, we see writ large the micro-politics of counselling as a preferred solution to personal problems. Along with magazines and talk shows, counselling and the other 'psy' disciplines (Donzelot, 1979) encourage us to turn our gaze on ourselves and our partners.

Of course, this is not to criticize counselling. Like many other caring professionals, counsellors enable us to achieve our ends. At the same time, like any discourse, the discourse of 'enablement' is both multi-faceted and, inevitably, involved in networks of power.

Notes

1. Of course, the relative silence of the analyst is often treated as a defining characteristic of the psychoanalytic method. I am reminded of a recent play by Terry Johnson performed in London. Johnson's *Hysteria* begins and ends with Freud saying that if you think he is going to break the silence, then you are mistaken!

2 Unlike Kinnell and Maynard (1996), perhaps because our research covers many centres, we also find non-directive styles of AIDS counselling based on the Interview Format (see also Peräkylä, 1995). Chapter 7 of this book shows, in addition, a counselling method based not primarily on information-giving but on highly directive, personalized advice-giving.

3. Extract 6.6, Chapter 6 (p. 121) is very much a case in point. In this Extract, C abstains throughout from actually delivering advice about safer sex. Nonetheless, his extended sequence of hypothetical questions leaves P in little doubt about the 'message' he is implying.

4. An important opening has been made by Barrett-Leonard (1981), who wants to treat empathy as an interactional process, rather than as a quality of individuals or relations. But he also shares the above-mentioned model of communication in which communication is between two private selves, mediated through the public sphere.

5. I am most grateful to Anssi Peräkylä for this way of formulating the practical import of our research.

6. Anssi Peräkylä (personal communication) has raised the provocative question of whether I am implying that all counsellors, whatever they do, are always skilful. I see that we might reach this (presumably absurd) conclusion by an over-mechanistic reading of conversation analysis's emphasis on the local functions of any turn-at-talk. It is obviously important to distinguish between this analytic version of 'skilfulness' and more practical versions which, quite properly, in their own terms, seek to identify skill 'deficits'. The only sense in which the latter version may be limited would be when its users failed to relate their identification of professional 'skills' to what-we-all-do-in-common in everyday conversation.

7. See Table 1.3, p. 14.

Appendix 1:
The History of the Research Project

The study discussed here emerged out of my work as a medical sociologist. Between 1979 and 1985, I worked on data from British outpatient consultations which involved parents and children. At the same time, I also conducted a small study of adult oncology clinics, comparing National Health Service (NHS) and private consultations conducted by the same doctor. This research was reported in a number of papers (Silverman, 1981, 1983, 1984; Silverman and Bloor, 1989) and brought together in a book (Silverman, 1987). In that book, I focused on how apparently 'patient-centred' medicine can work in many different directions, one of which can be quite coercive.

In 1987 I was given permission to sit in at a weekly clinic held at the Genito-Urinary Department of an English inner-city hospital (Silverman, 1989a). The clinic's purpose was to monitor the progress of HIV-positive patients who were taking the drug AZT (Retrovir). AZT, which seems able to slow down the rate at which the virus reproduces itself, was then at an experimental stage of its development.

Like any observational study, the aim was to gather first-hand information about social processes in a 'naturally occurring' context. As in the present study (see Chapter 2) no attempt was made to interview the individuals concerned, because the focus was upon what they actually did in the clinic rather than upon what they thought about what they did. The researcher was present in the consulting room at a side angle to both doctors and patient.

Patients' consent for the researcher's presence was obtained by the senior doctor. Given the presumed sensitivity of the occasion, tape-recording was not attempted. Instead, detailed handwritten notes were kept, using a separate sheet for each consultation. The sample was small (15 male patients seen in 37 consultations over seven clinic sessions) and no claims were made about its representativeness. Because observational methods were rare in this area, the study was essentially exploratory. However, an attempt was made to link the findings to other social research about doctor–patient relations.

As Sontag (1979) has noted, illness is often taken as a moral or psychological metaphor. The major finding of this early study was the moral baggage attached to being HIV positive. For instance, many patients used a buzzer to remind them to take their medication during the night. As one commented: 'It's a dead giveaway. Everybody knows what you've got.' However, despite the social climate in which HIV infection is viewed, there was considerable variation in how people presented themselves to the medical team. Four styles of 'self-presentation' (Goffman, 1955) were identified which I called 'cool', 'anxious', 'objective' and 'theatrical' (see Silverman, 1989a). But there was no simple correspondence between each patient and a particular 'style' of self-presentation. Each way of presenting oneself was available to each patient within any one consultation, where it might have a particular social function. So the focus was on social processes rather than on psychological states.

Along the way, I also discovered how an ethos of 'positive thinking' was central to many patients' accounts and how doctors systematically concentrated on the 'bodies' rather than the 'minds' of their patients. This led on to some practical questions about the division of labour between doctors and counsellors.

About the time I was writing up this research, Kaye Wellings, who was then working for the publicly funded Health Education Authority (HEA), approached me about the possibility of extending my research to HIV counselling. Until that time, the HEA had been funding research on the effectiveness of 'safer sex' messages carried in the mass media. In the light of the explosion in the number of HIV tests in the UK in the late 1980s, Kaye thought it might be useful to take a longer look at the effectivess of the health promotion messages being delivered in counselling people around the HIV-antibody test. I was interested in such a study for two reasons. First, it was the logical development of my study of medical interviews with AIDS patients. Second, it offered the opportunity to pursue my interest in looking at how communication between professionals and their clients worked out in practice – as opposed to the injunctions of textbooks and training manuals. Consequently, I submitted a research proposal and received funding from the HEA for 30 months beginning in late 1988.

As it turned out, receiving the funding was only the first part of what became a battle to recruit HIV testing centres for the research. It must be remembered that the late 1980s was a time when AIDS health workers were being flooded by patients and by requests from researchers anxious to study AIDS care. Apart from such overload, two other factors complicated access. First, obviously, were the multiple ethical issues involved in studying consultations where patients were asked to reveal the most intimate aspects of their behaviour. Second, extra patients and government worries about the AIDS 'pandemic' had brought sudden huge increases in resources to the previously 'Cinderella' branch of medicine treating patients with sexually transmitted diseases. Following the usual pattern, these resource changes produced 'turf' battles between different professions and different centres involved in the AIDS field (see Silverman, 1990).

All this meant that many months were taken in obtaining research access. One leading British centre turned me down, offering the understandable reason that they were already overloaded with researchers. At another such centre, a doctor gave me access but the counsellors subsequently proved very resistant to me observing or tape-recording their HIV consultations. Eventually, a compromise was reached whereby I myself was required to request patients to agree to participate in the research. Predictably, very few agreed in these circumstances.

Just as I thought that I had been funded for a study that I could never carry out, my luck began to turn. Riva Miller and Robert Bor agreed to offer me access to their counselling work with, respectively, haemophiliacs and the general population at the Royal Free Hospital (RFH) in London. This was a major breakthrough in two respects: Miller and Bor had just produced a major book (Miller and Bor, 1988) on using the 'systemic' method in AIDS counselling, and they had a video archive of the work of their clinics going back to the early 1980s.

On the basis of my access at the RFH, a major pharmaceuticals company, Glaxo Holdings plc (now Glaxo Wellcome) agreed to fund a two-year study (subsequently increased to three years) of the video archive. I was then lucky enough to recruit Anssi Peräkylä from Finland as Glaxo Research Fellow to work on this archive. Anssi had already conducted distinguished ethnographic work in hospital settings. Following his appointment, he more or less taught himself conversation analysis and had finished his PhD on the RFH data in three years, as well as publishing many articles both jointly with me and/or Bor and on his own. Gradually, other centres joined the project and data were also obtained directly from centres in the USA and Trinidad, as well as from Douglas Maynard's US HIV counselling materials (see Chapter 8).

As the research started to take off, great attention had to be paid to the ethical issues involved. We ended up with a method of recruitment whereby counsellors themselves explained the research to patients (often with the aid of written materials) and invited them to participate. Consent was sought on the understanding that the anonymity of all patients would be strictly protected by concealing their names (and other identifying information) in reports or publications. In addition, only Peräkylä, myself and a limited number of trained researchers and transcribers would have access to the audiotapes. The RFH videotapes were given additional protection – Peräkylä himself transcribed them, so access to them was limited to Peräkylä and myself, and the videos were never to be publicly shown or indeed to leave the premises of the RFH.

The methodology we used is discussed at length in Chapter 2. In this Appendix, I will only mention a few practical matters that may be of interest to researchers. In a multiple centre study I could not, as in my earlier work, be physically present as all the data were gathered. Instead, the audiotapes were simply sent to me by each of the centres for analysis. Soon we were inundated by data to be passed on to our main transcriber, Dr David Greatbatch, himself a distinguished CA researcher.

However, given the high quality of transcription required and our limited resources, it became totally impracticable to transcribe all the tapes. Instead, a few interviews were transcribed from each centre. On this basis, what I can best call 'candidate hypotheses' were developed about particular features in the talk, for instance how health advice was delivered and received. Peräkylä and I would then transcribe multiple instances from many more interviews where relevant phenomena seemed to occur.

In this way, the initial hypotheses were refined and subject to the test of 'deviant cases' which we actively sought out in our data. Overall, our method had much in common with the traditional method of 'analytic induction' commonly used by anthropologists and ethnographers (see Silverman, 1993: Ch.7).

Feedback and implementation

During the course of the research, we held many workshops for HIV counsellors – including many who had not participated in the study. To give some idea of the extent of this 'feedback', between 1989 and 1994 I ran four workshops on the research for counsellors in London (two at hospitals, one at Goldsmiths' College and one at the Royal Society of Medicine), as well as three workshops in Australian centres, three in Trinidad and Tobago, and one each in the USA, Finland and Sweden. In addition, each participating centre was given a detailed report of our findings.

The practical implications of our research are discussed in Chapter 10. I would only add my personal sadness that, despite my best efforts, the HEA was not able to push our findings into the public debate about health promotion and HIV. I hope that this book in some way manages to make good that deficiency.

Appendix 2:
The Data-Base

The overall total of interviews obtained was 195. These interviews derived from 11 HIV testing centres (seven UK, three US and one Trinidad).

In the present study, the following data have been excluded from this corpus:

Interviews in British genito-urinary medicine clinics where the professional is a medical doctor: these were excluded because they usually followed the standard model of a medical history-taking and so were not directly relevant to our interest in counselling. Indeed, in the British pattern, if patients requested an HIV test, they were then passed to a health adviser for pre-test counselling.[1]

Two UK hospital centres were excluded for the simple reason that funds ran out before their data could be transcribed.

Two non-UK centres were also excluded. One US centre was excluded because of the very limited data obtained. The Trinidad data, although fascinating, is, regretfully, also almost entirely excluded from this book. The tapes had to be locally transcribed because of the dialect used and I was really only confident in analysing them with the help of a linguist from the University of the West Indies, Dr Valerie Youssef (but see Youssef and Silverman, 1992).

Having excluded the material above, this book is based on the analysis of 93 HIV counselling interviews. Of these, 65 are pre-test, 16 post-test and 12 are with people living with HIV or AIDS. Only a limited amount of data from the Royal Free Hospital's Haemophilia Centre has been used here (largely in Chapter 9). This centre was the focus of Peräkylä's research and is fully reported by him elsewhere (Peräkylä, 1995).

To this data I have added, for comparative purposes, some material from a US family therapy centre collected by Gale Miller and analysed with him (discussed in Chapter 9).

Table A.1 sets out details of the data obtained from each centre discussed in this book. The code for each centre (e.g. UK1) is used before each data extract discussed.

Table A.1 *HIV counselling data-base: interviews at each centre*

Centre	Pre-test	Other	Counsellor
UK1 GUM	10	0	HA
UK2 GUM	12	1 (+)	HA
UK3 GUM	13	0	HA
UK4 Clinic	9	1 (+)	HA
UK5 HC	0	10 (+)	SW, Dr
US1 Clinic	0	16 (post-test)	C
US2 Clinic	21	0	C

GUM = Hospital Department of Genito-Urinary Medicine
HA   = British health adviser
SW   = Social worker
Dr   = Doctor
C   = Counsellor
(+) = person living with HIV or AIDS
HC   = Haemophilia centre

I now provide some information about each of the centres included in the study. Further general details about the organization of HIV counselling are provided in Chapter 1.

Centres in this study

UK1,2 and 3

These centres are all British sexually transmitted diseases clinics in Departments of Genito-Urinary Medicine in big city hospitals. The counsellors are called health advisers and are nearly all nurses, many with experience of 'contact-tracing' for sexually transmitted diseases. With the emergence of HIV and AIDS, they have taken on the role of pre- and post-test HIV counselling as well as being health adviser to seropositive patients seen in the department. To complement their earlier experience, they have attended AIDS training courses run at a national centre. Patients are either referred to these counsellors from a doctor in the clinic or self-refer for an HIV test.

UK4

This centre is also in a British hospital but, unlike the other British centres, it is not associated with the hospital's GUM Department but with a Department of Infectious Diseases. Patients make telephone appointments for an HIV test and are counselled by staff from a range of backgrounds, including clinical psychology, who are all trained in 'systemic' methods. Many consultations are routinely videotaped.

UK5

This is a haemophilia centre in a British hospital, associated with UK4. Like UK4, it employs a range of staff who are trainers or training in 'systemic' methods. All patients may have become exposed to HIV through the transfusion of infected blood products. The centre had provided counselling for haemophiliacs and their families for many years before the HIV epidemic was identified. Counselling was part of clients' routine visits to the centre for assessment and treatment of haemophilia. Some clients represented in our data had been coming for counselling at the centre for twenty or more years.

Clients were expressly invited to include their 'significant others' in counselling sessions. Depending on clients' age, their significant others might be parents, partners and/or friends. While there were always at least two counsellors present, one counsellor always took the leading role in counselling sessions. The other counsellors only asked questions through the lead counsellor. Although the counsellors come from diverse professional backgrounds (social work and medicine), they all practise a theoretically based counselling method derived from the systemic methods of family therapy (see Miller and Bor, 1988; Bor et al., 1992).

US1

This is a clinic in a major US city. Data have been taken from a gay men's health clinic and from a general walk-in HIV clinic. Staff are mainly volunteer counsellors whose training has elements of 'systemic' methods. In the gay men's clinic, the counsellors share the sexual orientation and gender of their clients. This centre only offers post-test counselling. Prior to that, each patient participates in a group question-and-answer session about the HIV test, fills out a questionnaire with details of their concerns and has blood taken. Blood testing is anonymized by a coding process. Each patient is asked to provide a set of numbers which are then used to set up a 'code' for their blood sample (and hence for their own test result).

US2

This is an HIV test centre in another US urban area. This centre does do one-to-one pre-test counselling. However, like US1, patients here fill in a questionnaire prior to the interview to which counsellors refer. Other similarities to US1 are the use of volunteer counsellors and anonymized blood testing. Data from this centre are also discussed in Kinnell and Maynard (1996). Doug Maynard has kindly provided me with this data-set.

US3

This is the only non-AIDS-related counselling discussed in this book. It is a family therapy centre, a private agency located in a city in the United States. Clients bring a wide variety of troubles, including marriage dissolution, eating disorders and problems in school. The therapists practise brief therapy, meaning that they emphasize finding solutions to their clients' troubles (not deep insight into their causes) in a minimum of sessions. Brief therapy is implemented by the use of a therapeutic team. Clients meet with a therapist in an interviewing room and one or more therapists (the team) observe from an adjoining observation room. Team members could and occasionally did communicate with the interviewer by means of an in-house telephone system. Typically, their communications consisted of requests for further information from clients or a recommendation that the interviewer utilize a different interviewing strategy. The interviews focused on clients' reasons for seeking therapy, the establishment of therapeutic goals, and whether clients were achieving their goals.

Note

1. The doctors' interviews are currently being analysed by Vicki Taylor who is working for a PhD, under my supervision, at Goldsmiths' College. Vicki is particularly interested in how doctors and counsellors organize a request for blood samples for non-AIDS related sexually transmitted diseases.

Appendix 3:
Simplified Transcription Symbols

Symbol	Example	Explanation
[	C2: quite a [while Mo: [yea	Left brackets indicate the point at which a current speaker's talk is overlapped by another's talk.
=	W: that I'm aware of = C: =Yes. Would you confirm that?	Equal signs, one at the end of a line and one at the beginning, indicate no gap between the two lines.
(.4)	Yes (.2) yeah	Numbers in parentheses indicate elapsed time in silence in tenths of a second.
(.)	to get (.) treatment	A dot in parentheses indicates a tiny gap, probably no more than one-tenth of a second.
_____	What's up?	Underscoring indicates some form of stress, via pitch and/or amplitude.
::	O:kay?	Colons indicate prolongation of the immediately prior sound. The length of the row of colons indicates the length of the prolongation.
WORD	I've got ENOUGH TO WORRY ABOUT	Capitals, except at the beginnings of lines, indicate especially loud sounds relative to the surrounding talk.
.hhhh	I feel that (.2) .hhh	A row of h's prefixed by a dot indicates an inbreath; without a dot, an outbreath. The length of the row of h's indicates the length of the in- or outbreath.
( )	future risks and ( ) and life ( )	Empty parentheses indicate the transcriber's inability to hear what was said.
(word)	Would you see (there) anything positive	Parenthesized words are possible hearings.
(( ))	confirm that ((continues))	Double parentheses contain author's descriptions rather than transcriptions.
. , ?	What do you think?	Indicate speaker's intonation (. = falling intonation; , = flat or slightly rising intonation).
-	becau-	Hyphen indicates an abrupt cut-off of the sound in progress.

| ^ | dr^ink | A 'hat' or circumflex accent indicates a marked pitch rise. |
| ---> | 1 ---> | Arrows in the margin point to the lines of transcript relevant to a point made in the text. |

References

Aggleton, P. (1989) 'Evaluating Health Education about AIDS', in P. Aggleton, G. Hart and P. Davies (eds), *AIDS: Social Representations, Social Practices*. Lewes: Falmer Press. pp. 220–36.

Atkinson, J. M. and Drew, P. (1976) *Order in Court*. Atlantic Highlands, N.J.: Humanities Press.

Atkinson, J. M. and Heritage, J. (eds) (1984) *Structures of Social Action*. Cambridge: Cambridge University Press.

Atkinson, P. (1995) 'Some Perils of Paradigms', *Qualitative Health Research*, 5: 117–24.

Baldock, J. and Prior, D. (1981) 'Social Workers Talking to Clients: a Study of Verbal Behaviour', *British Journal of Social Work*, 11: 19–38.

Barkham, M. and Shapiro, D. A. (1986) 'Counselor Verbal Response Modes and Experienced Empathy', *Journal of Counselling Psychology*, 33(1): 3–10.

Barrett-Leonard, G. T. (1981) 'The Empathy Cycle – Refinement of a Nuclear Concept', *Journal of Counselling Psychology*, 28: 91–100.

Beardsell, S., Hickson, F. and Weatherburn, P. (1995) *HIV Testing Services in North Thames (East)*. London: North Thames Regional Health Authority.

Beck, E. et al. (1987) 'HIV Testing: Changing Trends at a Clinic for Sexually Transmitted Diseases', *British Medical Journal*, 295: 191–3.

Bergmann, J. (1992) 'Veiled Morality: Notes on Discretion in Psychiatry', in Drew and Heritage (1992b). pp. 137–62.

Bernstein, B. (1971) *Class, Codes and Control, Vol. 1: Theoretical Studies towards a Sociology of Language*. London: Routledge.

Bloor, M. (1978) 'On the Analysis of Observational Data: a Discussion of the Worth and Uses of Inductive Techniques and Respondent Validation', *Sociology*, 12(3): 545–57.

Boden, D. and Zimmerman, D. (eds) (1991) *Talk and Social Structure*. Cambridge: Polity Press.

Bond, T. (1990) *HIV Counselling: Report on National Survey and Consultation*. London: British Association for Counselling/Department of Health.

Bor, R. (1989) 'AIDS Counselling', *AIDS Care*, 1(2): 184–7.

Bor, R., Miller, R. and Goldman, E. (1992) *Theory and Practice of HIV Counselling: a Systemic Approach*. London: Cassell.

Bourdieu, P. (1979) *Outline of a Theory of Practice*. Cambridge: Cambridge University Press.

Brown, P. and Levinson, S. (1987) *Politeness: Some Universals in Language Usage*. Cambridge: Cambridge University Press.

Bryman, A. (1988) *Quantity and Quality in Social Research*. London: Unwin Hyman.

Cade, B. and O'Hanlon, W. H. (1993) *A Brief Guide to Brief Therapy*. New York: W.W. Norton.

Carballo, M. and Miller, D. (1989) 'HIV Counselling: Problems and Opportunities in Defining the New Agenda for the 1990s', *AIDS Care*, 1(2): 117–23.

Chester, R. (1987) *Advice, Support and Counselling for the HIV Positive: a Report for DHSS*. Hull: Department of Social Policy and Professional Studies, University of Hull.

Cicourel, A. (1964) *Method and Measurement in Sociology*. New York: Free Press.

Clavarino, A., Najman, J. and Silverman, D. (1995) 'The Quality of Qualitative Data: Two Strategies for Analyzing Medical Interviews', *Qualitative Inquiry*, 1(2): 223–42.

Clayman, S. C. (1992) 'Footing in the Achievement of Neutrality: the Case of News-interview Discourse', in Drew and Heritage (1992b). pp. 163–98.

Coxon, A. (1989) 'Who's Doing What and To Whom . . .', *The Times Higher Education Supplement*, 17 November.

Cuff, E. C. (1980) Some Issues in Studying the Problem of Versions in Everyday Life. (Manchester Sociology Occasional Papers, No. 3), Department of Sociology, Manchester University.

Denzin, N. and Lincoln, Y. (eds) (1994) *A Handbook of Qualitative Research*. London: Sage.

de Shazer, S. (1982) *Patterns of Brief Family Therapy: An Ecosystemic Approach*. New York: Guilford Press.

Dingwall, R. (1980) 'Orchestrated Encounters', *Sociology of Health and Illness*, 2: 151–73.

Donzelot, J. (1979) *The Policing of Families*. London: Hutchinson.

Drew, P. and Heritage, J. (1992a) 'Analyzing Talk at Work', in Drew and Heritage (1992b). pp.3–65.

Drew, P. and Heritage, J. (eds) (1992b) *Talk at Work*. Cambridge: Cambridge University Press.

Drew, P. and Holt, E. (1988) 'Complainable Matters: the Use of Idiomatic Expressions in Making Complaints', *Social Problems*, 35(4): 398–417.

Drew, P. and Wootton, A. (eds) (1988) *Erving Goffman: Exploring the Interaction Order*. Cambridge: Polity Press.

Ellickson, J. L. (1983) 'Representational Systems and Eye Movements in an Interview', *Journal of Counselling Psychology*, 30(3): 339–45.

Emerson, R. M. and Messinger, S. L. (1977) 'The Micro-Politics of Trouble', *Social Problems*, 25: 121–35.

Feltham, C. (1995) *What is Counselling?* London: Sage.

Fenton, T. (1987) 'AIDS and Psychiatry: Practical, Social and Ethical Issues', *Journal of the Royal Society of Medicine*, 80: 271–5.

Foucault, M. (1973) *The Birth of the Clinic*, trans. Alan Sheridan. New York: Pantheon.

Foucault, M. (1977) *Discipline and Punish*, trans. Alan Sheridan. New York: Pantheon.

Foucault, M. (1979) *The History of Sexuality: Volume 1*, trans. Robert Hurley. Harmondsworth: Penguin.

Foucault, M. (1980) *Power/Knowledge*, ed. and trans. Colin Gordon. New York: Pantheon.

Garfinkel, E. (1967) *Studies in Ethnomethodology*. Englewood Cliffs, NJ: Prentice-Hall.

Goedert, J. (1987) 'What is Safe Sex? Suggested Standards Linked to Testing for Human Immunodeficiency Virus', *New England Journal of Medicine*, 316(21): 1339–42.

Goffman, E. (1955) 'On Face-work: An Analysis of Ritual Elements in Social Interaction', *Psychiatry: Journal for the Study of Inter-personal Processes*, 18(3): 213–31.

Goffman, E. (1974) *Frame Analysis*. New York: Harper & Row.

Goffman, E. (1981) *Forms of Talk*. Oxford: Basil Blackwell.

Goldenberg, I. and Goldenberg, H. (1991) *Family Therapy: An Overview*. Pacific Grove, CA: Brooks/Cole.

Greatbatch, D. (1988) 'A Turn-taking System for British News Interviews', *Language in Society*, 17: 401–30.

Green, J. (1989) 'Counselling for HIV Infection and AIDS: the Past and the Future', *AIDS Care*, 1(1): 5–10.

Greenblat, C. (1989) 'An Innovation Programme of Counselling Family Members and Friends of Seropositive Haemophiliacs', *AIDS Care*, 1(1): 67–75.

Gubrium, J. (1989) 'Local Cultures and Service Policy', in J. Gubrium and D. Silverman (eds), *The Politics of Field Research: Sociology beyond Enlightenment*. London: Sage. pp. 94–112.

Gubrium, J. (1992) *Out of Control: Family Therapy and Domestic Disorder*. London: Sage.

Gubrium, J. and Silverman, D. (eds) (1989) *The Politics of Field Research: Sociology beyond Enlightenment*. London: Sage.

Heath, C. (1988) 'Embarrassment and Interactional Organization', in Drew and Wootton (1988). pp. 136–60.

Heath, C. (1992) 'The Delivery and Reception of Diagnosis in the General Practice Consultation', in Drew and Heritage (1992b). pp. 235–67.

Heaton, J. M. (1979) 'Theory in Psychotherapy', in N. Bolton (ed.), *Philosophical Problems in Psychology*. London: Methuen. pp. 179–98.

Henry, K. (1988) 'Setting AIDS Priorities: The Need for a Closer Alliance of Public Health and Clinical Approaches towards the Control of AIDS', *American Journal of Public Health*, 78(9): 1210–12.

Heritage, J. (1984) *Garfinkel and Ethnomethodology*. Cambridge: Polity Press.

Heritage, J. and Greatbatch, D. (1991) 'On the Institutional Character of Institutional Talk', in Boden and Zimmermann (1991). pp. 93–137.

Heritage, J. and Sefi, S. (1992) 'Dilemmas of Advice: Aspects of the Delivery and Reception of Advice in Interactions between Health Visitors and First Time Mothers', in Drew and Heritage (1992b). pp. 359–417.

Hill, C. E. et al. (1988) *Therapist Techniques and Client Outcomes: Eight Cases of Brief Psychotherapy*. London: Sage.

Hodgkin, P. (1988) 'HIV Infection: the Challenge to General Practitioners', *British Medical Journal*, 296: 516–17.

Horvath, A. O. and Greenberg, L. S. (1986) 'Development of the Working Appliance Inventory', in L. Greenberg and W. Pinshof (eds), *The Psychotherapeutic Process: A Research Handbook*. New York: Guilford Press. pp. 529–56.

Hughes, D. (1982) 'Control in the Medical Consultation', *Sociology*, 16: 359–76.

Hutchby, I. (1995) 'Aspects of Recipient Design in Expert Advice-Giving on Call-In Radio', *Discourse Processes*, 19: 219–38.

Jefferson, G. (1980) 'On "Trouble-premonitory" Response to Inquiry', *Sociological Inquiry*, 50 (3/4): 153–85.

Jefferson, G. (1984) 'Notes on a Systematic Deployment of the Acknowledgment Tokens Yeah and Mm-hm', *Papers in Linguistics*, 17: 197–216.

Jefferson, G. (1985) 'On the Interactional Unpackaging of a "Gloss"', *Language in Society*, 14: 435–66.

Jefferson, G. (1988) 'On the Sequential Organization of Troubles-Talk in Ordinary Conversation', *Social Problems*, 35: 418–41.

Jefferson, G. and Lee, J. (1981) 'The Rejection of Advice: Managing the Problematic Convergence of a "Troubles-Telling" and a "Service Encounter"', *Journal of Pragmatics*, 5(5): 399–422.

Jefferson, G. and Lee, J. (1992) 'The Rejection of Advice: Managing the Problematic Convergence of a "Troubles-Telling" and a "Service Encounter"', in Drew and Heritage (1992b). pp. 521–48.

Kinnell, A. M. and Maynard, D. W. (1996) 'The Delivery and Receipt of Safer Sex Advice in Pre-Test Counseling Sessions for HIV and AIDS', *Journal of Contemporary Ethnography*, 24(4): 405–37.

Kirk, J. and Miller, M. (1986) *Reliability and Validity in Qualitative Research* (Qualitative Research Methods Series, Vol. 1). London: Sage.

Kofmehl, A. M. (1992) 'Doing a "Proposal of the Situation" in the Delivery and Receipt of Safer Sex Advice'. MSc thesis, Department of Sociology, University of Wisconsin-Madison.

Kuhn, T. S. (1962) *The Structure of Scientific Revolutions*. Chicago: University of Chicago Press.

Levinson, S. C. (1983) *Pragmatics*. Cambridge: Cambridge University Press.

Lipchik, E. (1988) *Interviewing*. Rockville, MD: Aspen Publications.

Lynch, M. (1985) *Art and Artifact in Laboratory Science*. London: Routledge.

McKeganey, N. (forthcoming) 'Being Positive: Drug Injectors' Experiences of HIV Infection', Social Paediatric and Obstetric Research Unit, University of Glasgow.

McLeod, J. (1994) *Doing Counselling Research*. London: Sage.

Marshall, C. and Rossman, G. (1989) *Designing Qualitative Research*. London: Sage.

Maurer, R. A. and Tindall, J. H. (1983) 'Effects of Postural Congruence on Clients' Perception of Counsellor Empathy', *Journal of Counselling Psychology*, 30(2): 158–63.

Maynard, D. W. (1985) 'On the Functions of Social Conflict Among Children', *American Sociological Review*, 50, 207–33.

Maynard, D. W. (1988) 'Language, Interaction, and Social Problems', *Social Problems*, 35: 311–34.

Maynard, D. W. (1989) 'On the Ethnography and Analysis of Discourse in Institutional Settings', in J. A. Holstein and G. Miller (eds), *Perspectives on Social Problems*, Vol. 1. Greenwich, CT: JAI Press. pp. 127–46.

Maynard, D. W. (1991) 'Interaction and Asymmetry in Clinical Discourse', *American Journal of Sociology*, 97(2): 448–95.

Maynard, D. W. (1992) 'On Clinicians Co-implicating Recipients' Perspective in the Delivery of Diagnostic News', in Drew and Heritage (1992b). pp. 331–58.

Maynard, D. W. (1996) 'On "Realization" in Everyday Life: The Forecasting of Bad News as a Social Relation', *American Sociological Review*, in press.

Maynard, D. W. and Clayman, S. (1991) 'The Diversity of Ethnomethodology', *Annual Review of Sociology*, 17: 385–418.

Mehan, H. (1979) *Learning Lessons: Social Organization in the Classroom*. Cambridge, MA: Harvard University Press.

Merritt, M. (1976) 'On Questions following Questions (in Service Encounters)', *Language in Society*, 7: 183–213.

Miller, D. (1987) 'Counselling', *British Medical Journal*, 294: 1671–4.

Miller, D. (1988) 'HIV and Social Psychiatry', *British Medical Bulletin*, 44(1): 130–48.

Miller, D. and Pinching, A. J. (1989) 'HIV Tests and Counselling: Current Issues', *AIDS*, 3 (Supplement 1): S187–93.

Miller, D. et al. (1986) 'Organizing a Counselling Service for Problems Related to AIDS', *Genitourinary Medicine*, 62: 116–22.

Miller, G. (1986) 'Depicting Family Trouble: A Micro-Political Analysis of the Therapeutic Interview', *Journal of Strategic and Systemic Therapies*, 5: 1–13.

Miller, G. (1987) 'Producing Family Problems: Organization and Uses of the Family Perspective and Rhetoric in Family Therapy', *Symbolic Interaction*, 10: 245–65.

Miller, G. (1990) 'Work as Reality Maintaining Activity: Interactional Aspects of Occupational and Professional Work', *Current Research on Occupations and Professions*, 5: 163–83.

Miller, G. (1994) 'Toward Ethnographies of Institutional Discourse: Proposal and Suggestions', *Journal of Contemporary Ethnography*, 23: 280–306.

Miller, G. and Holstein, J. A. (1995) 'Dispute Domains: Organizational Contexts and Dispute Processing', *Sociological Quarterly*, 36: 37–59.

Miller, G. and Silverman, D. (1995) 'Troubles Talk and Counseling Discourse: A Comparative Study', *Sociological Quarterly*, 36, 4: 725–47.

Miller, R. and Bor, R. (1988) *AIDS – A Guide to Clinical Counselling*, London: Science Press.

Mitchell, J. C. (1983) 'Case and Situational Analysis', *Sociological Review*, 31(2): 187–211.

Molotch, H. and Boden, D. (1985) 'Talking Social Structure', *American Sociological Review*, 50: 573–88.

Morrow-Bradley, C. and Elliott, R. (1986) 'Utilization of Psychotherapy Research by Practicing Psychotherapists', *American Psychologist*, 41(2): 188–97.

Nelkin, D. (1987) 'AIDS and the Social Sciences: Review of Useful Knowledge and Research Needs', *Reviews of Infectious Diseases*, 9(5): 980–7.

Nelson-Jones, R. (1982) *The Theory and Practice of Counselling Psychology*. London: Cassell.

Nelson-Jones, R. (1988) *Practical Counselling and Helping Skills*, 2nd edn. London: Cassell.

Parsons, T. (1951) *The Social System*. Glencoe, IL: The Free Press.

Peräkylä, A. (1993) 'Invoking a Hostile World: Patients' Future in AIDS Counselling', *Text*, 13: 291–316.

Peräkylä, A. (1995) *AIDS Counselling: Institutional Interaction and Clinical Practice*. Cambridge: Cambridge University Press.

Peräkylä, A. and Bor, R. (1990) 'Interactional Problems of Addressing "Dreaded Issues" in HIV Counselling', *AIDS Care*, 2(4): 325–38.

Peräkylä, A. and Silverman, D. (1991a) 'Reinterpreting Speech-exchange Systems: Communication Formats in AIDS Counselling', *Sociology*, 25(4): 627–51.

Peräkylä, A. and Silverman, D. (1991b) 'Owning Experience: Describing the Experience of Other Persons', *Text*, 11(3): 441–80.

Peterman, T. and Curran, J. (1986) 'Sexual Transmission of Human Immunodeficiency Virus', *Journal of the American Medical Association*, 256(16): 2222–6.

Peyrot, M. (1987) 'Circumspection in Psychotherapy: Structures and Strategies of Counselor–Client Interaction', *Semiotica*, 65: 249–68.

Prior, L. (1987) 'Policing the Dead: A Sociology of the Mortuary', *Sociology*, 21(3): 355–76.

Quinn, T. (1988) 'Human Immunodeficiency Virus Infection among Patients Attending Clinics for Sexually Transmitted Diseases', *The New England Journal of Medicine*, 318(4): 197–203.

Rawls, A. W. (1987) 'The Interaction Order Sui Generis', *Sociological Theory*, 5: 136–49.

Richards, T. (1986) 'Don't Tell Me on a Friday', *British Medical Journal*, 292: 943.

Rogers, C. R. (1957) 'The Necessary and Sufficient Conditions of Therapeutic Personality Change', *Journal of Consulting Psychology*, 21: 95–103.

Rogers, C. R. (1975) 'Empathic: An Unappreciated Way of Being', *The Counselling Psychologist*, 5(2): 2–10.

Sacks, H. (1972) 'On the Analysability of Stories by Children', in J. Gumperz and D. Hymes (eds), *Directions in Sociolinguistics*. New York: Holt, Rinehart & Winston. pp. 325–45.

Sacks, H. (1974) 'On the Analyzability of Stories by Children'. in R. Turner (ed.), *Ethnomethodology*. Harmondsworth: Penguin. pp. 216–32.

Sacks, H. (1984) 'On Doing "Being Ordinary"', in J. M. Atkinson and J. Heritage (eds), *Structures of Social Action*. Cambridge: Cambridge University Press. pp. 413–29.

Sacks, H. (1992) *Lectures on Conversation*, 2 vols, ed. Gail Jefferson with an Introduction by Emmanuel Schegloff. Oxford: Basil Blackwell.

Sacks, H., Schegloff, E. and Jefferson, G. (1974) 'A Simplest Systematics for the Organization of Turn-taking in Conversation', *Language*, 50(4): 696–735.

Sadler, C. (1988) 'Sexually Transmitted Diseases: More than Tea and Sympathy', *Nursing Times*, 84(49): 30–2.

Salt, H. et al. (1989) 'Paradoxical Interventions in Counselling for People with an Intractable AIDS-Worry', *AIDS Care*, 1(1): 39–44.

Schegloff, E. A. (1968) 'Sequencings in Conversational Openings', *American Anthropologist*, 70: 1075–95.

Schegloff, E. A. (1980) 'Preliminaries to Preliminaries: "Can I Ask You a Question?"', *Sociological Inquiry*, 50(3/4): 104–52.

Schegloff, E. A. (1981) 'Discourse as an Interactional Achievement: Some Uses of "Uh huh" and Other Things That Come Between Sentences', in D. Tannen (ed.), *Georgetown University Round Table on Languages and Linguistics 1981*. Washington, DC: Georgetown University Press. pp. 71–93.

Schegloff, E. A. (1991) 'Reflections on Talk and Social Structure', in Boden and Zimmerman (1991). pp. 44–70.

Schegloff, E. A. and Sacks, H. (1973) 'Opening up Closings', *Semiotica*, 7: 289–327.

Selvini-Palazzoli, M., Boscolo, L., Cecchin, G. et al. (1980), 'Hypothesizing, Circularity, Neutrality: Three Guidelines for the Conductor of a Session', *Family Process*, 19: 3–12.

Shernoff, M. (1988) 'Integrating Safer-Sex Counselling into Social Work Practice', *Social Casework*, June: 334–9.

Sherr, L. (1989) 'Health Education', *AIDS Care*, 1(2): 188–92.

Silverman, D. (1973) 'Interview Talk: Bringing Off a Research Instrument', *Sociology*, 7(1): 31–48.

Silverman, D. (1981) 'The Child as a Social Object: Down's Syndrome Children in a Paediatric Cardiology Clinic', *Sociology of Health and Illness*, 3: 254–74.

Silverman, D. (1983) 'The Clinical Subject: Adolescents in a Cleft-Palate Clinic', *Sociology of Health and Illness*, 5, 3: 253–74.

Silverman, D. (1984) 'Going Private: Ceremonial Forms in a Private Oncology Clinic', *Sociology*, 18, 2: 191–202.

Silverman, D. (1987) *Communication and Medical Practice: Social Relations in the Clinic*. London: Sage.

Silverman, D. (1989a) 'Making Sense of a Precipice: Constituting Identity in an HIV Clinic', in

P. Aggleton, G. Hart and P. Davies (eds), *AIDS: Social Representations, Social Practices*. Lewes: Falmer Press. pp. 101–26.

Silverman, D. (1989b) 'Telling Convincing Stories: A Plea for Cautious Positivism in Case-Studies', in B. Glassner and J. Moreno (eds), *The Qualitative–Quantitative Distinction in the Social Sciences*. Dordrecht: Kluwer.

Silverman, D. (1989c) 'The Impossible Dreams of Reformism and Romanticism', in J. Gubrium and D. Silverman (eds), *The Politics of Field Research: Sociology beyond Enlightenment*. London: Sage. pp. 30–48.

Silverman, D. (1990) 'The Social Organization of HIV Counselling', in P. Aggleton et al. (eds), *AIDS: Individual, Cultural and Policy Perspectives*. Lewes: Falmer. pp. 191–211.

Silverman, D. (1993) *Interpreting Qualitative Data: Methods for Analysing Talk, Text and Interaction*. London: Sage.

Silverman, D. (1994a) 'Analyzing Naturally-occurring Data on AIDS Counselling: Some Methodological and Practical Issues', in M. Boulton (ed.) *Challenge and Innovation: Methodological Advances in Social Research on HIV/AIDS*. London: Falmer Press. pp. 69–94.

Silverman, D. (1994b) 'Delicate Boundaries: Bernstein, Sacks and the Machinery of Interaction', in S. Delamont, P. Atkinson and W. B. Davies (eds) *Discourse and Reproduction: Essays in Honor of Basil Bernstein*, Creskill, NJ: Hampton Press.

Silverman, D. (1994c) 'Describing Sexual Activities in HIV Counselling: the Co-operative Management of the Moral Order', *Text*, 14(3): 427–53.

Silverman, D. and Atkinson, P. (forthcoming) 'Kundera's Immortality: The Interview Society and the Invention of the Self', *Qualitative Inquiry*.

Silverman, D. and Bloor, M. (1989) 'Patient-Centred Medicine: Some Sociological Observations on its Constitution, Penetration and Cultural Assonance' in G. L. Albrecht (ed.), *Advances in Medical Sociology*. Greenwich, CT: JAI Press. pp. 3–26.

Silverman, D. and Bor, R. (1991) 'The Delicacy of Describing Sexual Partners in HIV-Test Counselling: Implications for Practice', *Counselling Psychology Quarterly*, 4(2/3): 177–90.

Silverman, D. and Gubrium, J. (1994) 'Competing Strategies for Analyzing the Contexts of Social Interaction', *Sociological Inquiry*, 64(2): 179–98.

Silverman, D. and Peräkylä, A. (1990) 'AIDS Counselling: the Interactional Organization of Talk about "Delicate" Issues', *Sociology of Health and Illness*, 12(3): 293–318.

Silverman, D., Bor, R., Miller, R. and Goldman, E. (1992a) 'Advice-Giving and Advice-Reception in AIDS Counselling', in P. Aggleton, P. Davies and G. Hart (eds), *AIDS: Rights, Risk and Reason*. London: Falmer Press. pp. 174–91.

Silverman, D., Peräkylä, A. and Bor, R. (1992b) 'Discussing Safer Sex in HIV Counselling: Assessing Three Communication Formats', *AIDS Care*, 4(1): 69–82.

Sonnex, C. et al. (1987) 'HIV infection: Increase in Public Awareness and Anxiety', *British Medical Journal*, 295: 193–5.

Sontag, S. (1979) *Illness as Metaphor*. Harmondsworth: Penguin.

Stoller, E. J. and Rutherford, G. W. (1989) 'Evaluation of AIDS Prevention and Control Programs', *AIDS*, 3 (Supplement 1): S289–96.

Strong, P. M. (1979a) *The Ceremonial Order of the Clinic: Parents, Doctors, and Medical Bureaucracies*. London: Routledge.

Strong, P. M. (1979b) 'Sociological Imperialism and the Profession of Medicine', *Social Science and Medicine*, 13A: 199–215.

Strong, P. M. and Dingwall, R. (1989) 'Romantics and Stoics', in J. Gubrium and D. Silverman (eds), *The Politics of Field Research: Sociology beyond Enlightenment*. London: Sage. pp. 49–69.

Tannen, D. (1987) 'Repetition in Conversation: Towards a Poetics of Talk', *Language*, 63(3): 574–605.

Taylor, C. (1986) 'Foucault on Freedom and Truth', in D. Hoy (ed.), *Foucault: A Critical Reader*. Oxford: Basil Blackwell. pp. 69–102.

Ten Have, P. (1991) 'Talk and Institution: A Reconsideration of the "Asymmetry" of Doctor–Patient Interaction', in Boden and Zimmerman (1991). pp. 138–63.

Thompson, C. and McIver, A. (1988) 'HIV Counselling: Change in Trends in Public Concern', *Health Bulletin*, 46: 237–45.

Discourses of Counselling

Waitzkin, H. (1979) 'Medicine, Superstructure and Micropolitics', *Social Science & Medicine*, 13A: 601–9.
Watney, S. (1987) *Policing Desire*. London: Methuen.
Watson, R. (1987) 'Interdisciplinary Considerations in the Analysis of Pro-terms', in G. Button and J. R. E. Lee (eds), *Talk and Social Organization*. Clevedon, UK: Multilingual Matters. pp. 261–89.
Wellings, K., Field, J., Johnson, A., Wadsworth, J. and Bradshaw, S. (1990) 'Notes on the Design and Construction of a National Survey of Sexual Lifestyles', in M. Hubert (ed.), *Sexual Behaviour and Risks of HIV Infection*. Brussels: Facultés Universitaires Saint-Louis.
West, C. (1983) ' "Ask Me No Questions . . ." An Analysis of Queries and Replies in Physician–Patient Dialogues', in S. Fisher and A. D. Todd (eds), *The Social Organization of Doctor-Patient Communication*. Washington, DC: Center for Applied Linguistics. pp. 75–106.
Wittgenstein, L. (1968) *Philosophical Investigations*, trans. G. E. M. Anscombe. Oxford: Basil Blackwell.
Wittgenstein, L. (1969) *On Certainty*. trans. D. Paul and G. E. M. Anscombe. New York: Harper & Row.
World Health Organization (1988) *Guidelines for the Development of a National AIDS Prevention and Control Programme* (WHO AIDS Series 1). Geneva: WHO.
Youssef, V. and Silverman, D. (1992) 'Normative Expectations for Medical Talk', *Language and Communication*, 12(2): 123–31.

Subject Index

Author Index